Sacred Cows
and
Golden Geese

Sacred Cows and Golden Geese

The Human Cost of Experiments on Animals

C. Ray Greek, MD
and Jean Swingle Greek, DVM
Foreword by Jane Goodall

CONTINUUM

NEW YORK   LONDON

2001

The Continuum International Publishing Group Inc
370 Lexington Avenue, New York, NY 10017

The Continuum International Publishing Group Ltd
Wellington House, 125 Strand, London WC2R 0BB

Printed in the United States of America

Library of Congress Cataloging-in-Publication Data

Greek, C. Ray
    Sacred cows and golden geese: the human cost of experiments on
animals / C. Ray Greek, Jean Swingle Greek; foreword by Jane
Goodall.
      p. cm
    Includes bibliographical references.
    ISBN 0–8264–1226–2 (hc. : alk. paper)
    1. Animal experimentation. I. Greek, Jean Swingle. II. Title
HV4915.G73 2000
179'.4—dc21
                                                        99–057157

*To all our teachers and students,
from whom we have learned so much*

Contents

Foreword

by Jane Goodall, PhD

*S*acred *Cows and Golden Geese* bears an important message. It challenges the widely held belief that the use of living animals in biomedical research is absolutely necessary for the advancement of human medical knowledge. The authors, Drs. Jean and Ray Greek, show that the use of live animals in medical research is unethical, not with relation to the suffering of the animals as more commonly held, but because faulty science underpins it. This leads, in the long run, to human as well as animal suffering.

For years I have been criticizing the ethics of using animals on the grounds of their proven sentience and sapience. For nearly forty years I have had the privilege of working with and learning from our closest living relatives, the chimpanzees. As we have gradually discovered how like us they are (or we like them), the line that was once seen as so sharp between humans and the rest of the animal kingdom has increasingly blurred. Chimpanzees have vivid personalities, a complex social life, humanlike cognitive abilities, and emotions similar to ours. They are capable of compassion, they can show true altruism, and they have a sense of humor. Not surprisingly, they are also physiologically very like humans as well. That is why these closest relatives of ours have been—and still are—used as "models" in the study of human diseases. With no regard for their humanlike behavior, hundreds have been condemned to life imprisonment (up to sixty years) in five-foot by five-foot laboratory cages. And the only reason this is tolerated by anyone is because we have been told, repeatedly told, that only by testing drugs and vaccines on these humanlike bodies can we find ways of alleviating human suffering.

For the same reason, we tolerate the shocking abuse of many other sentient beings. If anyone other than white-coated scientists treated monkeys, dogs, cats, rabbits, pigs, and so forth as they do behind the locked doors of the animal lab, he or she would be prosecuted for cruelty. But, say the animal experimenters, it is for the good of humans. If animal experimentation were stopped, we are told, so too would human medical progress. How else could we learn about the nature of human diseases, find new cures and vaccines, perfect new medical technologies? This is the argument that is repeated, again and again, by the animal experimenters.

In most cases, people will choose to sacrifice any animal to save or improve the quality of a human life. In other words, in a scenario of "them" or "us," humans will always prevail. And this is hardly surprising. No matter how much a woman may love dogs or chimps, she will choose to sacrifice a dog or a chimp if told that this will save her child. Evolution has programmed us to make choices that ensure our genes will be represented in future generations. We choose in favor of our own children over the children of other people or other creatures. This is why those fighting for animal rights by using ethical and philosophical arguments, although they have made progress in changing attitudes toward animals, can never hope to bring all animal experimentation to an end by using these arguments alone.

However, what if it can be shown that the use of animals, in very many instances, provides misleading results? How often are potentially healing drugs withheld from humans because they harm animals? By contrast, how often are drugs that do not harm animals used on humans with disastrous results?

We dedicate vast amounts of research energy and research dollars to inflicting humanlike diseases on animals and seeking ways to treat them. Scientists use the data this generates to write papers in order to get new grants. What is less generally realized, unless one carefully follows the scientific journals, is how seldom these animal "breakthroughs" are useful in curing the "real" diseases in their human form.

And why is this? Although in many ways animals show physiological similarities to humans, they are different. Even chimpanzees, with immune systems so like ours, do not respond as humans do to a variety of diseases. Of all the hundreds of chimpanzees that have been infected with the human HIV retrovirus, for example, none have developed the typical symptoms of human AIDS. (Even in the two—yes, only two—who apparently died of AIDS, the course of the disease was very different.) Yet millions of dollars have gone into AIDS research using chimpanzees as (very inappropriate) models. Millions and millions more dollars have been used to infect animals even less like us.

Of course, thousands of people comprise the vast animal experimentation industry—the manufacturers and salesmen for cages, animal food, lab equipment paraphernalia, and specially bred genetic lines of experimental animals, the animal care staff, and all the scientists themselves. They would be out of a job if the animal research carpet were pulled from under their feet. All these people are, for obvious reasons, very anxious to preserve the status quo. This, presumably, is why those who are searching for alternatives to the use of live animals in experimentation so often get the cold shoulder from the scientific establishment. This is why there are no Nobel Prizes for alternative techniques. And this is why it is so much harder to get a new non-animal procedure approved than a new procedure involving animals.

I have a growing conviction that many animal data are not only obtained unethically, at huge cost in animal suffering, but are also unscientific, misleading, wasteful (in terms of dollars and effort) and may be actually harmful to humans. I constantly read through journals on alternatives to animal experimentation in my quest for good, solid, scientific facts to substantiate this conviction. Here, at last, is a book that exhaustively examines and synthesizes the literature on this subject. The facts are set out clearly and quite without sentimentality. The arguments presented here are not those of most animal rights activists that play on emotions to generate sympathy for animals. Nor are they the arguments of moral philosophers, based on logic. Instead the authors use factual, scientific arguments to explain how, in their view, the infliction of suffering on animals in medical research is not a biomedical evil, necessary to save human lives, but a real betrayal of the scientific method. Animal experimentation is unethical and cruel. It hurts animals, it is expensive, and it is so often detrimental to the very species it professes to be helping—our own.

Jean and Ray Greek are singularly well qualified to write this book since they are well versed in the science of medicine, both from the human and the animal perspective. Their specified aim in writing *Sacred Cows and Golden Geese* is to bring this whole issue into the domain of the general public. And because it is so clearly written, and the issues discussed so logically, those who read it will be in a far better position to evaluate the scientific pros and cons of animal experimentation. It will, for this reason, be invaluable for animal rights activists who have not, to date, considered the scientific arguments against animal experimentation. It should be read by all students who plan a career in medicine. It should find a place in all libraries, including high school libraries. Only when the general public has a better understanding of the issues can we expect a ground swell of opposition to animal experimentation. This will force science to direct its collectively awesome intellect into different pathways in its search to alleviate human suffering.

Acknowledgments

Since we have drawn from the medical and scientific literature, we are indebted to those who published the original articles in the peer-reviewed journals, wrote the books, and assembled the government reports. We are also deeply grateful to colleagues who pointed us in the right direction. Ned Bukuymichi, Murry Cohen, Stephen Kaufmann, Hugh LaFollette, Tony Page, Brandon Reines, Niall Shanks, Robert Sharpe, and others have written excellent critiques and reviews, and we have profited from their work.

We gleaned much direction from groups such as Animal Aid, the American Antivivisection Society, the Medical Research Modernization Committee, the National Antivivisection Society, the New England Antivivisection Society, the Physicians Committee for Responsible Medicine, and numerous physicians, veterinarians, and PhDs.

This book would not have been possible were it not for our agent Julie Castiglia. She took two untrained and unproven writers and guided them into making a readable book.

We are immensely grateful to Continuum International and our editor, Evander Lomke, for recognizing the imperative message of this book.

We are truly honored that Dr. Jane Goodall generously lent her name by writing the foreword, and grateful that so influential a scientist involved herself in this work.

Finally, we would like to thank our many friends who read and critiqued the countless rewrites; they are as glad as we to see this book published: André, Barbara, Bina, Jean, Jennifer, Jerry, Jonathan, Julie, Larry, Lauren, Lynn, Mark, Neva, Pam, Rick, Susan, and Turney. There are probably many others whose names we can not remember now that we are actually writing this acknowledgment, and for that we apologize.

Special Acknowledgement

To writer and editor Tershia d'Elgin for her excellent skills and blithe spirit.

chapter 1

Introduction

Comparative medicine may not be everyone's idea of a riveting dinner topic, but it is ours. This book grew out of our meal-time conversations during the 1980s. Those were the years of our professional education . . . one of us as a veterinarian, and the other as an anesthesiologist.

When our animal and human patients exhibited the same symptoms, discussion became most heated. This was because diagnoses and treatment plans for animals frequently differed for humans. Pitting the veterinarian's dictates on the one hand against the physician's on the other, we would each get huffy and self-righteous, then whip out our textbooks to prove our accuracy. Many references later, sure enough, according to the books, we were both right.

Well, this was puzzling! These discrepancies flew in the face of what we had been taught to revere. Animal experimentation was an inviolable convention—a political *sacred cow*. Everything we had been taught, from fetal pigs forward, suggested that animals were just like humans, a bit furry and funny looking perhaps, but otherwise just the same.

Like everyone, we had been convinced by many familiar determinants: animal experimentation for human medical research had a time-honored history. Milestones supposedly garnered from animal studies were constantly in the media. As medical students, we were well familiar with the government's requirement for animal assays in drug development and its financial rewards to research institutions. Certainly, grant money for such projects was vital to the incomes of our teachers and universities. Indeed, our medical training pivoted on assumed anatomic, biochemical, and physiological characteristics shared by man and beast.

This sizable and persuasive rationalism averred that animals were ideal test beds for human therapies. So, why then was Ray's human patient with high cholesterol developing coronary heart disease and Jean's dog with high cholesterol experiencing a thyroid disorder? Why do women who have had hysterectomies need to fight osteoporosis while neutered cats live longer, healthier lives? And why are humans not vaccinated for parvo and dogs for rubella? Our dinner conversations suggested that most animal diseases simply do not occur in humans. Conversely, the major killers of humankind are extraordinarily rare among the four-legged set.

Plainly, if there was parity, it was not universal. Sure, the basics are the same. Fundamental cell activity and metabolic processes—the stuff of research decades ago—correspond in animals and humans. Still, we thought, why did scientists use animals back when human autopsy, tissue culture techniques, or human observation could have provided the same information? Some animal experimentation led to developments. But in how many cases were the animals *necessary*? Animals can be used to grow viruses, but so can petri dishes and human tissue cultures. All mammalian blood—animal and human—has components in common, so why not use human blood for totally accurate results? Moreover, when it came to present-day research—mostly involving microbiology on the most complex levels—why scrutinize species whose physiologic response to disease, disease manifestation, and disease incidence so clearly deviates from human response? Logic, it seemed to us, even back then when we had but few comparisons, was somehow amiss.

Both of us had performed animal experimentation. We knew from experience how similar the gross anatomy of animals and humans is, and how dissimilar are the details. For example, all mammals have a four-chambered heart that pumps blood, but our own education taught that at the cellular level mammals react very differently to medications. All land mammals have four limbs, but attempts to test surgeries of the aorta on dogs fail because dogs' circulation is different in part due to their walking on four extremities while we walk on two. Animals and humans both secrete gastric juices and other chemicals. However, the gastric fluid in dogs' stomachs is much more acidic than ours. This is why Fido can gobble down uncouth matter without upsetting his stomach, and humans cannot.

Scientists have a name for one-to-one correspondence between all elements in two or more living systems. *Isomorphism.* Clearly, animals are not isomorphic with humans. With systems as complex as the human body, very small dissimilarities not only negate isomorphism but also have radical implications. Grossly, animals are alike, that is why we are all part of the animal kingdom. We differ on the cellular and molecular level, and, importantly, *that is where disease occurs.*

We, the tireless medical students, became more inquisitive. We asked the kind of questions everyone asks when confronted with the subject of animal experimentation. No one really wants to torture animals, but look where a history of animal experimentation has led us. Where would we be today without the antibiotics, the scanners, the modern surgical techniques, and the host of medications used daily to treat everything from heart disease to arthritis to cancer? If animal-models are not employed, what or who will be? Few people aspire to be the first patient of an inexperienced surgeon or the first person to take a new drug. Moreover, we rationalized, is it not reassuring to know that new advances have been thoroughly tested on animals, found not only safe, but also effective?

But how safe, how effective are these animal-modeled advances? Investigating further, we learned that though cardiac-bypass surgery was practiced extensively on animals, when first tried on humans, the patients actually died. Penicillin kills guinea pigs and is not effective in rabbits. Were these troubling examples common ones? Or were they exceptions to the rule? Apparently not, we found. Roughly fifteen percent of all hospital admissions are caused by adverse medication reactions. And legal drugs, which made their way to the public via animals, kill approximately 100,000 people per year. That is more than all illegal drugs combined and costs the general public over $136 billion in health care expenses.[1]

We found the actual merit of using animal tissues—in the culture medium, as heart valves or for insulin, or to produce monoclonal antibodies, and so forth—was by no means as advantageous as we had been led to believe. There were heavy risks, sometimes resulting in human illness and even death. And no one was mentioning the less dangerous treatments these therapies delayed. Likewise underestimated was the potential for animal-borne viruses that might mutate into a more deadly and contagious form in the human body. When we began to collect data, the fatally infectious protein particles called *prions* (which could inhabit all animal tissue and which medicine has no way to thwart) had yet to reveal themselves. Now that prions have been front page news, from the incidences of Mad Cow disease, everyone should know that mining animals for treatments is courting disaster. But they do not.

We had been led to believe that the majority of medical advances had come about as the result of research carried out on animals. Now we wondered was this truth or propaganda?

We do not deny that we are both "animal lovers," to some extent motivated by our affection for animals and our concern for their well being. However, more essentially, we are both medical doctors and scientists. For ten years, Ray performed the most demanding branch of anesthesiology in cardiopulmonary and transplantation surgeries. Jean became one of the top veterinary dermatologists in the world. We have both published extensively in the scientific literature. Our lifestyle and careers are grounded in science. Logic, reason, data, causal relationships, verifiability, repeatability, and all other tenets of the scientific paradigm—these provide the hard scientific foundation for our choices, both personal and professional.

We were finding, through scientific research, that extrapolating data from animals to humans is either *misleading, unnecessary, dangerous,* or all three.

The strongest tenet that arises from science is predictability. To be reliable, a model should have predictive value. That is science. In medicine, strong models assume four factors: the same symptoms, the same postulated origin of disease, the same neurobiological mechanism, and the same treatment response. The truth is that though certain animals may fulfill some of the same criteria as humans in some incidences, no animal consistently fulfills all four. This means that animals are not strong models for human disease.

It also means that all data recovered from animal model experiments must be *scaled*. Scaling is a scientific term that, generally, refers to "the fudge factor." Since we are all putting our lives and the lives of our loved ones in the hands of supposedly rigorous science, is not a model that requires so much fudging grossly inadequate—especially since humans themselves provide the perfect model?

Given all these peculiarities, we began to ponder just how humans do benefit from animal experimentation. We asked physicians how it had specifically contributed to their field. Surgeons denied knowledge of any specific contributions, but referred us to pediatricians. Pediatricians knew of no significant achievements in pediatrics that relied on animals, but referred us to psychiatrists. Psychiatrists pointed out the drawbacks to studying psychosis in mice and suggested we contact the internists. And it continued. Each specialist, though unaware of true animal-model successes in his own field, was convinced that other specialists were reliant on this protocol. They too had bought what was fast appearing to us as a bill of goods.

Delving deeper through the scientific literature, searching for the substantive development history of explicit drugs, technologies, and techniques, we found a broad gap between prevailing thought and actual incident. Commonly attributed to animal experimentation, the development of drugs and technologies did *not* rely on animals. We began to collect data on these disparities. Of course, we were not the first to question the relevance of animal experimentation. And as we researched we uncovered to what extent it had been criticized.

Among our predecessors we found many men and women who had dared to refute the animal model. They expressed doubts on the order of these from Dr. M. Beddow Bayly, who in 1961 wrote:

> The paramount need for a clear and documented account of past achievements arises from the prevalent custom of those medical authorities who set out to support and defend the practice of experimenting on living animals so far to distort historical facts as to create the impression in the mind of the public that every single medical diagnosis and treatment had depended for its discovery and application on vivisection . . . Happily, even the briefest perusal of

the available evidence shows falsity of these claims and provides historical proof of the supreme value of clinical observation and experiment when contrasted with the doubtful and often misleading practice of animal experimentation.[2]

In other words, Dr. Bayly felt as we had begun to feel—that most advances were due to clinical observations by doctors and nurses on their human patients.

So there we were, with our growing pile of data. It reflected how many ways and for how many years, we had all been duped. Agreeing with the Dr. Baylys of the world and troubled by the utter lack of scientific grounding in animal experimentation, we wanted to know why it persisted. Perhaps we had missed something? We decided to go to the animal experimenters themselves and ask why and how animal experiments were important.

The animal experimentation lobby has very persuasive arguments. Time after time we thought, "Surely this is an advance that must be credited to the animal model." However, once we actually looked up the true origins of the advance in the scientific literature, we either found a clinical discovery, serendipity, or some other non-animal based discovery had previously revealed the knowledge, which animal experimenters later "validated" in animals. Animal experimentation lobbyists or public-relations people did not, of course, mention these preemptive revelations.

The incidences where actual medical history deviated from that presented by pro-animal experimenters grew and grew. They are what *Sacred Cows and Golden Geese* is about—in part. Our other subject, and indeed underlying theme, is why animal experimentation continues.

Anyone who asks "why" has only to follow the money to find an answer. Like the goose who laid the golden egg, animal experimentation is a source of infinite financing. Tracing the funding dollars, we found a medical-research system corrupted by lobbying groups, opportunistic scientists, irresponsible drug companies, unlearned public officials, and clogged bureaucracies, all profiting off the animal model's golden eggs.

Science is a lot of things, but fundamentally, it is not public relations. It is not bureaucracy. It is not trends. It is not professional societies, nor special-interest groups. It is not a commodity. Though public relations, trends, organizations, bureaucrats, and money may drive it, science is not any of these. However, science is shaped by our perceptions, just as our experience of the sun is affected by the earth's atmosphere. The dollars go where the concern rests.

What we found, in our search for the source of continued animal experimentation, was not "science," but mass confusion kept in spin by mass deception. The general public has more confidence in hype than in facts, possibly because the facts, being largely in scientific journals, are mostly unavailable and inscrutable.

The other reason that animal experimentation continues is simply the momentum of convention. It is a bit like Newton's first law of motion— objects in motion tend to remain that way. Animal experiments continue because they have occurred for a long time, as we explain in the next chapter.

The purpose of this book, therefore, is threefold.

First, it exposes the scientific fallacy of reliance on the animal model for human medical research. We now know that animal experimentation has failed miserably, at tremendous expense, and has done real harm to human patients. True advances in medical knowledge have not come from animals. When, on rare occasion, advances took place through animal experimentation, they were not *incumbent* on animals. Alternative methods—autopsies, *in vitro* research, clinical observation, epidemiology, mathematical modeling, and other human-based research modalities—could have resulted in the same achievements without injury to humans. Animal models are inaccurate, superfluous, and create risk to humans.

Second, we make this information available to the non-specialist. We have written this book largely without medical jargon. However, we do ask readers to judge the merits of the information we present by evaluating the references. We do not use any "animal-rights" arguments. To strengthen our position with emotional appeal, this book could have included pictures of monkeys with their brains wired, dogs with legs amputated or viscera dangling, or other heart-wrenching images. However, this is a book based on science and reason. Instead, we rely on the scientific facts and we rely on the voices of scientists who have personally experienced the ineptitude of the animal model, and who have come forward even when so doing may have jeopardized their livelihood.

Many of the scientists we quote make their living from animal experimentation though admitting to its fallacy. Common sense compels us to give credence to statements made by researchers who have come out against the very system that feeds their families, even if they later deny them. They may have made their statements not anticipating that they would be quoted. One candid admission is notable when the person who makes it has so much at stake. And in any event, checking our references will confirm the authenticity of their statements.

We ask readers to compare our arguments to those of the pro-vivisectionists whose spokespeople are vested in continuing animal studies. Clearly, those whose entire professional life hinges on continued animal studies, and those who risk disenfranchisement by peers will cling to the status quo as though to their very lives. Just as tobacco executives insisted, under oath, that cigarettes did not cause cancer nor were they addictive, those with a vested interest in animal experimentation will state that animal experiments are vital for new cures to be found. The animal experimentation industry spends millions annually to persuade the public that all medical advances are directly due to animal experimentation. As you will read, the facts do not support this claim.

Third, we encourage all scientists, researchers, veterinarians, and physicians to come forward and speak out on the failure of animal experimentation as revealed in their own field. Not until the volume of dissent rises high enough will there be significant change and an end to the corruption. And because modern research, particularly in regard to contagious illnesses, can potentially unleash epidemics of cataclysmic proportions, the need for change is more critical than ever.

The United States medical research establishment is no easy target. It is regarded as preeminent, both here and abroad. Our scientists have received more Nobel Prizes than scientists of any other country. Yet, today the United States ranks twenty-ninth in infant mortality, sixteenth in maternal death rates, fifteenth in life expectancy for women, and twenty-second in life expectancy for men.[3] These are astonishing statistics. In light of these, careful scrutiny of some of the factors that send medicine in this country askew is merited and overdue.

We anticipate criticism. Those who profit from animal experimentation are fierce opponents because they have everything to lose. Their arguments are very familiar to us because a good portion of our time is spent parrying their assault in writing, in debate, and in other public forums. We have heard their justifications for animal models in regard to drugs and medical procedures. By now, we know every one of their claims. We have countered them for the last six years.

A single book cannot contain the encyclopedic transgressions of animal experimentation. We were forced to prioritize, choosing subjects of most concern in today's medical climate, and saving the rest for a subsequent volume. Here, we explore how the animal model bears on the top three killers of Americans—heart disease, cancer, and stroke. AIDS is another high profile disease that demanded inclusion. Xenotransplantation, as the most pressing danger of clinging to the animal model, could not be postponed.

Reluctantly, we have postponed chapters on neurological and psychiatric diseases, pediatric diseases, and vaccines and infectious diseases other than AIDS. Also awaiting another book is animal experimentation's impact on surgery and anesthesiology as well as an examination of whether animals were necessary to Nobel Prize–winning science.

Hence, *Sacred Cows and Golden Geese* takes on many, but not all of animal experimentation's reputed hallmarks. It pulls back the veil of prevarication and downright falsehood pro-vivisectionists have used for years. Our countless references from the scientific literature expose and support the truth: animal experimentation has betrayed its promise to find human therapies and cures. The animal model harms people.

chapter 2

How It All Began

The Origins of Animal Experimentation in the West

The idea of the good of humanity was simply out of the
question, and would be laughed at, the great aim being to
keep up with, or get ahead of, one's contemporaries in
science.

—Dr. George Hoggan, former student of Dr. Claude
Bernard in the *Morning Post,* February 2, 1875

A certain logic does suggest using animals for human medical research. As mammals, humans have four limbs, just like mice, just like
dogs, just like apes. As mammals, we do not lay eggs. Nor do mice. Nor
do dogs. Nor do apes. They have four-chambered hearts, livers, lungs,
and so on. So do we. It is not incredible that we should conjecture based
on these apparent similarities. Granted.

Conjecture is one matter, but *scientific* conclusion is another.
Throughout history, and still, scientists have stated as absolute a theory
learned from animals, only to have the ensuing human data refute it.
Our boxloads of data illustrate that using animals for human medical
research is grossly unscientific, beyond any doubt. Mere experimentation
on animals is not scientific; anyone can do that. If the results are inapplicable, misleading, and dangerous, then the fundamental principles
supporting respectable knowledge-gathering crumble.

So, how did this puppy dog's tail–type science become so entrenched?
Here, tracing back, readers will find that the history of animal experimentation is one of ignorance, immense egos, Church-determined biases,
and bad news for animals and humans alike.

Galen's Legacy

Methods for acquiring medical knowledge commenced soundly enough.
In the fourth century B.C.E., Hippocrates fathered the concept of clinical

research. This august scholar taught that, by observing enough cases, physicians can predict the course of a disease, both in terms of its likely effect and vulnerable population. Hippocrates' methodology has stood the test of time. Clinical observation still provides our most accurate and usable medical information.

Then, in second century Rome, a still revered physician put Hippocrates' human-based medical research process substantially off course. An experimenter of great energy and resources, Galen, was physician to the gladiators and to Marcus Aurelius's son. Galen might have continued investigation of the human model, but this practice was stanched by moral opposition. There already existed a bishop of Rome and a state-supported Church protocol disallowing human autopsies. So, Galen cut into goats and pigs and monkeys purloined from North Africa's Barbary Coast instead.

Thus, Galen became the father of vivisection. (*Vivisection* literally means the cutting up of the living, but it refers to experiments conducted on animals.) Galen combined physiologic data from animals with his personal observation of humans to forge broad theories of physiology. He was a persuasive lecturer and prolific writer. More than five hundred written tracts on medicine and other subjects contributed to his historic importance.

Unfortunately, many of his theories fell short of accuracy. Galen's essential theory was this: Four bodily humors—blood, phlegm, yellow and black bile—govern all variables of health and disease. Likewise he believed that the liver manufactured blood. Though recognizing that blood travels, Galen fell short of concluding that it *circulated*. He described the heart as a warming machine for two separate types of blood and was convinced that veins and arteries were not connected. In his version of our blood's passage, it moved through invisible pores in the heart's intervening septum to the heart's left side, drawn by arteries that expanded like a bellows to draw fluid into them. Thus, according to Galen, the blood collected *pneuma*, drawn in by the lungs flowing both backward and forward from the heart."[1,2,3]

Galen also described blood vessels directly under the brain. This network of blood vessels is present in many of the animals Galen dissected, but is absent in humans.[4] He attributed cancer to the invasion of humors that resulted in inflammation.

To be fair, his was an era with little instrumentation and poor research conditions. That Galen erred is not surprising. Nevertheless, it must be said that medical knowledge in Asia was not likewise obfuscated, possibly because no Roman Catholic Church prohibited autopsy there. *Nei Sing*, the book that provides the basis for Chinese medicine, compiled nearly three thousand years before Galen, described the blood flowing from the heart in a continuous circle.[5] Human autopsy rather than animal dissection would have eliminated (and eventually did eliminate) this and many other of Galen's inaccuracies.

Even with evidence that Galen's shortcomings were largely due to animal experimentation, his contributions through vivisection are still considered sacrosanct. Animal experimentation fans often cite them. In the early 1990s, the American Medical Association (AMA) published a "White Paper," promoted as a history of animal experimentation's contributions. (Chapter 5 explains AMA motivations for this.) The publication is a feat of omission and distortion, as is apparent by its citations in this book, of which the following is the first: ". . . the Roman physician Galen used apes and pigs to prove his theory that veins carry blood rather than air."[6] As surgeon to the gladiators, certainly Galen's observations of humans were adequate to this conclusion. He did not require animals. Focusing exclusively on Galen's conclusion that blood travels around the body via vessels, the AMA and the animal experimentation contingency conveniently fail to mention the scope of Galen's errors and how they cast a shroud over medical progress, a darkness which did not lift for a millennium and a half.

Galen's errors, knitted together with the Church's prohibitions, suffocated medicine for centuries, both in terms of achievement and practice. Physicians adopted his frequently-amiss conclusions about the human body. The acceptance of Galen's doctrines, without equivocation, stymied the knowledge base about the human body and disease for 1,500 years. Doctors administered to the sick with treatments governed by Galen's four-humor theory—bloodletting and so forth—and tens of thousands of people died in the process.

The Church's influence over science in the pre–Renaissance era cannot be overemphasized:

> Negative attitudes toward dissection of the human body; the stranglehold of Galen, whose four humors, doctrines of qualities, and inaccurate anatomy virtually paralyzed progress in medical science for fourteen centuries . . .[7]

Since Church edict forbade autopsies in medieval Europe, animal dissection revealed bones, tendons, ligaments and other fundamentals about mammals, including humans. Tendons connect the muscle to the bone and ligaments connect bones to each other. Since the baseline of knowledge was low, the addition of such knowledge was obviously good. Autopsies would have elucidated the same information and more, but it did not. Moreover, there were massive downsides to obtaining knowledge from animal experiments. Only with the study of the human body, centuries later, were faulty information and medical practices corrected:

> [Galen] unhesitatingly transferred [extrapolated] his discoveries directly to humans, thus initiating many errors. The combination of

Galen's immense authority and the prohibition by the Church of postmortem dissections of the human body conserved these errors well into the sixteenth century.[8]

Formalized human dissection did not recommence for more than a millennium after Galen. Disquietude over what appeared to be errors in Galen's thinking nevertheless grew.

A Great Awakening, Renaissance Science

Finally, in the thirteenth century, Mondino de'Luzzi published what is believed to be the first text of human anatomy based on human dissection. But resistance was intense. Soon after, Paracelsus, a scientist who taught at the University of Basel, was dismissed for publicly burning Galen's work. Not until the Enlightenment, could humanity throw off its Church-bound ignorance and pursue the scientific method. We now know that Leonardo da Vinci actually discovered and documented arteries and arterial valves, but at the time his anatomical drawings did not receive sufficient attention.

Not until Andreas Vesalius was impetus sufficient to dislodge medieval thinking. In 1543, Vesalius, a Belgian anatomist and physician, began to dissect the human body and found, disturbingly enough, that most of what Galen had written was in fact erroneous. Not yet thirty, he published his results in De Corporis Humani Fabrica or Structure of the Human Body. Vesalius's book was published in the same year that Copernicus published his own startling and radical discoveries. Challenging the very foundations of civilization, those prescribed by the Catholic Church, these two books marked the beginning of the scientific revolution. But it was a troubled beginning.

Like d'Luzzi's text, Vesalius's actually represented human anatomy. All previously recognized publications were sheer speculation based on animal dissection. A pupil of the great artist Titian illustrated Vesalius's book. The written descriptions combined with the drawings proved to be truly paradigm shattering. One of Vesalius's more heretical findings was that both men and women had twelve ribs. This discovery shattered Church doctrine based on Genesis, that men had one less rib since Eve derived from Adam's rib.[9]

Church officials were infuriated. Galen's theories were edict and his many loyal supporters tried to prove the upstart Vesalius wrong. The Church accused Vesalius of heresy, a capital crime. Young Vesalius was forced to hide from his colleagues and the authorities of the Church, in fear for his life. Heated dispute ensued, and fortunately, truth eventually won out. Vesalius eventually became physician to Charles V, the Holy Roman Emperor.[10,11,12]

Once the scientific community overpowered the Church's objections, the acquisition of medical knowledge accelerated. From Vesalius on, anatomy based on human dissection was the norm during the Renaissance.[13] Where Vesalius left off, Gabriel Fallopius continued. Using human dissection, Fallopius described numerous structures including the fallopian tubes, the inner-ear anatomy, and the clitoris.[14]

Evidently, human autopsy provided better results than animal dissection. Galen's results were wrong because his methodology was wrong. This may seem obvious in retrospect, but at the time autopsy was very controversial. Human autopsy soon established itself as the method of choice for advancing knowledge at Europe's premier learning institutions. The systematic study of the human body via dissection began at the medical school in Bologna, which quickly distinguished itself as the premiere medical teaching facility. Other schools, like that at Salerno, previously the foremost medical school in Europe, faded into the secondary tier because their students were not so well versed in anatomy. Henceforward, universities changed their curricula to include human dissection. Pressure and competition between academics was such that the Church was forced to give way to modern advances, just as it had in other sciences after Galileo and Copernicus.

It was an exhilarating time with an open exchange of ideas over a growing body of knowledge. New information about "how humans work," all drawn *from humans*, cast aside Galen's stunting inaccuracies. It was, in every way, a *renaissance*. Eager students from elsewhere in Europe made their way to Italy to profit from this invigorating atmosphere.

One of these students at last expunged Galen's misinterpretation of blood circulation. As explained, the Chinese understood blood's action as early as 2,650 B.C.E. Although it may have been apparent to other experimenters previously, William Harvey is the Westerner now credited with the first accurate written description of the blood's circulation. An English physician who trained in the rigorous academic environment at Padua, Harvey observed the association of the heartbeat and pulse in human beings. His autopsies proved that blood circulated from the right heart through the lungs back to the left heart and into the arteries and veins, about which he wrote in 1628.[15] This certainly debunked Galen's "invisible pores in the heart." Harvey even hypothesized the capillaries.[16] Again citing the AMA's White Paper, pro-vivisectionists would have us believe that "Advances in knowledge made through these [animal] experiments included Harvey's demonstration of the circulation of blood in 1622."[17]

Searching the literature of the time, however, we found an opposing description of Harvey's methods. Dr. Lawson Tait, one of the most famous surgeons of the nineteenth century, thought of it differently:

That he [Harvey] made any contribution to the facts of the [blood circulation] case by vivisection is conclusively disproved . . . It is, moreover, perfectly clear that were it incumbent on anyone to prove the circulation of the blood as a new theme, it could not be done by any vivisectional process but could, at once, be satisfactorily established by a dead body and an injecting syringe.[18]

Harvey trained with an Italian physician named Hieronymus Fabricius of Aquapendente. Fabricius, by performing autopsies, had discovered that valves prevent blood from flowing away from the heart in veins. Fabricius then postulated that blood goes from the heart in arteries and returns via veins. Early on, Harvey actually placed a tourniquet around his own arm to establish on which side blood accumulated, and also injected water into a corpse's heart, forcing it from one side to another. The Church still censored human experimentation at the time. Publicly, Harvey claimed that the conclusions came from dissecting eighty different animals because he did not want to admit breaking an English law against experimentation on human corpses.[19,20]

Hence autopsies at last explained what we today consider a very basic phenomenon: Blood passes through the lungs to pick up oxygen. But regardless of how and why Harvey arrived at his conclusions, the truth is that it was, and is, possible to demonstrate the circulation of blood without using animals. Whether or not Harvey used animals does not mean that they were *necessary*. Even a superficial dissection of the human circulatory system would reveal the basic concepts demonstrated by Harvey in his experiments. Morticians prove it every day as they embalm cadavers.

During this epoch, Giovanni Morgagni popularized the autopsy. This was, naturally, the ideal method for correlating physical abnormalities and diseases. Morgagni employed this method, with some success specifically related to heart, lung, and liver disease. His high position at the medical school in Padua influenced the next generation of great medical thinkers attending that institution. Morgagni is remembered for his seminal work in pathology.[21]

Autopsies were to reveal most of the facts that we today consider obvious or take for granted about the human body. "For over a century, starting in the late 1700s, the autopsy occupied center stage in scientific medicine. Modern concepts of disease and health were developed from a rich harvest of observations collected from autopsies. Thousands of diseases were identified, treatments developed, and therapeutic misadventures corrected."[22]

Soon after Morgagni, in the late-eighteenth century, Marie François Xavier Bichat postulated that cancer was an overgrowth of tissue instead of inflammation.[23] It had taken sixteen centuries to reverse Galen's original concept of humor invasions. Bichat discovered that different organs have discrepant textures and are composed of different tissues. Postulating that specific diseases attack specific tissues, he advocated study of the function and constitution of normal and diseased tissues. These fields of observation are known as *pathology* and *histology*. This revolutionary thought was based on his autopsy experience. Ironically, even though Bichat himself was distrustful of the microscope, his findings pointed to the exigency for microscopic observation.

By the 1800s, the autopsy was thought indispensable to the practice and advancement of medicine.

What were the achievements that assured such an important place for the autopsy? Among them were thousands of diseases discovered and described, numerous classifications of lesions, countless associations between disease states and anatomic abnormalities, and innumerable ideas for medical and surgical treatment. A bare listing of these findings would comprise a virtual encyclopedia of medicine ... *Virtually the whole of modern medical knowledge was created through the study of autopsies.*[24] (Emphasis added.)

Medical science seemed to be moving out from under Galen's shadow at last. Then, tragically, history repeated itself.

Removing Humans from Human Medical Research

In the mid-nineteenth century, a French physiologist emerged to disturb the steady growth of medical revelation. His name was Claude Bernard. Bernard had turned to medical school only after failing as a playwright. A mediocre student, he obtained a position in a physiology lab. In as outrageous an act of recidivism as has ever occurred in the history of medicine, Bernard reinstigated animal experimentation. His energies turned vivisection into first a vehicle of elitism, then inevitably into establishment. Bernard succeeded in persuading the scientific community that if any disease could not be reproduced on animals in the laboratory, it simply did not exist—despite accumulated clinical (human) data to the contrary. Quite suddenly, lab research on animals was all the rage. The scientific community came to feel its methods were erudite, and even preferable to observation of humans. And, with abundant animals, it also made doing science more convenient. How did this happen?

In 1865 Bernard published *Introduction to the Study of Experimental Medicine*. In it he described the laboratory as the "true sanctuary of medical science."[25] He extolled laboratories, not bedsides, as offering the greatest insights into medicine and professed that lab animal experiments could do far more to heal sick patients than clinical observation:

I consider hospitals only as the entrance to scientific medicine; they are the first field of observation which a physician enters; but the true sanctuary of medical science is a laboratory; only there will he seek explanations of life in the normal and pathological states by means of experimental analysis. In leaving the hospital, a physician . . . must go on into his laboratory; and there, by experiments on animals, he will account for what he has observed in his patients, whether about the actions of drugs or about the origin of morbid lesions in organs and tissues. There, in a word, he will achieve true medical science . . . Experiments on animals, with deleterious substances or in harmful circumstances, are very useful and *entirely conclusive* for the toxicity and hygiene of man. Investigations of medicinal or of toxic substances also are *wholly applicable* to man from the therapeutic point of view; for as I have shown, the effects of these substances are the same on man as on animals, save for difference in degree. (Emphasis added.)[26]

He and his colleagues also explained why the animal experimenter is above compassion, in tones not unlike H. G. Wells's megalomaniacal Doctor Moreau,

The physiologist is not an ordinary man: He is a scientist, possessed and absorbed by the scientific idea he pursues. He does not hear the cries of animals, he does not see their flowing blood, he sees nothing but his idea, and is aware of nothing but an organism that conceals from him the problem he is seeking to solve.[27]

A pupil of Bernard's, Elie de Cyon, echoed his mentor's sentiment,

The true vivisector must approach a difficult vivisection with the same joyful excitement and the same delight wherewith a surgeon undertakes a difficult operation . . . He who shrinks from cutting into a living animal . . . will never become an artist in vivisection.[28]

Not exactly attitudes that foster compassion. Not surprisingly, Bernard also thought experimentation on humans was not immoral.[29] He occasionally performed his experiments at his home, even purloining the family pet. His wife and daughter were so appalled by his methods that they founded a humane society. They set up a home for stray dogs and scoured the streets, hoping to intercept lost dogs before Bernard did.[30]

The female Bernards were not alone in their horror. One of Bernard's students, Dr. George Hoggan, was one of the founders of the first antivivisection society in England in 1875, the Victorian Street Society. He wrote,

We sacrificed daily from one to three dogs, besides rabbits and other animals, and after four years experience I am of the opinion that not one of these experiments on animals was justified or necessary. The idea of the good of humanity was simply out of the question, and would be laughed at, the great aim being to keep up with, or get ahead of, one's contemporaries in science even at the price of an incalculable amount of torture needlessly and iniquitously inflicted on the poor animals.[31]

Recognizing that animal experimentation, though macabre and invalid, already had peer respect, Hoggan stated that no medical student or physician would dare challenge the vivisectors. They feared that they would be expelled from their profession and unable to earn a livelihood.

Hence, just as medicine was showing signs of recovering from deceptions sown by Galen's animal-based inaccuracies, Bernard snapped a lid on progress. Bernard and the socioeconomic conditions that proliferated because of the Industrial Revolution reinstated Galen's erroneous methods, and they still persist today.

To understand how animal experimentation again took hold, despite its many drawbacks, it is perhaps important to examine the philosophical mood of the times. Contrary to the open, expansionary sentiment of Renaissance Italy, a stricter and more conservative disposition permeated Europe and America during the Victorian age. Based on Bernard's precedent, would-be scientists understood that animal experimentation could provide both money and reputation. Those who lacked talent in a clinical setting could turn to lab investigations for income.

Philosophies surfaced to reinforce a logic for mining nonhumans for human insights. There were those who admitted animal experimentation did no good but pursued it because their preeminence as humans put them above the common laws of morality. Professor Leon Le Fort, head of the Faculté de Medicine in Paris explained thus,

Speaking for myself and my brethren of the faculté, I do not mean to say that we claim for that method of investigation [vivisection] that it has been of any practical utility to medical science, or that we expect it to be so. But it is necessary as a protest on behalf of the independence of science against interference by the clerics and moralists. When all the world has reached the high intellectual level of France, and no longer believes in God, the soul, moral responsibility, or in any nonsense of that kind, but makes practical utility the only rule of conduct, then, and not till then, can science afford to dispense with vivisection.[32]

First published in 1859, Darwin's *On the Origin of Species* shook the world. It sparked vehement dissent from religious groups and from scientists who struggled to squash its revelations into an interpretation that validated their thinking. According to Darwin's *actual* theory of natural selection, humans are not the perfect culmination of God's work. There is no slow upward progression of species leading to *Homo sapiens*. Humans are not the paragon. Rather, evolution is about mutation and adaptation. Therefore, other species are equally ideal, equally successful *other* animals. It is plain now that Darwin's theory accounted for the failures of animal experimentation. That animals are not defective first drafts of humans makes them unlikely test beds for human medicine.

At the time, however, Darwin was widely misinterpreted. People grappled with his findings, trying to match them to prevailing sentiment and scientific activity. The Church, interpretations of the Bible, and indeed most humans clung doggedly to their anthropocentrism and the idea of our dominion over nature. High thinkers even went so far as to exume the works of French biologist Jean Baptiste Lamarck, ignored in his time nearly a century before, because they supplied a more pleasant interpretation of evolution.

Lamarck's less troubling philosophy arranged God's creatures hierarchically. He had written that evolution was like a tree, each branch more advanced than the one below it. Dogs, cats, goats, whales, apes, and so on—all were nature's failed attempts to produce man. Whereas Darwin proved that speciation is not a tree, but an intensely complicated bush that never ceases to grow, Lamarckism kept man at the pinnacle. For God-fearing scientists, Lamarck's theory was a lot more reassuring.

Bernard, for his part, rejected evolution altogether and remained a creationist. His experiments were predicated on the assumption that animals were below humans but similar enough to draw data from. He overlooked that nature fashioned each species differently. Not surprisingly, these differences account for many of the research failures covered in this book, all of which took place after Bernard.

Researchers continued to use animals in their attempts to get to the bottom of human physiology and disease. As the Industrial Revolution dawned, animal experimentation labs tooled up as its medical research manifestation.

Senselessly, human clinical observation took a back seat to lab work with animals. Since Bernard's time, patient observation has been considered strictly anecdotal until confirmed on animals in the lab. Recognize that the word "anecdotal" has a negative connotation among scientists. It refers to unusual occurrences, generally observed in a clinical setting and carefully described. Even today, applying the adjective "anecdotal" derogates observations that have not been repeated in a laboratory. From the outside, we can see how preposterous this is. We can agree that actual medical problems and effective therapies in humans are meaningful, whether or not they can be perpetrated on another batch of mammals.

Nevertheless, Bernard held that those seeking the cause of life or the essence of disease through humans were "pursuing a phantom." He said,

"The words life, death, health, disease, have no objective reality."[33] Rather startling didactic for a medical professional.

It is not disease that is the phantom. It is animal-model data in transit to human application. During this forced voyage from laboratory cage to *Homo sapiens*, the data dies. It loses its substance. Scientists grab at this specter trying to mine it for worth against cancer, against heart disease, against degenerative disease, against mental illness. Always it is elusive.

The Tenacious Mistake

No matter how elusive the comparison, no matter how unsound the practice, the phantoms of animal experimentation proliferated, seeping into every branch of medicine and haunting every human-based finding. Apparent progress based on animal experimentation reinforced the efficacy of the lab protocol, as it still does. That the progress later proved to be no progress at all did not however stem the trend. (This happens all the time today. When a therapy proves effective in mice, it is front page news. Television specials. Public radio interviews. When, a few months later, the therapy proves induplicable, it is a news footnote, an after-mention, unnoticed by the public at large.)

In the nineteenth century, respected scientists, chief among them Louis Pasteur and Robert Koch, lent credibility to the animal experimentation convention when their vivisection work resulted in ostensible discovery. In reality, animal experimentation actually misled their investigations, most notably in the field of virology, as Koch later emphasized.

Pasteur, who was actually a chemist and not a physician, made three great contributions to medicine—sterilization, pasteurization, and the germ theory of disease. None relied on animals.

Most people of the mid-nineteenth century believed that deadly diseases occurred as a result of *spontaneous generation*—that is, the diseases sprang from nowhere. Questioning why wine goes bad, Pasteur found that living organisms, yeasts, occupied the wine. The wine deteriorated if the yeast was not killed prior to storage. This discovery led to further study and the suggestion that humans were as susceptible as wine to tiny infectious organisms. Pasteur used his influence to convince physicians to sterilize their surgical instruments and work in a cleaner environment.

Based on observation and thought, not research on animals, Pasteur formed a fresh tenet to replace spontaneous generation, which he called the *germ theory of disease*. He postulated that disease was communicable because of small living organisms spread from person to person by contact. Today, we immediately accept this. But in Pasteur's epoch, the idea that tiny organisms could kill large mammals was incredible.

Pasteur's substantial evidence and his own eloquence ultimately convinced his peers.

Many call the germ theory of disease the greatest single contribution to medicine ever. The importance of Pasteur's finding to our discussion is this: The germ theory forced people to recognize imperceptible influences, influences smaller than the gross similarities we share with animals. Recognition of this aspect is essential to understanding the inadequacies of animal experimentation.

There was an essential flaw in Pasteur's earliest assessments. He believed that all species could become ill from the same microbe. As we now know, and as Pasteur may have eventually deduced, those who do become ill do not necessarily become ill in the same way. Not yet realizing this, Pasteur used animals as pseudo-humans as he attempted to craft a rabies vaccine. He took spinal column tissue of infected dogs and made what he thought was a vaccine. Unfortunately, the vaccine did not work seamlessly and actually resulted in deaths. Yet, this gross failure somehow did not detract from reverence for the animal-lab process.[34] In truth, the only successful animal experimentation Pasteur did was for the benefit of animals. He studied anthrax in ungulates and cholera in chickens and found vaccines to prevent them.[35]

Robert Koch, another esteemed bacteriologist of the day, reinforced Pasteur's germ theory. Koch extolled six assumptions, which came to be known as "Koch's postulates." He stated that these six criteria must be met to implicate a specific pathogen as causing a particular disease:

- The organism must be present in every case of the disease.
- The organism should not be present in other diseases.
- The organism should be isolated from a sick individual.
- The organism should be purifiable.
- The organism should induce the same disease when inoculated into an animal.
- The animal should be able to pass on the organism to other animals via a culture medium.[36,37,38]

Initially, Koch demonstrated his postulates by isolating *Bacillus anthracis*, the causative agent for anthrax, a fatal disease of cattle. This was the first isolation of bacteria ever. Koch isolated it in mice. When Pasteur went on to vaccinate sheep with a weakened form of the bacteria successfully, it did certainly suggest the efficacy of Koch's postulates. There, however, felicitous parallels ceased. Koch's own subsequent work ultimately proved that not only were animal experiments unnecessary, but that they could be quite misleading.

In the 1870s, Koch isolated *Mycoplasma tuberculosis*, the causative agent for tuberculosis, then a horrific scourge on the scale of cancer or AIDS today. He used samples from human tissue for tuberculosis and for cholera, to which he then turned his attention.[39,40,41] Koch traveled to India in his capacity as the head of the German Cholera Commission. In 1884, he reported on the progress of experiments on fifty white mice,

> Although these experiments were constantly repeated with material from fresh cholera cases, our mice remained healthy. We then made experiments on monkeys, cats, poultry, dogs and various other animals that we were able to get a hold of, but we never were able to arrive at anything in animals similar to the cholera process.[42]

Eventually, Koch put away the mice and discovered the causative organism by using a microscope and examining material from human victims of the disease. He was also able, through epidemiological methods, to identify how the disease was transmitted in contaminated water, on eating utensils and so on. Ultimately, Koch concluded,

> Should it prove possible later on to produce anything similar to cholera in animals, that would not, for me, prove anything more than the facts which we now have before us. Besides, we know of other diseases which cannot be transferred to animals, e.g., leprosy, and yet we must admit, from all we know of leprosy bacilli, that they are the cause of the disease . . . We must be satisfied that we verify the constant presence of a particular kind of bacteria in the disease in question and the absence of the same bacteria in other diseases.[43]

The same sort of realization, though even more of a jolt, issued from Koch's tuberculosis work. Attempting, over time, to develop a vaccine against tuberculosis based on animals, Koch had injected *tubercle bacillus* into frogs, turtles, mice, guinea pigs, and monkeys. The bacterium killed the frogs and turtles; however Koch was ultimately able to cultivate a vaccine from mice.[44]

Hopeful tuberculosis sufferers flocked to Berlin to participate in Koch's new "cure." Disaster struck. The human trials of Koch's vaccine were ruinous because in humans the disease takes a different form.[45] In fortunate patients, the mouse-modeled vaccine simply did not work. In other previously recovered patients, the vaccine caused the disease to flare up.[46,47,48] Scientists acknowledged,

> Tuberculosis in human beings and tuberculosis in animals *are distinctly different*, although caused by the same microorganism. The disease in animals is relatively simple in character, and fairly predictable in its course, whereas in the human being it is far more complex; so one must not assume that a drug that is effective in the laboratory animal will be equally effective in man.[49] (Emphasis added.)

Clearly, two of Koch's postulates, the ones involving animals, were erroneous. Personally witnessing the amount of havoc they could produce, Koch retracted them. His experience proved that when a known disease-causing organism or pathogen, is injected into animals, the response it elicits depends on the species. Other deadly diseases in humans cause no illness whatsoever when injected into animals. Even then *The Lancet* published, "Thus we can not rely on Koch's postulates as a decisive test of a causal organism."[50]

Not long before he passed away, Koch himself wrote: "An experiment on an animal gives no certain indication of the result of the same experiment on a human being."[51] Despite Koch's recantation, scientists clung stubbornly to the animal model.[52] Though Koch's two postulates regarding animals are inaccurate, *and Koch himself disclaimed them*, all six postulates are part of every high school biology curriculum and every modern student of bacteriology still memorizes them. Few medical students are advised of Dr. Koch's own disclaimers.

As indicated, animal experimentation played havoc with vaccine development. The animal-model protocol was also demonstrating its drawbacks in other areas of research. Nonetheless, proponents of animal experimentation regularly distort historical accounts of Pasteur and Koch's work to suggest that their discoveries did issue from the animal lab.

Despite what was fast becoming the "machine of animal experimentation," clinical observation and autopsies abided as the most important methods for true discovery. Not surprisingly, the great advances came about in spite of lab animals, not because of them. Whenever a discovery occurred, researchers dispatched to the lab to "validate" it. The animal assay became a sort of automatic response to any suggested medical achievement. If vivisectionists could not validate the achievement, then their so-called science invalidated the finding, clinical evidence to the contrary.

Examining the history of early endocrine investigation exposes the absurdity and danger of this animal experimentation part of the sequence. Physicians used to believe that the proper functioning of organs was entirely dependent on the nervous system. The discovery of the endocrine system proved that this was too simplistic. Our endocrine glands produce a variety of hormones. Hormones travel throughout the body like messengers, acting to regulate the functions of other organs. For instance, clinical observation led to the discovery that the pituitary gland was involved in abnormalities involving the sex glands.[53]

The adrenal glands are located on top of the kidney. They are a component of the endocrine system. The adrenal glands secrete a number of hormones including steroids and adrenaline, also known as *epinephrine*. In 1855, Thomas Addison described five patients in whom tuberculosis had invaded and crippled the adrenal glands. After the human findings were known, researchers hastened to the lab to remove animals' adrenal glands. However, they were unable to reproduce the same symptoms. Unfortunately, this failure in what Bernard had called the "true sanctuary of science" stuck, effectively negating Addison's clinical observations. For thirty years, Addison's disease was ignored. Not until 1882, did James F. Goodhart associate adrenal atrophy with the symptoms Addison had described.

Since Addison was the first to describe its symptoms, Addison's disease now bears his name. We now know that Addison's disease occurs when human adrenal glands are not able to produce specific hormones required to regulate our electrolytes—potassium, sodium, and other similar elements. It is life threatening, causing vomiting, diarrhea, and ultimately death from heartbeat irregularities.

In 1893, a physician named George W. Oliver tested adrenal secretions on his son. He described a decreased diameter of the radial artery accompanied by increased blood pressure. As we know, adrenaline prepares us for "fight or flight." It increases blood pressure and decreases the lumen of arteries, thus diminishing the amount of blood going through them. This is why people with heart disease experience chest pain or angina if they are suddenly frightened. Take note: This was discovered in a human.

What do animal-experiment advocates remember? This: Oliver then went to physiologist Edward A. Shafer's lab and "validated" on dogs the results he had seen on his son. Although the role of the adrenal glands was based on clinical observation from start to finish, and although animals only reproduced data already known, many sources still credit Shafer's animal experiments with revealing the role of the adrenals. Once again animal experiments were counted more valuable than human observation.[54-63]

The female reproductive organs, the ovaries, are also a part of the endocrine system. Dr. Robert T. Morris demonstrated ovarian function in a surgical procedure on women in 1895. A researcher named Emil Knauer reproduced the procedure in rabbits in 1896. Whom does history credit? Knauer, in yet another example of clinical observation and discovery falsely attributed to a lab-animal scientist.[64-67]

The predilection for experimental zoology was so strong around the turn of the century that animal experimenters actually held more sway than physicians in the medical community. Not just these scientists, but many scientists of the epoch piggybacked on knowledge that had been documented in humans much earlier.

Gastric physiology, the study of digestion, is another case in point. As long ago as 1833, U.S. Army surgeon and physiologist William Beaumont had the good fortune to observe gastric activity inside a patient named Alexis St. Martin, the recipient of a shotgun blast to the abdomen. Most would have died as a result of this trauma, but St. Martin lived to the age of 82, with a large hole in his belly. Through this hole,

Beaumont made detailed observations, describing gastric motility, gastric juice composition, and influences over the secretion of gastric juice in humans. Claude Bernard, upon hearing of this work, proceeded to "validate" it in animals.[68]

Another of Beaumont's subjects, known as "Tom," had eaten some very hot food as a child and suffered from a very tight stricture in his esophagus. This too allowed Beaumont to observe numerous functions of the GI tract.[69,70] Beaumont passed away in 1853.

Over fifty years later, Ivan Pavlov, the Russian physiologist, received the 1904 Nobel Prize following the publication of his articles about the enervation to the stomach and other mechanisms of gastric function. Pavlov observed animals' digestive systems, even though Beaumont had already observed and documented these revelations in humans many decades before.

Observations of Beaumont's subject, "Tom," eventually led A. J. Carlson to conceive of a new surgical procedure. By placing balloons into the esophagus of patients with strictures, he was able to dilate the esophagus, thus allowing the patient to swallow normally. This procedure is still performed today. Carlson first experimented on animals like most researchers of his day. But the experimentation could have been avoided without any risk to his patients, thanks to Beaumont's work. Animal experiments conducted since then have been entirely unnecessary since, unfortunately, accident victims like Tom and St. Martin abound.

While Pavlov was exacerbating his dogs' stomachs, a truly accurate description of gastric physiology issued from Walter Canon. In the early-twentieth century, Canon developed the technique of radiographing a patient after the patient had swallowed radio-opaque substances, thus outlining the esophagus and stomach. He described various physiologic changes in the GI tract based on this technique. Neither the development of this technique nor the experiments that followed necessitated animals. Canon did perform some experiments on animals but only to "validate" human data.[71]

Window to the Microcosms

Even though animal experimentation presented a persistent impediment, medical progress pushed on, thanks to contributions like Canon's. The bulk of this technological ingenuity we cover in later chapters. It is important at this juncture, however, to discuss one critical leap toward our understanding of living systems, and that is the advent of the microscope. Magnification produced a medical revolution. The ability to see cells and even cell components rendered reliance on the animal model even more ridiculous. Finally, scientists could acquire hard data in regard to complicated human cell function and directly observe how it reacted to disease and therapies. We no longer had any reason at all for applying disease and therapies to nonhumans for purposes of divining human outcome.

Curved surfaces were recognized as having optical properties as long ago as 300 B.C.E. People had been examining items under actual magnifying lenses since the fourteenth century, with better resolution all the time. In the productive atmosphere of renaissance Italy, Marcello Malpighi, invented the first real microscope in 1650. And just a few years later, in 1665, the English scientist Robert Hooke published his *Micrographia,* the first textbook of microscopy. Based on his observations of cork, Hooke described dead cells. This was landmark work. Shortly thereafter, the Dutch scientist Anton van Leeuwenhoek published a paper, identifying living cells in detail. Without the aid of animal experiments, he described bacteria and spermatozoa.

After this first flush of discovery, progress slowed. Acceptance of a cell theory was delayed because researchers, in typical fashion, at once tried to identify cell components using animal tissue. They used chick embryo sac cells since these are translucent. (Until techniques for processing tissues for microscopic examination were developed, translucency was desirable.) These atypical cells do not have a cell wall or membrane, and the cells were therefore difficult to distinguish. Using human tissue from surgery and autopsy might have prevented these and other errors based on animal cells.

The watershed invention was the modern microscope, built by J. J. Lister, the son of the famous British physician, Baron Joseph Lister, in 1828. The younger Lister's invention of a true magnifying device led directly to the cell theory upon which modern biology and medicine is based. Finally, researchers were able to confirm the existence of cells because they could observe the cell walls of plants. Plants, not animals provided the material for the confirmation. Though Lamarck and others had written that life depended on cellular tissue, German botanist Matthias Schleiden and German zoologist Theodor Schwann formulated the cell theory with particular clarity in 1839. Seeing underlying structural similarities between plant and animal cells, they stated that all living organisms consist of cells and are capable of reproducing themselves. The obvious upshot of the cell theory is this: Whole organisms can be understood through the study of their cellular parts. This revelation is of tremendous importance to medical discovery, and also to our argument discrediting animal experimentation. It also bears repeating that the cell theory would very likely have been realized much earlier if investigators had used human tissue from autopsies.

More comprehensive evidence regarding cell composition and cell function followed. It was one hundred years after Bichat identified gross discrepancies between body tissues. A German pathologist, Rudolf Virchow, expanded on this idea in 1858, introducing his theory that all cells come from preexisting cells. In his description of leukemia, it became apparent that diseases occur on a cellular level. Thus, Virchow demonstrated that the cell theory applies to diseased tissue as well as to healthy tissue—that is, that diseased cells derive from the healthy cells of normal tissue. He concluded that only by studying tissue under the microscope could we correctly deduce our nature. Virchow's contributions ushered in modern medicine.

Virchow's ideas led directly to knowledge of cell division and cell differentiation. Peering into a microscope, scientists saw in broadening detail the many differences between human cells and the cells of other species. It was clear that though all cells—plant and animal—have characteristics in common, the cells of each species are distinct and they demonstrate different susceptibility to diseases. They are not identical when healthy. The diseases that assault them are not the same, and even when they are similar, they assault them differently. Sir William Osler, a physician and educator of tremendous influence who had studied under Virchow, carried the illuminations of human cell research forward toward the twentieth century.

One can understand how this knowledge undermined any apparent relevance of animal experimentation. Watching cells under a microscope, scientists implicitly grasped that medicine had advanced beyond drawing parallels between all creatures with four-chambered hearts. Now, they had evidence that not all four-chambered hearts are alike. They could clearly see that human heart tissue cells react differently to medications and diseases from cells of a pig's heart or a chimpanzee's heart.

In the late-nineteenth century, Hans Gram, Paul Ehrlich, and Robert Koch used tissue samples from humans to develop dyes and techniques for selectively staining cell parts. Employing the stains, scientists refined their detection of tiny cell structures and their diagnoses of diseases. Again using human tissue, Ehrlich discovered a new white blood cell, the mast cell, while using the new dyes. The mast cell is involved with allergic reactions.[72,73,74] With increasing amplification, and more technology, scientists were to learn more and more about the ways we differ from animals and even each other.

Throughout history and today, please observe the same pattern: each new development brings better methods for more detailed observations. And with each method the merit of animal experimentation diminishes. With expanding medical ingenuity, similarities between humans and animals fade, becoming less significant, while remaining differences between humans and animals become even more important.

In other words, even on the gross level (the visible level) there are differences between species. On the cellular and molecular levels these differences are magnified exponentially. For example, there are few visible differences in the way blood gets around in mammals. Blood circulates in horses as it circulates in pigs as it circulates in humans. But for scientists hoping to elucidate something as precise as human coronary-artery disease, plumbing animals for knowledge is an exercise in frustration. Likewise, there is a vast difference in recognizing that the pancreas is involved in metabolism in all mammals and stating that pancreatic cancer in a mouse is the same as pancreatic cancer in a human. The comparisons just have not held up, as we describe throughout this book.

Millions of variables skew results *even within the human species.* Is the patient male or female? How old was the patient when afflicted? What sort of lifestyle supports or undermines the patient's health? Does the patient have any concurrent illnesses? Are other medications taken that impact the course of the disease? Does the illness run in the family? Some scientists have remarked that the only accurate model of your illness and its most effective therapy is *you.*

Most humans are sufficiently similar that if penicillin cures my skin infection, it will probably cure yours, too. Yet, there are exceptions even to this. What if your skin infection is due to a virus, whereas mine was bacterial or fungal or parasitic? What if you are allergic to penicillin? There are also differences in the disease itself as it manifests in different people.

Race and gender, too, influence susceptibility to disease and receptivity to therapies. Some races are more vulnerable than others to high-blood pressure. People with light-colored skin are more prone to certain types of skin cancer than people with dark skin. Men and women react differently to pain medications. Pain medications that work on kappa receptors (central nervous system tissue that helps fight pain) work better in women. Why? Researchers believe it is because testosterone, found in greater quantity in men, inhibits pain medications that act on kappa receptors. Women normally have lower hemoglobins, probably because of menstruation. This protects them from iron-induced myocardial damage, a predisposing factor for heart attack. Men and women have different reactions to selective serotonin re-uptake inhibitors, such as Prozac. Women are much more likely to experience sexual dysfunction than are men. Very few non-Jewish people suffer from Tay-Sach's disease. Sarcoidosis is much more prevalent in black people than white people. So is gastric cancer. Very few non-black people suffer from sickle cell anemia.

Differences such as these proliferate. The need to learn all these differences accounts, in large part, for the long duration of medical training. People are different from each other. If each person responds differently to illness and medication, imagine the variability of animals in regard to people. Multiply these complications by a million when you try to extrapolate information from one species to another.

Yet, people still believe that we should use animals as models, particularly primates, because of their genetic material's proximity to our own. This common argument in favor of vivisection is actually very flawed.

To explain, chromosomes bear the basic units of heredity, called *genes*. These genes are passed down from generation to generation, and they also govern day-to-day function of living and reproducing cells. The essential genetic material is DNA, or deoxyribonucleic acid. Eighty-four percent of the DNA in New World monkeys and humans is the same. Most scientists agree that between 97 and 99 percent of our DNA is the same as the great apes. This sounds good. But further inspection reveals the inadequacy of the argument.

What the animal experimenters fail to mention is twofold. First, remember how physicians used to believe that the nervous system alone governed the smooth functioning of our organs until they discovered the important and more complex role of the endocrine system? When there is a major leap in our understanding that reveals increased complexity of systems, it tends to diminish the role of simplistic former explanations.

We now know that proximity in DNA is only a small part of the picture, leaving unexplored the vast infinitesimal spectrum of *base-pair sequences*. The DNA of humans is composed of billions and billions of base pairs, about which we have known very little until recently. *It is not the number of pairs in common that are important but rather the specific pairs and sequences of the ones that are not.* The specific pairs and sequences are what makes you a human and Fido a dog. The base pairs tell the body to form amino acids, which are the building blocks of the body.

To give an idea of how complex this is, look at one important enzyme, cytochrome-C. It is composed of 104 amino acids in a very specific sequence. Monkeys have the same cytochrome-C sequence as humans except for one amino acid. There are twelve differences between humans and horses and 22 differences between humans and fish. The fact that only one amino acid is different in monkeys means that we are more similar to them than we are to fish. It does not negate the fact that monkeys are different from humans. It is very, very small changes like this in our DNA that separate the various animal species. Very small differences on the DNA level translate into very large differences between species and even within species. (For example, one change in the DNA base sequence at a particular gene results in sickle cell anemia. Just one change. The same is true for cystic fibrosis.)

Moreover, approximately 97 percent of our DNA is unaccounted for in terms of function. So, the DNA argument in favor of animal experimentation is highly misleading. It is like saying, "we are all alike except where we are different." It is these differences that make the results of the study of animals inapplicable to humans.

Animal experimentation overwhelms our view of tiny degrees such as base-pair sequences. Coming chapters disclose how often and at what cost it has persuaded researchers into circuitous and dangerous detours that seem never to lead to viable human application. We also explore the technology and alternative-research methods that have moved our knowledge along, in spite of using animal models.

chapter 3

Legislated Ineptitude

There is no doubt that the best test species for man is man. This is based on the fact that it is not possible to extrapolate animal data directly to man, due to interspecies variation in anatomy, physiology and biochemistry.

—Dr. MacLennan and Dr. Amos, Clinical Sciences Research Ltd., UK, *Cosmetics and Toiletries Manufacturers and Suppliers,* 1990; XVII:24

Twisted Reason in the Drug Development Process

Swept along by interplay between arrogance, ignorance, fear, and greed, like most senseless conventions, the protocol requiring animal testing all but established itself. It moved of its own momentum for a while, was eventually systematized, and then finally congressionally mandated.

As described, the scientific atmosphere of the early-twentieth century was already infatuated with the benefits of animal experimentation—the control, the immediacy, the prestige, the money—thanks to Claude Bernard and others. Then, a single episode, in 1937, effectively routinized animal testing for medications in the United States. In 1937, people received elixir of sulfanilamide, a new sulfa drug antibiotic dissolved in *diethylene glycol,* a chemical similar to antifreeze. One hundred and seven people died, most of them children.[1] Scientists administered the medicine to animals and they too died. This single occasion of parity convinced the scientific community that animals should henceforward be used for testing all medications. That *diethylene glycol* just happened, coincidentally, to be fatal to humans and other creatures, could not possibly prove that *all* chemicals react the same in all species. Nevertheless, that erroneous conclusion prevailed.

Even in the thirties, however, there was some scientific dissent. In a publication of that epoch, a physician stated, ". . . the results of drug experiments upon animals are, as far as their application to man is concerned, absolutely useless and even misleading."[2]

In 1938, Congress passed the Food, Drug, and Cosmetics Act, demanding that drug manufacturers provide proof that their medications were safe. Congress bestowed responsibility for overseeing the act to the Food and Drug Administration, a division of the Department of Health and Human Services.

Then World War II broke out. New drugs proliferated as the government hastened medications through the manufacturing process and out into the war zones. The urgency for antibiotics and vaccines gripped the engine of pharmaceutical development and spun it furiously. It became a perpetual motion machine.

Pharmaceutical companies grasped at any and every substance, natural or synthetic, which even hinted of a marketable therapeutic effect, then tried it out on animals. When lab animals did not manifest ill side-effects or die, drug companies jammed the substances through human trials, most of which were too abbreviated to provide substantial data in regard to possible side effects. In an effort to maximize their profits from these often jury-rigged medications, pharmaceutical companies patented them. With a patented monopoly of seventeen years, they could continue selling the therapies at high prices.

Up until this time, people had been largely self-medicating, purchasing medicines from the corner pharmacy either on their own or at the family doctor's suggestion. The advent of these new alleged cures meant that the friendly neighborhood pharmacist was no longer mixing up a few milligrams of assorted compounds in his mortar. Pharmaceutical companies created their own cures and then scurried to establish confidence in their products from physicians. Through heavy marketing, complimentary leather bags, *Merck Manuals*, even free trips and ample samples, drug companies made sure the medical world heard of and used their products.

In 1951, legislation introduced by then-Senator Hubert Humphrey who had been a pharmacist, mandated that most drugs would require prescriptions. This event strengthened the symbiosis between physicians and drug companies. Patients were more reliant than ever on their physicians. Physicians could make more money. By helping physicians earn more money, pharmaceutical companies got richer. Theirs became a moneymaking symbiosis of which the patient was both beneficiary and victim.

The Thalidomide Years

As the fifties wore on, alarming side effects from these supposed miracle cures began to emerge. Probably the most notorious of all tragic side effect stories is that of thalidomide, a drug intended to ameliorate morning sickness that was also—as an antispasmodic, antihistamine, and sedative—a component in cough syrup and analgesics of the time.

A German pediatrician named Widikund Lenz was the first to suggest a link between thalidomide and teratogenesis. ("Teratogenesis" comes from the Greek word *teras*, meaning malformation or monstrosity. Teratogenesis is the chemical induction of malformation in a developing fetus, and in the case of thalidomide the birth defect was phocomelia. Chemicals that produce birth defects are "teratogenic.") Mothers who had taken thalidomide gave birth to babies with often shocking deformities. Most lacked developed limbs. The first recorded case of phocomelia secondary to thalidomide occurred on Christmas Day, 1956, but in 1957 the drug was released anyway.[3] A clinician from Australia, W. G. McBride, confirmed thalidomide's dangers. Alarmed, he, Lenz and others wrote letters to the distinguished medical publication, *The Lancet*, reporting phocomelia in infants of mothers taking thalidomide.[4]

As the incidences of deformity increased, scientists frantically attempted to reproduce teratogenesis from thalidomide in animals of all varieties. They gave thalidomide to scores of animals looking for proof in animals of what they already *knew* occurred in humans—that thalidomide could cross the placenta and drastically damage unborn offspring—and they could find none. Since animal testing had not indicated a problem with thalidomide, its use persisted. Hence, animal testing delayed the recall of this highly teratogenic drug.

Finally, one breed of rabbit, the White New Zealand rabbit, was affected, and then only at a dose between 25 to 300 times that given to humans. Eventually some monkeys gave birth to hideously deformed offspring too, but it took ten times the normal dose to make this happen.[5,6,7] Two scientists summarized the thalidomide testing as follows:

An unexpected finding was that the mouse and rat were resistant, the rabbit and hamster variably responsive, and certain strains of primates were sensitive to thalidomide developmental toxicity. Different strains of the same species of animals were also found to have highly variable sensitivity to thalidomide.[8]

Animal tests provided no real predictive value for any animal except the one being tested. Writing on chemically induced birth defects, James L. Schardein remarked,

In approximately 10 strains of rats, 15 strains of mice, 11 breeds of rabbits, 2 breeds of dogs, 3 strains of hamsters, 8 species of primates and in other such varied species as cats, armadillos, guinea pigs, swine and ferrets in which thalidomide has been tested, teratogenic effects have been induced only *occasionally*.[9] (Emphasis added.)

Schardein went on to write:

> It is the actual results of teratogenicity testing in primates which
> have been most disappointing in consideration of these animals'
> possible use as a predictive model. While some nine subhuman pri-
> mates (all but the bush baby) have demonstrated the characteristic
> limb defects observed in humans when administered thalidomide,
> the results with 83 other agents with which primates have been
> tested are less than perfect. Of the 15 listed putative human terat-
> ogens tested in non-human primates, only eight were also terato-
> genic in one or more of the various species . . . The data with respect
> to "suspect" or "likely" teratogens in humans under certain circum-
> stances were equally divergent. Three of the eight suspect teratogens
> were also not suspect in monkeys or did not induce some devel-
> opmental toxicity.[10]

Eighty-three agents, fifteen suspected human teratogens, nine monkey
species and data too divergent to draw from! While scientists quite literally monkeyed around, Dr. Lenz's assumption, which was based on
obvious and graphic epidemiological evidence in the form of hundreds
of babies born with flippers or no limbs at all, was largely ignored for
five more years. In that interval, until thalidomide was recalled in 1962,
over 10,000 additional children were born crippled.[11] By consistently
providing a false negative result, animal studies claimed an active role
in magnifying this tragedy.

The pro-animal testing contingency still maintains that thalidomide
was *not* tested on animals prior to its release. Two scientists, Jack H.
Botting and Adrian Morrison, so stated in a *Scientific American* article
supporting animal testing, February 1997: "Scientists never tested thalidomide in pregnant animals until after fetal deformities were observed
in humans." To the complacent reader this seems persuasive proof in
favor of testing drugs in animals. However, it is a gross misstatement.
Since animal testing was already the established protocol, Botting and
Morrison's claim is unlikely, even taken at face value. And according to
a German medical journal of the epoch, toxicity tests on animals were
conducted prior to thalidomide's release.[12] And some of these were conducted on pregnant rodents and phocomelia did not occur. It is controversial whether tests specific to teratogenicity were performed, though
data from Germany suggest they were.[13] Even *Time* magazine February
23, 1962, stated that thalidomide was released "after three years of animal tests."[14]

In any event, animal-modeled teratogenicity tests could never have
been conclusive. In which animal would scientists have put their store?
Mouse? Rabbit? Guinea pig? Primate? And in what dose? Further, administration of any drug to any species will at some juncture eventually

induce nonspecific birth defects. Any drug. These tests could not have provided the kind of results required. As one scientist stated,

> There is at present no hard evidence to show the value of more extensive and more prolonged laboratory testing as a method of reducing eventual risk in human patients. In other words the predictive value of studies carried out in animals is uncertain. The statutory bodies such as the Committee on Safety of Medicines which require these tests does so largely as *an act of faith* rather than on hard scientific grounds. With thalidomide, for example, it is only possible to produce specific deformities in a very small number of species of animals. In this particular case therefore, it is unlikely that specific tests in pregnant animals would have given the necessary warning: the right species would probably never have been used. Even more striking, the Practolol *adverse reactions have not been reproducible in any species except man.*[15] (Emphasis added.)

Only immense trial and error and enormous doses of thalidomide produced teratogenesis in isolated species. *As was scientifically demonstrated, no amount of animal-testing could have prevented the thalidomide disaster.* And it is a notable irony that the very lack of side effects in animals tested with thalidomide allowed thalidomide to make it to market in the first place and then stay there in the face of *human* studies.

Yet again, the obvious—why did they not use human tissue to predict human response? As is usually the case, research on human tissue *in vitro* could have averted the thalidomide disaster.[16] This incidence shows not the benefit of animal testing, but how animal testing sent treatments calamitously astray. It also illustrates the agility of those with a vested interest in animal experimentation, such as Botting and Morrison, for changing history to suit their agenda.

The Deadly Decree

The thalidomide disaster heightened paranoia regarding the drug industry. The paranoia was well founded, but the solution in America strayed from reason. Senator Estes Kefauver, who had already distinguished himself by pushing legislation against organized crime, shouldered a new cause with Senator Hubert Humphrey, namely to overhaul the Food, Drug, and Cosmetic Act. The FDA was badly in need of revision. Naturally, Kefauver was much opposed in his efforts by lobbyists from the pharmaceutical industry, which was not eager to have its profitability checked in any way. His legislation, the Kefauver-Harris Act, which would not be passed until 1961 during the thalidomide furor, demanded that medications be not only safe, but also effective—a much overdue directive. Unnecessarily and disastrously, it would also mandate animal testing. Dramatic, but ill-informed, the Kefauver-Harris Act seemed to declare, "Rodents, cats, dogs, primates . . . but not our children!"

Plenty of scientists were aware of obstacles in the animal model in the early sixties. Studies had already demonstrated that animal testing of new medications in no way accurately reflected human complications or efficacy. The prestigious scientific journal *The Lancet* published, "We must face the fact that the most careful tests of a new drug's effects on animals may tell us little of its effect in humans."[17]

This sentiment was echoed frequently in coming months.[18] In one study of the time, scientists compared known side effects of six drugs in rats, dogs and humans. The study restricted observations to *visible* side-effects. Side effects such as headaches, which are difficult to identify in animals, were not included. Of the 78 adverse side effects seen in humans, only 36 or 46 percent of these were reported in the animals, approximately the same results as one would expect from flipping a coin.[19] This was not news to pharmacologists, who were aware of the lack of parity since the birth of pharmacology.[20]

By mandating animal testing, Kefauver-Harris made it possible for drug companies to continue their slovenly development processes; as long as their compounds passed through plenty of lab animals, they could claim due diligence.

Animal testing persisted and still persists because it provides a legal sanctuary for pharmaceutical companies. In fact, it is itself fundamentally malpractice. There is *always* less than a fifty-fifty chance that a medication tested on animals will provide the same results in humans . . . usually *much less*. This is not science. It is expensive and dangerous gambling.

Insulin, the Animal Experimenters' "Poster Drug"

Achievements in administering to diabetics provided another boost to the animal testing protocol during the first half of the last century. Pro-animal experiment contingencies hailed the advent of animal insulin, as a diabetic treatment, as support for continued lab animal study.

Certainly, animals have figured largely in the history of diabetic research and therapy. Again, however, there are profound holes in the assumption that animal experimentation was necessary. A discussion of this interlude provides another example of how a rush to commercialize compromised human lives and confounded the path to medical breakthrough.

Diabetes is a very serious disease. Even today it affects ten to fourteen million Americans. It is a leading cause of blindness, amputation, kidney failure, and premature death. Much remains mysterious about diabetes, but what is understood is that it impairs delivery of the body's main fuel, glucose. Our digestive system breaks down food into glucose, a simple sugar. Normally, the hormone insulin (a protein composed of 51 amino acids), produced in the pancreas, ushers the glucose, or blood sugar as it is called, along through the bloodstream. Fat cells, muscle cells and other cells have insulin receptors. When insulin attaches to a receptor, it triggers chemical reactions inside the cell that allow glucose to enter.

In diabetics, blood cannot deliver glucose to cells because without insulin, cell membranes reject the glucose. When diabetes develops in childhood, it is because the pancreas, an organ of the digestive and endocrine systems, fails to produce sufficient insulin. Adult-onset diabetes is different. There is an adequate supply of insulin, but the cells stop responding to it readily. There are numerous types of diabetes, but in all types insulin receptors do not function properly, even in the presence of adequate glucose. Glucose accumulates in the bloodstream, raising blood sugar levels dangerously high.

Let us consider when and how animal studies entered into the exploration of this tragic condition. In the first century C.E., Araeteus and Celsus described a disease of frequent urination, unquenchable thirst, and wasting. In the seventeenth century, Thomas Willis observed that the urine of people suffering from this disorder contained sugar. As early as 1788, Thomas Cawley and others performed autopsies on deceased diabetic patients and found consistent changes in the pancreas. Cawley also described other patients with pancreatic lesions that developed diabetes. Subsequent autopsies continuing into the twentieth century repeatedly confirmed Cawley's findings.[21] In 1833, another physician named Bright discovered pancreatic cancer in a diabetic patient, establishing another link between the disease and pancreatic dysfunction.[22,23] In 1869, scientists identified the Islets of Langerhans, insulin-producing pancreatic cells that are affected in diabetic patients. In short, many pancreatic conditions, such as pancreatic cancer and pancreatitis (inflammation of the pancreas) were already known to produce diabetic symptoms, reinforcing the disease's link with the pancreas before the twentieth century with its predilection for animal experimentation.

In 1870, a physician named A. Bouchardat renounced the practice of feeding extra sugar to patients in compensation for sugar loss in the urine. By contrast, he recommended diet changes and exercise. This then-revolutionary idea continues to be a mainstay of diabetic therapy today. In 1875, Bouchardat also noted the association of diabetes with lesions of the pancreas.

In 1895, Hansemann reviewed the literature and found seventy-two cases of diabetes accompanied by lesions of the pancreas.[24] However, based on dog experiments he concluded that diabetes had nothing to do with the pancreas.

Dr. Pierre Marie found the association between acromegaly, a pituitary disorder, and sugar in the urine, thus connecting sugar metabolism and the pituitary gland in 1882. Another doctor, Atkinson, published data in 1938 that revealed 32.8 percent of all acromegalic patients suffered from diabetes. Bouchardat had published similar findings in 1908. For some reason, the scientist who validated this in dogs, Bernardo Houssay, ended up winning the Nobel Prize in 1947. Obviously, it is hardly fair to say dogs were responsible for his kudos, since sizable knowledge predated Houssay's experiments and any number of human-based methods would have produced the same findings.

It was not until animal experimenters entered the picture that the hitherto nicely progressing course of knowledge regarding the pancreas and diabetes ran amok. Considerable documentation around the turn of the century confirms this.[25] Claude Bernard conducted experiments on dogs that produced sugar in the urine. Remember, this had already been observed in humans. However, the condition in quadrupeds led Bernard to conjecture that diabetes was a liver disease, linking sugar transport to the liver and glycogen. He also conducted many experiments on animals' central nervous system in an attempt to establish a link there. Granted the liver is involved in carbohydrate metabolism and injuries to the brain can result in hyperglycemia (elevated blood sugar levels), but this is not insulin resistance at the cellular level or a lack of insulin production from the pancreas. These animal studies threw diabetes research off the track for many years. Because of animal studies, many scientists did not believe the pancreas to be involved in diabetes nor that a hormone such as insulin existed. One scientist, Pfluger, stated that the pancreas does not "play any part at all in the origin of diabetes, whether, in fact, there is such a thing as pancreatic diabetes."[26]

In the 1880s, intending to "validate" what had already been established in humans, scientists—most notably Joseph von Mering and Oskar Minkowski—feverishly began removing pancreases from dogs, cats, and pigs. Sure enough, the animals did become diabetic.

In the early 1920s two scientists, J. J. R. Macleod and Frederick Banting, were given credit for isolating insulin by extracting it from a dog. For this they received a Nobel Prize. Macleod admitted that their contribution lay not in discovering insulin (for which they are often credited), but in providing evidence from the animal lab.[27]

Macleod and Banting were not *obligated* to extract insulin from a dog, because certainly there was ample tissue from humans. They did so because it was a convention of the time. In that same year Banting and another experimenter named Charles Best gave dog insulin to a human patient, a fourteen-year-old boy, with disastrous results. When accepting the Nobel Prize, Banting stated that the dog insulin had resulted in a "marked reduction" in the child's blood glucose level. In fact, it only went down an insignificant twenty-five percent and was accompanied by severe side effects. A second dose was not given due to the ineffectiveness and sequellae of the first. J. B. Collip, a biochemist in Macleod's team, said that the administration of the dog insulin was "absolutely useless." Note what scientists said about the dog experiments in 1922: "The production of insulin originated in a wrongly conceived, wrongly conducted, and wrongly interpreted series of experiments."[28] Even Banting and Best's *supporters* said they were "unqualified to do good work."[29]

Years later scientists such as Pratt reviewed the entire insulin isolation experiments that occurred in Toronto and concluded that Banting and Best's dog experiments had not been vital. It was the chemistry of Collip and Macleod that had isolated and purified insulin.[30] M. Bliss states, "Banting and Best did not discover insulin . . . It is particularly important to repeat that Banting's great idea, duct ligation [on dogs] played no essential part in the discovery."[31] Banting and Best experimented on some dogs and by sheer happenstance persuaded people who had knowledge of *in vitro* research to look for insulin and purify it.

Collip, Macleod and other scientists modified the process of isolating and purifying insulin using *in vitro* techniques and later mass-produced insulin from pigs and cattle by reaping it in slaughterhouses. The real credit for purifying insulin should have gone to Collip who used chemistry to purify the insulin. The existence of insulin was already well known. It was its purification that allowed harvest from slaughterhouses and administering to humans. Note what Bliss states about Macleod's opinion of the entire Banting and Best role in the purification of insulin: "In Macleod's mind, the whole importance of Banting and Best's experiments had been in convincing Macleod and the others of the team [Collip] that the internal secretion [insulin] was there to get."[32]

In other words, providing evidence of the existence of insulin from the dog lab was the convincing factor, another case of scientists not being convinced of something just because it was seen in humans. In the forthcoming years, scientists refined the substance. J. J. Abel, in 1926, purified pure insulin from animals. H. C. Hagedorn introduced protamine insulin, a longer lasting form, in 1936. Some lab animal work with the new insulin suggested that it caused birth defects.[33] Fortunately for diabetics, this is not the case in humans.

Discussion of harvesting insulin from animals also introduces a very important distinction of relevance to the vivisection debate. The pro-vivisection community uses the concepts of (a) animal experimentation and (b) harvesting animal parts for use in humans interchangeably. However, these activities are not the same and they produce different risks. Further, animal experimentation as it misleads science is the topic of this book; harvesting animal parts is not. We do not deny that some animal parts can be made to function in humans. But what the vivisection community often understates is the risk of those organs or chemicals.

Animals tissue can be used for human benefit without misleading science—heart valves from pigs, insulin from cows and pigs, the production of monoclonal antibodies from mice, and so on. However these tissues and chemicals have risks, and as occurred with insulin, their ready availability delayed safer therapies. We explore these concepts in more detail in Chapters 8 and 11 when discussing cancer and xenotransplantation.

It is true that without insulin harvested from slaughterhouses many diabetics would have lost their lives. It is also true that the harvest delayed the synthesis of far safer human insulin. Science and industry does not search for solutions to problems that are not apparent and hence do not appear profitable. Synthetically produced human insulin might have been developed much more quickly had science and industry not decided that animal insulin was just as good. Furthermore, animal insulin's availability shrouded the discovery of important diabetes-contributing factors, which we will discuss. Whereas animal insulin helped many diabetics, others suffered severe side effects, and it potentially endangered many more.

Though it is true that beef and pork insulin saved lives, they also created an allergic reaction in some patients. Beef insulin has three amino acids that differ from humans while pork insulin has only one. Although this sounds negligible, remember that it takes very little amino acid discrepancy to undermine health. (Only one deviant amino acid is enough to produce a life-threatening disease, such as cystic fibrosis or sickle cell anemia.) Injecting animal-derived insulin also presented the considerable danger of contracting *zoonoses* (viruses, bacteria, and other microorganisms that cross from one species to another). Had researchers then recognized these potentialities as well as the gulf of differences between ruminants and humans, the exigency for human insulin would have resulted and it would have been developed sooner.

The ready availability of animal-derived insulin and the animal model in diabetes research has continued to encumber the investigation of diabetes throughout this century.

Whereas ample resources were devoted to studying animal models, human diabetic observation limped along with little subsidy. The ability to treat patients suffering from diabetes *without* giving them insulin injections was discovered entirely by chance. In 1942, M. Janbon noticed that when patients were given sulfonamides their blood sugar dropped precipitously. In 1954 patient observation again paid off. Dr. H. Franke was giving patients a new sulfonamide when he too observed symptoms of hypoglycemia. Dr. J. Fuchs then confirmed the observation by taking the medication himself.[34] Today, the administration of oral anti-hyperglycemics, which arose from serendipity and this human self-experimentation, entirely dispenses with the need for insulin injections in many patients.

Not until 1955 was the structure of *human* insulin revealed. By the 1970s scientists had established the DNA sequence of the insulin gene, and in the next decade spliced the gene into *E. coli*, thus creating a limitless supply of synthetically-produced human insulin. A combination of *in vitro* research and technological breakthrough allowed the development of human insulin and insulin preparations that last longer in the body.

Once geneticists located the genetic source of diabetes, genetic breeders scurried to cook up a special mouse for diabetic study. Not surprisingly, this non-obese diabetic (NOD) mouse has certain drawbacks. Unlike the human genome, the mouse genome contains *two* unlinked insulin genes. Drs. M. A. Atkinson and E. H. Leiter commented that,

> Our understanding of the pathogenic mechanisms underlying Type 1 diabetes development in NOD mice is now quite advanced. However, this understanding has been accompanied by the realization that when this mouse is used as a surrogate for humans, genus-specific differences that restrict their interpretation are unavoidable.[35]

In other words, the model does not work, and the differences are profound. NODs lack certain human-immune-system components. The NOD mice also resist diabetic ketoacidosis (DKA). DKA is the most serious manifestation of diabetes; it is what leads to diabetic coma and frequently to death, so the fact that that rather important clinical sign is missing is considerable.

Other models fare no better. Streptozotocin (STZ) knocks out the Islet of Langerhans cells in the pancreas in mice. B. Rodrigues et al., writing about STZ-induced diabetic lab animals in *Experimental Models of Diabetes* state,

> In conclusion, numerous types of experimental diabetes are available . . . However, with the different animal models of diabetes, there will always be physiological, pathological, and morphological differences between models. Moreover, an unavoidable reality is that none of these animal models of diabetes are perfectly equivalent to the human disease state.[36]

Scientists attempt to pass off the STZ-induced rat as a twin of the human diabetic. Yet problems very quickly arise. For example, *the STZ rat does not require insulin to survive* as humans do. Nor is it sensitive to renal toxicity brought about by exposure to the antibiotic gentamycin. But physicians discovered that humans are, particularly diabetics who have compromised renal function to begin with. Sharma and colleagues noted that "... this model does not exactly reproduce the structural hallmark of diabetic nephropathy [kidney disease]."[37]

"Not exactly"? Remember, most of the people we quote have a vested interest in animal experimentation. "Not exactly" is really sciencespeak for "this does not predict anything for humans."

The animal models actually differ *dramatically.* The *STZ injected rat does not require insulin to survive,* and other diabetes models, the Zucker rat for one, do not even suffer from elevated blood glucose.[38] C. Ioannides et al., state,

> None of these models of insulin-dependent diabetes mellitus (IDDM) mimics all the characteristics encountered in the human form of the disease ... Animals in which diabetes has been chemically induced may survive for several months in the absence of an exogenous supply of insulin, and in this respect they differ markedly from the human disease ... [39]

Humans cannot survive months without insulin. Certainly this suggests some very substantial discrepancies. Likewise referring to IDDM experimental models, another authority writes, "No animal model of diabetes mellitus is a perfect model of the disease; hence a wide variety of models continue to be employed."[40]

Nonhuman models misled the development of non-insulin therapies, such as oral antihyperglycemics, for diabetes. The FDA recently approved troglitazone and Parke Davis marketed it as Rezulin. Troglitazone has been linked to severe hepatotoxicity and liver failure and associated with as many as 155 deaths.[41] This is not an isolated incidence. Repeatedly, the animal model has thwarted diabetes research, due to the great differences in digestion and metabolic processes between species. The pancreas continues to be a difficult organ for animal experimenters today, but this has not slowed animal-modeled attempts. In 1992, researchers had this to say about animal models of pancreatitis:

> ... the most important role of experimental models in animals is their use in investigating aspects of pathogenesis, morphology and diagnosis. Whether the induction of experimental acute pancreatitis by whatever means imitates the etiology in humans seems to be most doubtful ... As long as we do not know the true causative factors and their pathogenic principles in human acute pancreatitis, it remains speculative whether these models have a comparable pathogenesis ... Finally, human acute pancreatitis seems to be a different disease than the one induced in experimental animals.[42]

Due in part to dollars misallocated to animal labs, diabetes is still stunningly enigmatic. Most clinicians believe that strict glucose control through insulin injections offers advantages over a less regimented treatment plan and we agree. However, insulin is a treatment, *not a cure*, for diabetes. The exact biochemical process through which insulin regulates blood sugar is still not known. Neither have researchers discovered how that lack of regulation results in diabetes. As one scientist has stated, "Since the discovery of insulin in 1921, many physicians and patients alike have had the erroneous impression that the horrific disease diabetes mellitus has been conquered."[43]

Even in the 1920s, after insulin had been purified and was being given to diabetics, many heralded it as a cure.[44] The insulin-centric nature of our investigation and treatment of diabetics may have produced a forest-for-the-trees kind of oversight. Importantly, even though as many as twenty to thirty percent of children are genetically predisposed to diabetes, most do not develop the disease.[45] That is a pretty staggering discovery. It means other factors such as diet, exercise, and as yet unknown determinants bear significantly on susceptibility.

The availability of insulin obfuscated more important and other factors. Clearly, diet and exercise can decrease or eliminate the amount of insulin needed for many patients and relieve them of the risks associated with taking insulin. Programs that reduce fat in the diet and increase exercise show dramatic benefits and enable some patients to get off antihyperglycemic medications in less than a month.[46] By controlling glucose levels and maintaining lower blood sugar, these diabetes patients also decrease the risk of complications.[47,48]

Bad Busywork but Not without a Lesson

The insulin story is only one example of ways the animal model has insinuated itself into medical history. Added to the politics and distortion surrounding the thalidomide catastrophe, one can see how the ranks tightened for using lab animals. Their use was handy in so many ways—financially, first of all.

The fact that animal testing became mandatory means that those who want it to persist can, with justification, say that animal studies have played a role in every discovery of the last decades. That is to say, yes, animals have figured in discoveries because lab animals are ubiquitous, but the discoveries did not *rely* on them.

It would take institutions, scientists, and bureaucrats who were entirely dedicated to circuiting the well-entrenched animal testing protocol to get a drug to market without having animal studies fit into the equation somewhere. Imagine how laborious this would be. How would one find scientists who had not done animal studies in school or afterwards? Where is a research institution without lab animals? Why would a pharmaceutical company in a hurry to get a drug on the market go to this trouble?

Pharmaceutical companies have tried-and-true protocols for hastening along drug development. Ever since Kefauver-Harris, government agencies have required toxicity data on all chemicals and drugs prior to the release of a substance into circulation. This data tells them what quantity of a medication will kill. Of course, no one would suggest using humans for this.

Hence, a test called the "LD50" became the standard toxicity data-gathering method. And what is this LD50? It stands for "Lethal Dose Fifty Percent." Incremental doses of a chemical are administered to animals—usually dogs and rats—until fifty percent of the subjects die. That dosage is then designated the LD50. The sheer volume of the substance can cause the deaths. Of all the tests described in the book, the LD50 is arguably the most stupid because, as we repeat, rats, dogs, and people do not, and cannot, react the same to medications. As is obvious even to the uninformed, a lot of variables such as the age, weight, and gender of the animal, the environmental conditions, and so on torque the outcome, rendering it invalid even for the species tested. But never mind that. The government still wants the data. Agencies for many years required the LD50 before a drug company could release a new substance.

Over the course of the last four decades, many drugs which were approved and labeled by virtue of tests like the LD50, had drastically different effects in humans. The breadth of difference between species became more and more visible. Take, for example, forty-five drugs tested in 1978. Only twenty-five percent of those effects predicted by animals transpired in humans.[49] As usual, animal tests did not predict the actual side effects to humans. They also raised concerns that the side effects occurring in animals would not materialize in humans. What use was this animal model, if it was not predictive?

It is not easy for vested parties to admit that their sacred, highbrow professions are really just grand scale speculation with human health at stake and animals as currency. Nevertheless, Dr. Ralph Heywood, director Huntington Research Center stated, ". . . the best guess for the correlation of adverse reactions in man and animal toxicity data is somewhere between five and twenty-five percent." Only five to twenty-five percent![50,51] Those odds make animal testing even *more* hit and miss than tossing a coin.

Until ten years ago the LD50 test was still part of almost all regulatory guidelines for safety assessment of chemicals worldwide. At a 1987 congressional hearing on the subject, highly accredited toxicologists testified that the LD50 is not a biological constant and does not address toxicity to organs.[52,53]

Some government agencies are gradually seeing the light. The FDA no longer requires the LD50 and will accept *in vitro* tests for genotoxicity, photogenotoxicity, drug-protein binding, drug metabolism, skin penetration, and bioavailability, as well as skin irritation or photoreactivity.

Even though the FDA does not require the LD50, because they accept it, the testing continues. It is a protocol research institutions are familiar with, and they may not be tooled up to provide alternatives. (The EPA still requires the LD50.)

Yes, animal testing for medications is itself an institution, unshakable despite its inexhaustible drawbacks. Even an FDA official confessed that "most of the animal tests we accept have never been validated. They evolved over the last twenty years, and the FDA is comfortable with them."[54]

And so are pharmaceutical companies. We must not overlook the ancillary benefits of animal testing that fall outside government requirements. Think how the litigious atmosphere has thickened since Kefauver-Harris. Malpractice litigation feeds what is now a *bastion* of animal experimentation. The United States has not yet addressed the issues of frivolous lawsuits and outrageous judgments with tort reform, so billions of dollars in animal testing and experimentation persist. The pharmaceutical companies, while privately acknowledging that animal testing does not work, continue to lobby for and use it because their attorneys can get up in front of juries and say, "See. My client did due diligence with bunnies, guinea pigs, or rats. So don't levy damages against us."

On the other hand, knowledge that the animal testing convention is a false refuge for pharmaceutical companies is burgeoning, and it may be that the legal profession will play a part in unraveling it as a shelter. Judges have, on occasion, ruled that studies on animals were "untrustworthy and lacking in probative value," had "dubious significance in the light of epidemiological data," and "[animal] teratology studies are of scant utility in drawing conclusions about whether a substance will cause birth defects in humans."[55] Ironically then, the legal system that legislated animal testing into being may eventually topple it.

Meanwhile, what are the historical and long-term consequences of this legislated protocol that protects drug companies, not human beings? Appalling, as you will read in subsequent chapters.

chapter 4

The "Pathetic Illusion" of Animal-Modeled Drugs

> In part because of possible major differences in responses to
> drugs in animals and man, the knowledge gained from studies
> in animals is often not pertinent to human beings, will almost
> certainly be inadequate, and may even be misleading.
>
> —Dr. Arnold D. Welch, Department of Pharmacology,
> Yale University School of Medicine in *Responses*
> *in Man*, 1967

Most medications derive from one big contradiction: Our government demands that we test all medications on animals prior to continuing to human trials, and it admits that applying animal data to humans is a "leap of faith."[1] No wonder, then, that each year tens of thousands of people get sick from legal pharmaceuticals. And many of them die. And no wonder our diseases go uncured.

The government's requirement yields only two tangibles—a very accurate picture of the compounds' effect on lab animals, whether positive or negative, and a legal safe harbor for the government and drug companies. When drugs cause illness and death in humans and there is an inquiry, all those involved in development and approval of the drug can point to copious animal testing and claim due diligence. The animal testing provides no surety whatsoever about what these chemicals do to humans. Even those in favor of the animal model are wary. In fact, the most widely respected textbook on the animal experimentation subject, the *Handbook on Laboratory Animal Science*, itself states,

> Uncritical reliance on the results of animal tests can be dangerously
> misleading and has cost the health and lives of tens of thousands

of humans, as in Ciba Geigy's clioquinol scandal, the Opren disaster of Distra Products Ltd., or ICI's Eraldin calamity.[2]

And human trials are still necessary. Those who say we test on animals to avoid testing on people are wrong. Once animal studies are complete, all new medications are evaluated on humans. The first people to take a new substance are being experimented on as surely as if they were guinea pigs locked in a laboratory.

Open up a rat, a dog, a pig, and a human, and you will find much the same terrain but with differences. These visible differences have an impact when it comes to assimilating drugs. Consider the most commonly used species in toxicology research, the rat. Rats have no gall bladder. They excrete bile very effectively. Many drugs are excreted via bile so this affects the half-life of the drug. Drugs bind to rat plasma much less efficiently. Rats always breathe through the nose. Because some chemicals are absorbed in the nose, some are filtered. So rats get a different mix of substances entering their systems. Also they are nocturnal. Their gut flora are in a different location. Their skin has different absorptive properties than that of humans. Any one of these discrepancies will alter drug metabolism. And these are only differences on a gross level.

Smaller differences, being largely chemical, are more difficult to observe. Therein lies a greater dilemma. Medications do not act on the macro-organism—the large, visible level of, say, keeping organs in the right arrangement or bones in the right place. Medications act on the microscopic level. They interrupt and/or initiate chemical reactions, altering molecular activities that are far too small for the human eye to observe. Indeed, medications' actions are not apparent, even with high-tech instrumentation, until they occur.

The discrepancies between diverse mammals are largely microscopic. Imponderably intricate, they are born of millions of years of speciation, adaptation, and mutation. The more modern science reveals about genes, cell function, ion channels, proteins, and so on, the more apparent is the complex gulf between species. And the more ludicrous the existing requirement for animal testing becomes.

The other, even more obvious, problem with the animal model is that animals cannot communicate about their well-being. They cannot say, "I have a stomachache" or "my head hurts," or even "I ache all over." Hence, until animals manifest grand scale malaise in a lab, observations are all guesswork. Or as experts in toxicity write,

The only universal model for a human—that is, one which would best predict what would happen at a given endpoint across the full range of chemical structures, concentrations, etc.—is other humans.[3]

Is it possible that we are not only receiving inaccurate data about the side effects of medications, but also not receiving access to certain drugs that do not produce those side effects that animal models claim? Are we missing good medications because of animal testing? Logic suggests that the answer to these questions is *yes*.

As it is now, animal testing for medications has created and continues to create catastrophe. Animal experiments fail to predict the lethal side effects of many drugs and also prevent good medications from reaching the marketplace. These two outcomes are called "false negatives" and "false positives," as we will explain. The critical word here is false. Animal models for human medicine are false.

Different chemicals have diverse effects on different species. Therefore, the belief that "simply doing enough animal testing will predict all human toxicity" is, as Dr. Louis Lasagna of the University of Rochester so eloquently put it, a "pathetic illusion."[4]

When compounds demonstrate therapeutic effect on an animal, therapeutic effect without ill side effect, they proceed to human clinical trials. There, very often—our research shows anywhere from 52 to 100 percent of the time—they fail, frequently by wounding or killing people. Animal testing has made it look as if given compounds will not injure humans, but they do, as the many examples later in this chapter indicate. Test results such as these are called "false negatives," an important term in the trial process. Thalidomide is a perfect example of a "false negative."

The second catastrophic impact of animal testing is this: compounds that show evidence of therapeutic effect in the human arena are tested on animals. When they bring on injurious side effects in animals, they are withheld from development for humans. More people stay ill. More people die. When it later turns out that humans do not experience the side effects as animals did and also that they actually benefit from the medication, then the animal modeled test results are called "false positives"—a second significant drawback to the animal testing protocol.

In this chapter we show many examples in both categories. These examples only begin to reflect the scope of the historic failure of testing potential human remedies on non-humans.

Cures Worse Than Illness

Ushering drugs to market through animal testing is treacherous. Legal drugs kill more people per year than all illegal drugs combined. An article from an April 1998 *Journal of the American Medical Association* described a study that concluded that deaths from adverse reactions to medications are the fourth leading killer of Americans.[5] (This study's findings are controversial and should not be misinterpreted as condemning all medications, but suffice it to say that medications are killing many patients.) In 1994 adverse drug reactions killed an estimated 106,000 Americans. It is well accepted that approximately 100,000 deaths per year and approximately fifteen percent of all hospital admissions are caused by adverse medication reactions. This costs the general public over $136 billion annually.[6]

As noted, thalidomide is but one high profile disaster. In fact, medical history is strewn with comparable hazardous medications and human fatalities—all traceable to drug development's dependency on the animal model.

The following short histories begin to suggest how drastically human physiology differs from that of lab animals used by pharmaceutical companies in drug development.

- Diethylstilbestrol (DES), a synthetic estrogen, is an example of a medication brought to market on the basis of false negative results in animals. Doctors prescribed DES to pregnant women to prevent miscarriage. No human clinical trials were done. All safety data was gathered from animals. The drug not only failed to do that which it was designed to do. It did just the opposite, causing increased spontaneous abortions, premature births, and neonatal death. Despite clinical data dating from 1953 stating that the drug was dangerous, it remained on the market until 1971. By then teratogenic results manifested. DES increased the risk of vaginal and cervical cancer in the patients' daughters. Even the granddaughters of patients were affected. Only clinical studies revealed this.

  In 1938, researchers found that DES caused breast cancer in some male mice, but the type of cancer varied with the strain of mouse, rendering the data useless. In hindsight, this data has been proffered as "proof" that animal tests predicted the DES-induced cancers. Think how crazy this is: breast cancer in isolated breeds of male mice held as a model for cervical cancer in the daughters of human patients! What a stretch! Human outcome was known. To dose dozens of species without effect, then find a single manifestation is hardly a substantial "ah-ha!" Just as we explain in chapter 11 on cancer, cancer in animals does not predict cancer in humans. Nor does the inability to induce animal cancer assure human safety. Human data yielded the only reliable assessment of DES.[7,8,9,10] One physician writes, "It is well-known that animal effects are often totally different from the effects in people. This applies to substances in medical use as well as substances such as 245y and dioxin."[11]

- Ticlid (ticlopidine), an anti-stroke medication, was relabeled following more than a hundred cases of a life-threatening blood condition known as thrombotic thrombocytopenic purpura.

- Rexar, an antibiotic, was withdrawn by Glaxo as it had been linked with severe cardiovascular events and seven deaths.
- Celebrex, an arthritis drug, a COX-2 inhibitor, was linked to ten deaths and eleven cases of GI hemorrhage in its first three months on the market.
- Zimeldine, the first SSRI (selective serotonin reuptake inhibitor), caused a paralyzing illness known as Guillain-Barre syndrome, not predicted by animal tests, and was withdrawn. This delayed the marketing of Prozac, which proved safe.[12]
- Enbrel (etanercept), a treatment for rheumatoid arthritis, has been associated with serious infections and deaths. The manufacturer, Immunex, is re-labeling the drug.[13]
- Zafirlukast (Accolate), a common medication used to treat asthma, has recently been linked, by human studies, to a rare and sometimes fatal condition known as Churg-Strauss syndrome. Despite extensive testing on animals, this complication did not manifest until Accolate was released to the general public. If larger clinical trials were mandatory, perhaps like situations would not arise.[14]
- Birth control pills, as we now know, can cause life threatening blood clots in some women. To the best of our knowledge, scientists have still not been able to reproduce this finding in animals, certainly not for lack of trying! Extensive animal tests revealed no such problem. In fact, dog testing predicted that the pill would actually decrease the likelihood of clotting.[15] Scientists said this about the animal studies of birth control pills:

  > [Of] the conditions in humans associated epidemiologically with an increased risk in pill users . . . none . . . was predicted by toxicity tests in experimental animals . . . The increase risk of thromboembolic disorders [stroke], which is primarily associated with the estrogen component of the pill, has no analogue in animals. Changes in blood coagulation parameters have only been observed in dogs, but in them they have been due to a specific progestin-related increase in plasma fibrinogen. . . . It is apparent that most of the salient findings in animal experiments have lacked analogues in humans, and most of the adverse and beneficial effects associated with the use of contraceptives have not been predicted by toxicity tests.[16]

- Chloramphenicol, an antibiotic, caused life threatening aplastic anemia.[17,18,19,20] Chloramphenicol is a good example of a drug that varies tremendously from species to species. Dogs do well with it, but cats die from it. Cows tolerate it well, but horses do not tolerate it at all. Like all antibiotics, it lingers in tissue after death. It is so toxic to susceptible people that its use has been outlawed in animals used for food. The tiny amount consumed from ingesting a hamburger made from a treated cow will cause death in a susceptible person, unless that person receives a bone marrow transplant. The aplastic anemia could have been predicted by *in vitro* testing with human cells.

- Fialuridine (FIAU), a medication anticipated to counteract hepatitis B, caused liver damage in seven out of fifteen people. Five eventually died and two more needed liver transplants.[21] But it worked well in woodchucks.[22,23] Even knowing the hazards of Fialuridine in humans, it was difficult to develop these effects in animals.

A retrospective evaluation of the material available in 1993 still supports [the original decision] . . . There was nothing in the preclinical [animal] toxicity studies that was suggestive of the tragic episode that transpired in the [Fialuridine] clinical trial. Furthermore, unfortunately, there is nothing to indicate that other laboratory animal studies would have been more appropriate or capable of better prediction of the fatal outcome.[24]

This is typical of the type of medication differences between humans and animals. Incidents like this prompted scientists to state, "Every species has its own metabolic pattern, and no two species are likely to metabolize a drug identically."[25]

- Isuprel (isoproterenol), a medication used to treat asthma, proved devastatingly toxic for humans in the amounts recommended based on animal studies. Thirty five hundred asthmatics died in Great Britain alone. It is still difficult to reproduce these results in animals.[26–31] Scientists had this to say about the futility of animal experimentation and isoproterenol: "Intensive toxicological studies with rats, guinea pigs, dogs and monkeys at dosage levels far in excess of current commercial metered dose vials . . . have not elicited similar results."[32]
- Flovent (fluticasone propionate), another asthma treatment, recently needed relabeling after some recipients came down with systemic eosinophilia. Many manifested vasculitis consistent with Churg-Strauss syndrome. Bronchial complications of this nature range from mild to life threatening.
- Methysergide, a treatment for migraine, led to retroperitoneal fibrosis, or severe scarring of the heart, kidneys, and blood vessels in the abdomen.[33] Scientists have been unable to reproduce this in animals.[34]
- Suprofen, an arthritis drug, was withdrawn from the market when patients suffered kidney toxicity. Prior to its release researchers had this to say about the animal tests: ". . . excellent safety profile. No . . . cardiac, renal [kidney], or CNS [central nervous system] in any species."[35,36]

- Surgam, another anti-inflammatory arthritis drug, was supposed to have a stomach protection factor, which would prevent stomach ulcers, a common side effect of many arthritis drugs. Although the drug appeared promising in animal tests, ulcers occurred in human trials. Scientists stated after human trials, that ". . . animal data could not safely be extrapolated to man."[37,38]

- Selacryn was a diuretic, thoroughly tested on animals. Diuretics are commonly prescribed to patients in heart failure to prevent fluid overload. When a heart no longer keeps up with the demands placed on it, fluid can collect in the lungs, causing death. It was withdrawn in 1979 after twenty-four people died from drug induced liver failure.[39,40]

- Perhexiline, a heart medication, was withdrawn when it produced liver failure. Animal studies had not predicted this. When the unexpected reaction occurred, researchers rushed back to the lab to attempt to reproduce it in animals. Even knowing that they were looking for a particular type of liver failure, they could not induce it in animals. One scientist stated, "At this point we simply have been unable to induce hepatic disease in any species [with this drug]."[41] Any species except man, that is.

- Domperidone was designed for nausea and vomiting. It made the heart beat irregularly and had to be withdrawn. Scientists were unable to reproduce this in dogs even with seventy times the normal dose.[42,43]

- Novantrone (Mitoxantrone), a cancer treatment, produced heart failure in humans. It was extensively tested on dogs, which did not manifest this effect.[44,45]

- Carbenoxalone was supposed to prevent formation of gastric ulcers. Instead it caused people to retain water to the point of heart failure. Scientists retrospectively tested it on rats, mice, monkeys, and rabbits, without reproducing this effect.[46,47]

- Cleocin (Clindamycin), an antibiotic, causes pseudomembranous colitis (a bowel condition). Scientists tested clindamycin in rats and dogs every day for one year without producing the side effect. Rodents tolerate doses ten times greater than the human dosage. Its use is routine in cats but kills horses.[48,49,50]

- Beta-blockers are commonly used for high blood pressure and headaches. Different beta-blockers act differently on different species. Pronethalol is tolerated in animals but can cause human hearts to fail. Inderal (Propranolol) is tolerated in humans but causes collapse, vomiting, and heart lesions in some animals.[51]

- When the Valium-type drugs first came out scientists had this to say about the possibility of their being habit-forming, "animal experiments . . . do not indicate the potential for development in the human of dependence at therapeutic dose levels."[52] When millions of people became addicted, they acquiesced that "animal studies . . . do not predict clinical dependence potential reliably."[53]

- Linomide (roquinimex), tablets for the treatment of multiple sclerosis, went to clinical trials based on experiments on animals. Pharmacia & Upjohn discontinued these tests after several patients suffered heart attacks.
- Cylert (pemoline) is a medication used to treat Attention Deficit Hyperactivity Disorder in children. It caused liver failure in thirteen children. Of these eleven either died or needed a liver transplant. Abbott Laboratories has recalled it in Canada and is relabeling it in the United States.
- Eldepryl (selegiline), a medication used to treat Parkinson's disease, induced very high blood pressure, a symptom not manifested in animal testing. Veterinarians prescribe the same compound to treat senile dementia and endocrine disorders in animals; however, animals do not get Parkinson's.
- The medication combination of fenfluramine and dexfenfluramine was linked to heart-valve abnormalities and taken off the market in 1997. The *New York Times* quoted acting FDA Commissioner Dr. Michael Friedman, "No one had initially thought to examine patients' hearts . . . because animal studies had never revealed heart abnormalities."[54] They should have consulted the human data. Physicians in Belgium reported heart abnormalities in patients using the medications as early as 1994.[55] Animal experiments obfuscated human studies.
- Troglitazone, a Warner Lambert diabetes medication better known as Rezulin, was tested on animals without significant problems. On October 31, 1997, the company warned doctors of liver damage that could result from using the medication. In March 1998, they admitted that at least twenty-eight patients had died and seven had undergone liver transplants as result of liver damage caused by the medication.[56] According to a *Los Angeles Times* independent survey, as many as 155 people have died of liver failure secondary to taking Rezulin.[57]
- Seldane (terfenadine), an allergy drug, was tested extensively on animals. Although it did not cure allergies, it had no ill effect. It caused life-threatening heartbeat abnormalities in humans. Taking it with grapefruit juice increased blood levels thus raising the risk of dysrhythmia. Seldane is no longer on the market.
- The Wyeth Ayerst medication Duract (bromfenac sodium), a nonsteroidal anti-inflammatory, has caused fulminant hepatitis and liver failure. Four people died and eight more underwent liver transplantation because of taking the drug.[58]

• The antibiotics Omniflox and Floxin, so well described by Stephen
  Fried in his book *Bitter Pills*, progressed through animal testing
  only to inflict horrifying consequences in humans. Omniflox
  was recalled secondary to deaths, and Floxin was found to
  cause seizures and psychosis in humans, one of whom was Stephen Fried's wife.

How did scientists learn that these drugs were murderous? Not
through animal testing. Epidemiology, clinical observation, and autopsy
proved these medications were deleterious. The ill effects of using diethylene glycol as an ingredient in medications were found by autopsy
and epidemiology. The complications of phenacetin causing necrotizing
papillitis and interstitial nephritis; the anesthetic halothane causing liver
damage; zoxazolamine (a muscle relaxant) causing lethal liver disease;
the complications of chemotherapy, and many more problems manifested through autopsy and clinical observation.

A book like Stephen Fried's *Bitter Pills* could be built around any one
of the drugs above. All had misguided development. All were envisioned
as highly profitable. All banked on Americans' trust in the medical profession and its adjunct, the pharmaceutical industry. All destroyed not
just one or two people's lives, but many lives. Our list leaves these personal tragedies undescribed, but emphasizes instead the magnitude of
the problem the animal model creates.

As long as the list of drugs referenced above is, it is not nearly exhaustive. These are only a fraction of the medications tested on animals
that went on to produce severe to life-threatening problems in humans.
A complete list would fill an encyclopedia.

In 1991, the FDA compiled its own report. The report—which
underscored the inaccuracies inherent in drug tests on animals—
tracked the history of all drugs approved in a ten-year interval, from
1976 to 1985. During that period, the FDA approved 209 new compounds for use in the United States after extensive animal testing. Of
the 209, nine drugs fell into a class of so-called orphan drugs. (Occasionally, pharmaceutical companies decide not to market a drug—
to "orphan" it—following FDA approval, because they determine it
will not be profitable.) Of the remaining 200, the FDA followed
all but two for side effects and effectiveness. Astonishingly, 102 of the
198 new medications, or 52 percent, were either withdrawn or relabeled secondary to severe unpredicted side effects.[59]

These side effects included lethal dysrhythmias (when the heart beats
irregularly, severely limiting the amount of blood pumped), heart attacks, kidney failure, seizures, respiratory arrest (inability to breathe followed by the heart stopping), liver failure, stroke, and many more.

Epidemiology provided the data that proved these medications were harming humans. The following are but a few examples of such drugs.

- Flosint, an arthritis medication, was tested on rats, monkeys and dogs; all tolerated the medication well. In humans, however, it caused eight deaths. Incidents like this led Dr. Guilio Tarro, a former associate of Dr. Albert Sabin, to comment, "I have finally come to the conclusion that no serious importance can be attached to any laboratory experiment on animals in the study of analgesics [pain medications], for the results cannot in any circumstances be extrapolated to human beings."[60]

- Nomifensine, an anti-depressant, was linked to kidney and liver failure, anemia, and death in humans.
- Amrinone, a medication used for heart failure, was tested on numerous animals and released without trepidation. Humans developed thrombocytopenia, a lack of the blood cells needed for clotting. This side effect occurred in a startling twenty percent of patients taking the medication on a long-term basis. Dr. C. T. Eason stated, "*A comprehensive program of animal studies* in mouse, rat, hamster, guinea pig, dog, and rhesus monkey completed prior to clinical trials *failed to predict* the occurrence of reversible, asymptomatic thrombocytopenia in up to twenty percent of patients receiving long term treatment with amrinone." (Emphasis added.)[61,62,63] Some of these patients died.
- Clioquinol, an antidiarrheal, passed tests in rats, cats, dogs and rabbits. It was pulled off the shelves all over the world in 1982 after it was found to cause blindness and paralysis in humans. After the animal tests, scientists had gone on record attesting that there is "no evidence that clioquinol is neurotoxic."[64] Small wonder that the authors of the *Handbook of Laboratory Animal Science* wrote: "Uncritical reliance on the results of animal tests can be dangerously misleading and has cost the health and lives of tens of thousands of humans . . ."[65] After this fiasco, scientists returned to the laboratory, hoping to figure out how they missed such a ghastly toxicity. Follow-up studies were unable to induce the neurotoxicity from clioquinol in laboratory animals.[66]
- Practolol (Eraldin), a heart treatment included in the report, caused twenty-three deaths despite the fact that no untoward effects could be shown in animals. In fact when it was introduced it was, ". . . particularly notable for the thoroughness with which its toxicity was studied in animals, to the satisfaction of the regulatory authorities."[67] Practolol caused blindness and death in humans. Even laboring long and hard after the

drug was withdrawn, scientists failed to reproduce these results in animals.

- Opren, also for arthritis, killed sixty-one people. Over 3,500 cases of severe reactions have been documented. Opren was tested on monkeys and other animals without problems.
- Zomax, another arthritis drug, killed fourteen people and caused many more to suffer.
- Enalapril, an angiotensin-converting enzyme blocker used to treat high blood pressure, may cause heart attacks, stroke, kidney failure, pancreatitis, blood dyscrasias and other problems.
- Tocainide, an antiarrhythmic, may cause blood dyscrasias. A blood dyscrasia occurs when bone marrow is unable to produce blood cells in appropriate numbers or proportions. A decrease in white blood cells disables the body's defense against infection. A decrease in platelets may lead to spontaneous bleeding and a decrease in red blood cells leads to anemia. None of these side effects was predicted from experiments on animals.
- Orap (Pimozide), an antipsychotic, led to seizures.
- Maprotiline and Wellbutrin (Bupropion), antidepressants, led to seizures.
- Halcion (triazolam), a hypnotic, had untoward central nervous system side effects.
- Ritodrine, a drug prescribed to avert premature labor, introduced pulmonary edema (fluid in the lungs leading to difficulty breathing and possibly death).
- Ridaura (Auranofin), a gold-containing medication, causes blood problems, especially thrombocytopenia and anemias. It is used for rheumatoid arthritis and other autoimmune disorders.
- Primacor (milrinone), a medication given when the heart is not pumping enough blood, worked well in rats but increased deaths in human patients by thirty percent.

The list continues. Like thalidomide, all of these medications exhibited "false negative" test results. Animal tests wrongly predicted that the medications were safe, but use in humans had very adverse results (death, liver failure and so forth). We are not against medications. Medications have revolutionized the practice of medicine. It is the *process* whereby a chemical becomes a licensed medication that is flawed. Testing medications on animals does nothing good and much that is bad. We further explore how medications are discovered and legalized in a later chapter.

The preponderance of animal testing pressures the FDA into approving bad drugs. In a more recent survey (1998), conducted by the Public Citizens' Health Research Group, nineteen medical officers at the FDA said twenty-seven new drugs approved by the agency in the past three years should not have been. Dr. Sidney Wolfe, director of the Public Citizens' Health Research Group, said standards are going down because the agency has been under pressure from the Congress to approve products more quickly.[68] Pharmaceutical companies use animal test evidence to evince approval for their drugs from the FDA.

Of 172 FDA officers interviewed, eight said there were fourteen instances in the last three years in which they had been told not to present their opinion to an advisory committee if it would reduce the likelihood of a drug's approval.[69] Whereas eight officers represent a small percentage of the total polled, it is likely that others were not entirely candid about pressures they may have received. Considering the revolving door between the FDA and industry, many drugs reach the marketplace due to reasons other than scientifically proven efficacy.

False negatives can also occur when a medication is tested in animals and fails to reveal good effects. Medications discarded as useless from the animal laboratory have frequently gone on to have applications in humans. For example,

> The anti-rheumatic action of phenylbutazone was never seen with reasonable dosages in various types of experimental inflammation, because of the different pharmacokinetics of the drug in animal and in man, and even less so have the antirheumatic effects of chloroquine or penicillamine experimental equivalents; the action of clonidine in migraine and the antidiuretic effect of thiazide diuretics in diabetes insipidus are two other examples to be quoted in this context.[70]

Can we actually credit experimentation on animals as having prevented the FDA from releasing a medication that would have been dangerous to humans? This is difficult to assess, obviously, since such drugs never progressed to market.

However, it is worth remarking that countries that do not rely on animal testing have no higher incidence of adverse-drug reactions than the United States, and frequently have access to the latest drugs years before we do. Dr. Roy Goulding, former head of the poison unit at Guys Hospital, London, had this to say,

> Today, the subject and practice of toxicology has become exalted to the eminence and influence of a religion. It is, moreover, an established form of worship, actively supported by the State. It has its creeds and its commandments, and its hierarchy of high priests, worshipers, adherents and novitiates. Again, like religion, it relies rather more on faith than on reason.[71]

Finally, as summed up by Dr. Herbert Hensel, Director of the Institute of Physiology at Marburg University,

In the opinion of leading biostatisticians, it is not possible to transfer the probability predictions from animals to humans . . . At present, therefore, there exists no possibility at all of a scientifically-based prediction. In this respect, *the situation is even less favorable than in a game of chance* . . . In our present state of knowledge, one cannot scientifically determine the probable effect, effectiveness or safety of medicaments when administered to human beings by means of animal experiments . . . The example of the Thalidomide disaster . . . illustrates this problem particularly clearly. Such a medicine-caused disaster could no more be prevented with adequate certainty through animal experimentation today than it could at that time.[72] (Emphasis added.)

Again the coin toss. Almost forty years after the inferno of thalidomide, the pharmaceutical and medical industries are still gambling with Americans' well-being. Heads, we pass the drug on to the unsuspecting public, tails, we do not. Of the drugs in the FDA Report that passed animal tests, over half were withdrawn or relabeled. A coin toss would be more cost effective. But no one could use that as indemnification in court, as they do animal experimentation.

By now, pharmaceutical companies have finessed mechanisms for dampening bad publicity such as that which surrounded thalidomide. They always point to the extensive animal testing that transpired during the development process. As we explain, this is negligent in the extreme. It is no comfort to a widow that hundreds of guinea pigs tried out the compound that killed her husband. Nor is it a solace that dozens of macaques never skipped a beat while taking a drug that caused massive cardiac arrest in a child. If these drugs had been initiated and tested on the human-based models such as human tissue, the drug companies could justifiably claim to have acted comprehensively. Yet, given the bulk of error, and the extant knowledge we now have about the many, many drawbacks to animal-modeled drugs, mortalities are not accidents. They are inevitabilities.

Delusions of Harm

"Normally, animal experiments not only fail to contribute to the safety of medications, but they even have the opposite effect." So stated Dr. Kurt Fickentscher of the Pharmacological Institute of the University of Bonn, Germany, in *Diagnosen*, March 1980. Here is another scientist emphasizing that animal tests not only fail to predict the bad effects. When they falsely predict side effects, it keeps good medications off the market. Koppanyi and Avery stated of many medications that are used to save lives today, "Had these drugs first been tested in animal experiments for their safety, some of them might never have reached clinical trial."[73] The truth is that all medications in use today can be found to cause a serious side effect in some animal. *Given that, if medications were withheld based on a negative side effect in animals, we would have no medications today.*

Pharmaceutical companies are very wary of releasing drugs that have extremely negative effects on their test animals for legal reasons. Therefore, they keep some of these compounds off the market. Again, as explained earlier, when an animal experiment predicts side effects that do not occur in humans, it is called a "false positive." It is the false positives that prevent potentially therapeutic medications from reaching afflicted humans who really need them.

For an idea of just how helpful these medications might be, we have only to weigh the personal benefit of several common painkillers—drugs that demonstrate false positives in animals but have outstanding therapeutic value in the human setting.

Look in your own medicine cabinet. When you get a headache, would you reach for a pain medication of which a single dose causes renal failure and death in cats? Perhaps. That medication is acetaminophen most commonly marketed as Tylenol. Leery now of Tylenol, you might prefer aspirin. Today, twenty-nine billion aspirin per year are sold in the United States and twice that number are sold worldwide. Aspirin is not only used for pain relief and fever reduction but for the prevention of strokes, heart attacks, and other illnesses. Aspirin causes birth defects in mice and rats and results in such extensive blood abnormalities in cats that they can only take twenty percent of the human dosage every third day.[74] How about ibuprofen, which most people know as Advil or Motrin? Ibuprofen causes kidney failure in dogs, even at very low doses.

When clinical success suggests itself for humans, researchers labor long and hard to find an animal whose response to the drug is favorable. Some animal, somewhere, will eventually produce the kind of results they are after. Some researchers even use fish! Once they know what kind of effect they are after, the cat (for example) is out of the bag.

Frequently, drugs used abroad have such overwhelming evidence of effectiveness and safety for human use that the FDA eventually approves them for use in this country. Sometimes the FDA requires abbreviated animal testing. Other times it demands the entire protocol, but releases the manufacturer from certain requirements. Prozac is a good example of this.

We found many other examples of valuable medications of which Americans were initially deprived because the mandate for animal testing prevents their development and distribution here.

- Depo-Provera, the contraceptive, was barred from release in the U.S. in 1973 because it caused cancer in dogs and baboons.[75]

Elsewhere in the world, women used it and found it safe. Not until 1993 did the FDA release the drug to the American public.

- Digitalis, a plant used by herbalists for centuries to treat heart disorders, was discovered without animal use. It is described later in this chapter. However, clinical trials of the drug were delayed when it caused high blood pressure in animals. Digoxin, an analogue of digitalis, was much later released and has saved countless lives. How many more could it have saved had it been released sooner?[76–79]

- Streptomycin, a popular antibiotic, is teratogenic in rats, causing limb malformations in offspring.

- FK 506, now marketed as Tacromilus, an antirejection agent, was almost shelved before proceeding to clinical trials.[80] After experimenting on dogs, researchers stated, "Animal toxicity was too severe to proceed to clinical trial."[81] Subsequent research with baboons yielded different results, once again proving that we cannot extrapolate results from one species to another. Test enough species and you are bound to find one that gives you the results you want. Scientists, experimenting on animals, also suggested that the combination of FK 506 with cyclosporin might prove more useful.[82] In fact, just the opposite was true in humans.[83]

- Corticosteroids, drugs like prednisone and cortisone, are prescribed by doctors for a wide variety of human complaints. Despite years of effectiveness and relative safety in humans, researchers are still experimenting on animals because the medications previously caused cancer in some rodents. Corticosteroids were not carcinogenic to other rodents including rats, or other species including monkeys. Also, steroids cause birth defects in some animals but not humans.[84,85] This is another example of different animals reacting differently to the same drug.[86,87] A textbook of toxicology states, "In general, tests on one species have limited value in predicting effects on another species. This is seen in regard to the drug cortisone which is teratogenic in mice but only in some strains of rats."[88]

  Corticosteroids were first used to treat brain edema (swelling) before their application in the treatment of spinal injuries. Although animal studies of steroids showed no effect on the swelling associated with spinal injuries, their effectiveness on humans with brain injuries led to widespread belief that they would be beneficial to people with spinal cord injuries.[89,90,91] Once again, if scientists had relied on animal data we would be without a very useful medication. Failure to reduce brain or spinal cord swelling immediately causes permanent damage.

Just as corticosteroids have indications in humans that are not present in animals, the converse is also true. Animal experiments suggested that these drugs would help septic shock, a severe bacterial infection of the blood.[92,93] Unfortunately, humans reacted differently, leading scientists to conclude that corticosteroids were ". . . ineffective for the prevention or treatment of shock associated with sepsis . . . [and] may make secondary infection worse."[94] Others agreed stating that ". . . extrapolation of data from experimental models to the clinical setting may be dangerous and misleading."[95]

The final analysis showed clearly that this treatment increased the death rate in cases of septic shock.[96] This variation from animals to humans should not be particularly startling. It happens all the time. The dose required to achieve therapeutic effects from corticosteroids in the cat is double that of the dog. The type and incidence of side effects also differs dramatically between these two seemingly similar species. Chronic steroid use damages the canine liver and causes diabetes in cats. In humans it causes adrenal suppression and osteoporosis. Though dogs also suffer adrenal suppression and osteoporosis from steroid use, they are less susceptible.

• Penicillin was delayed by animal testing and almost derailed altogether. Alexander Fleming saw penicillin kill bacteria in petri dishes in 1929 and tested it on rabbits. It did not work. We now know that rabbits excrete penicillin in their urine; it is eliminated before it can be effective. Based on rabbit work, Fleming put the drug aside, believing it to be useless as a systemic medication.[97] He later had a very sick patient and since he had nothing else to try, administered the penicillin. The rest is history. Interestingly H. W. Florey, co-winner of the Nobel Prize for penicillin administered penicillin to a sick cat at the same time Fleming was giving it to his sick human. Florey's cat died.[98] Fleming attributed the discovery to serendipity, saying, "Penicillin happened . . . It came out of the blue."[99]

Fleming might have thrown his penicillin away entirely if he had tried it first on guinea pigs or Syrian hamsters instead of rabbits. It kills them.[100] In addition, penicillin is teratogenic in rats, causing limb malformations in offspring.[101] Fleming stated, "How fortunate we didn't have these animal tests in the 1940s, for penicillin would probably never been granted a license, and possibly the whole field of antibiotics might never have been realized."[102]

Macfarlane, another early penicillin researcher, also credited serendipity in penicillin's discovery referring to "a series of chance events of almost unbelievable improbability."[103] And:

Mice were used in the initial toxicity tests because of their small size, but what a *lucky chance* it was, for in this respect man is like the mouse and not the guinea-pig. If we had used guinea-pigs exclusively we should have said that penicillin was toxic, and we probably should not have proceeded to try and overcome the difficulties of producing the substance for trial in man.[104] (Emphasis added.)

What if mice had not worked either? It was Fleming's application to a human patient that proved the drug's effectiveness.

Interestingly the other individuals awarded the Nobel Prize for penicillin, along with Florey and Fleming, Dr. E. B. Chain, stated this about testing medications on animals,

No animal experiment with a medicament, even if it is carried out on several animal species including primates under all conceivable conditions, can give any guarantee that the medicament tested in this way will behave the same in humans.[105]

- Prilosec (Omeprazole), a gastrointestinal medication, was almost canceled because of an effect in animals that did not occur in humans. The drug was delayed for years. Presently, millions now prefer it to the traditional H2 blockers like cimetidine.[106]
- Isoniazid is a commonly used medication for tuberculosis. It causes cancer in animals. Here is what one researcher said about isoniazid:

Presently, we recognize the ability of the effective antituberculosis drug, isoniazid, to induce lung adenocarcinomas [cancer] in a wide variety of mice that are susceptible to this tumor . . . Despite the fact that this drug has been effectively and extensively used since 1953, a period of 24 years, I know of no convincing evidence of its carcinogenic effect in man . . . Unfortunately, we know of no sure way to differentiate accurately between those drugs and other chemicals which induce cancer in both animals and man and those which although effective in animals, are ineffective in man.[107]

- Furosemide, commonly called Lasix, is another example of an important medication almost lost to the public due to animal studies. It is a diuretic, used to treat high blood pressure and heart disease. Mice, rats and hamsters suffer liver damage from this widely used drug, but people do not. The drug is metabolized differently in each species.[108,109,110]
- Fluoride, which causes cancer in rats, was initially withheld from dental use. A dentist made the discovery that fluoride may decrease the risk of dental decay. Observing patients who had mottled teeth from living in areas with a large concentration of fluoride in the water, he noticed that they had fewer cavities.[111]

Scientists carried out epidemiological studies and found the protective link between fluoride and caries. Fluoride has been added to our water for years, without hazardous effect.[112,113,114]

For development and distribution of these drugs in the U.S., pharmaceutical companies overcame the animal model mandate only through perseverance. What of the potentially thousands of curative substances that do not overcome this hurdle? Is it possible that we are not only not getting accurate data from animals on the side effects of medications (false negatives) but also are not having access to certain drugs because of inaccurate predictions of side effects (false positives)? Are we missing good medications because of animal testing? Apparently so.

Dr. C. Dollery has this to say about missing good medications because of animal tests:

> For the great majority of disease entities, the animal models either do not exist or are really very poor. The chance is of overlooking useful drugs because they do not give a response to the animal models commonly used.[115]

All medications in use today can cause a serious side effect in some animal. As we have already explained, if researchers persevere, inculcating enough species with high enough dosages, illness will eventually result in one or more species. Hence, if we truly withheld any medication from the public based on its negative impact on non-humans, we would have no medications today. This fact alone destroys all justification for continuing animal testing.

The more we learn in regard to the physiological differences between humans and other animals, the more strained support for animal experimentation becomes. What use are animal tests if scientists' chances of predicting safety are no better than fifty percent? The troubled impact of the animal model on drugs covered in this chapter, albeit incomplete, is tragic enough to merit overhaul of drug development procedures.

The National Cancer Institute and other prestigious institutions have issued statements stating that they no longer *rely* on animal tests. They do not believe animal tests are protective, and they admit there are cases of safe medications being withheld because of animal-derived data.

However, despite these institutions and despite billions and billions of dollars in flawed, misleading, inconclusive science and who knows how many hundreds of thousands of human lives lost, the animal testing mandate persists. Intelligent scientists and reputable publications continue to support it. In the February 1997 issue of *Scientific American*, in their article defending animal experimentation, authors Jack H. Botting and Adrian Morrison nonsensically state, "In truth, there are no basic differences between the physiology of laboratory animals and humans."

Current estimates place the cost of developing, testing, and marketing each new drug at between 150 and 349 million dollars, the latter figure according to a 1993 report by the Congressional Office of Technology Assessment.[116] The drug companies pass the costs along to the patients and our insurance companies. Drugs are so outrageously expensive in the United States that the elderly and poor cannot afford them. In view of these staggering costs, measures should be taken to insure that only cost-effective and accurate tests are conducted. Not until the Congress and the FDA changes the way medications are evaluated prior to releasing the drug will tragedies stop and valuable therapies, previously withheld, reach the needy expeditiously.

More extensive preclinical testing on human tissue, more extensive clinical trials, and mandatory postmarketing drug surveillance would offer the general public much safer medications. These changes are long overdue and absolutely vital!

The only truly accurate knowledge about the positive and negative effects of medications on humans is acquired through *in vitro* testing, computer modeling, epidemiology, clinical observation, and autopsy of humans. Today's technology makes observations of compounds on human systems more and more easy. Nonetheless, animal testing persists. We explore why in the next chapter.

chapter 5

White Coat Welfare

Whenever people say, "We mustn't be sentimental," you can take it they are about to do something cruel. And if they add, "We must be realistic," they mean they are going to make money out of it.

—Brigid Brophy, British novelist and essayist in
Animals, Men and Morals

There are, in fact, only two categories of doctors and scientists who are not opposed to vivisection: those who don't know enough about it, and those who make money from it.

—Dr. Werner Hartinger, M.D., German surgeon, 1989

Today's medical research establishment has assumed a life of its own. Segmented but interconnected, it has tentacles extending into every aspect of our lives. Composed of researchers, medical associations, pharmaceutical companies, purveyors of research equipment, government agencies, publishers, lobbyists, and public relations companies, its aspects are sometimes good, sometimes bad, and frequently entirely neutral, *except for their cost*.

Gertrude Belle Elion was a Nobel laureate scientist, an esteemed figure in the medical research establishment. Now deceased, Elion used to insist that all her research be applicable, and she demanded the same of her peers. Elion time and again asked, "If we carry out these experiments, how will we use the information generated, and where will this lead us?"[1] Far too few scientists share Elion's stipulation, particularly in regard to animal experimentation. Their cavalier disregard for accountability corrupts the Hippocratic obligation to save lives and nurture health.

We have described how the predilection for animal experiments gathered steam and became law, and how the animal-model protocol protects drug companies and the government from liability in the event of unforeseen side effects or deaths from medical innovation. In addition, other businesses and the government also use animal experiments to prove or disprove claims against them.

Even though animal experimentation is now used to prop up questionable commerce for many contingencies, its ineptitude has never been a secret. Knowledgeable scientists and industry business people have always known that many animal tests are performed strictly because of the legal system. Even by 1964, Dr. James G. Gallagher, Director of Medical Research, Lederle Laboratories, stated,

> Another basic problem which we share as a result of the regulations and the things that prompted them is an *unscientific* preoccupation with animal studies. *Animal studies are done for legal reasons and not for scientific reasons. The predictive value of such studies for man is often meaningless—which means our research may be meaningless.*[2] (Emphasis added.)

Top personnel at leading pharmaceutical companies knew animal data was meaningless as long ago as 1964. Nonetheless, despite widely held doubt that animal testing provides any assurances whatsoever, no one has ever been eager nor even willing to give up this legal safe harbor.

This chapter examines the tightly knitted machinations that sustain animal-modeled medical research despite this meaninglessness. The rest of this book documents the deception, but here we explain just how medical research turned into this colossal, intransigent, and often corrupt force. By providing insight into the agendas that propel scientists, institutions, business, and government, we hope to illuminate possible justifications for their refusal to reform.

One only has to follow the money.

The Engine of Higher Education

Our ivory-towered research institutions are sacrosanct. Most Americans are idealistic about scientists in laboratory settings, picturing purists doggedly pursuing "true knowledge" in their respective fields. No one seems as respect-worthy as these disciplined white-smocked savants. Surely they must be impervious to mundane concerns such as money and prestige.

Well, scientists too have mortgages and children and dreams. Scientists are just like the rest of us, materialistic and opportunistic. They, too, struggle to survive and excel in a competitive world. As Irwin Bross, PhD, former Director of Biostatistics at the Roswell Park Memorial Institute for Cancer Research, put it: "They may claim to love truth, but

when it is a matter of truth versus dollars, they love the dollars more
... Money talks."[3]

Rivalry for research dollars is fierce. Less than fifteen percent of all
medical grant applications are funded. So, replace your image of altru-
istic savants with one of PhDs rattling their beakers while panhandling
for grants. You will be far closer to the truth. Researchers who do not
crank out papers with great regularity find themselves not only unten-
ured but also unemployed. "Publish or perish" may be a cliché. But it
is the pivotal admonition in academia.

With the threat of perishing omnipresent, people tend to choose the
path of least resistance. And what is the easiest and fastest way to produce and publish papers in medical science? Animal experimentation. It
is a time-honored convention. Laws require animal tests. Government
agencies and charities fund them. They generate, if not applicable results,
at least results. Scientific journals are fully receptive to publishing the
results. Publishing leads to promotions, and more grant money. And
quantity of experimentation wins over quality every time. The cynic who
quipped, "the rat is an animal which when injected, produces a paper"
was on target.

First, animal experimentation is tidy. The lovely thing about rats is
that you can go home on Friday night and rest assured that they will
still be in their cages when you get back on Monday. On the other hand,
clinical research on humans can be tricky, or as Judith Vaitukaitis said
in *Clinical Research*, "Nothing is more demanding, more difficult, more
frustrating, more time-consuming, and requires more creativity than clinical research."[4]

Clinicians have no control over their subjects, who may not return for
follow-up appointments nor follow instructions. Human subjects may
even be dishonest about their lifestyles. You can addict monkeys to crack
cocaine or heroin in your nice clean lab. If you want to study human
crack or heroin addicts, you may have to interact with potentially nasty
and even dangerous people.

In 1998, a National Institutes of Health panel noted with alarm de-
clining numbers of clinical research grant recipients. It attributed this
decline to several factors—the long timeframe required by many studies,
the complexity of working with human subjects and the difficulties of
involving and crediting multiple investigators.

Not only easier, animal experiments are also much quicker than human studies. A rat's generation time is weeks, not decades. By the time
a clinician publishes one good paper, an animal experimenter can publish at least five. The easiest way to publish is to take a concept already
published and change something, the type of animal used, the dose of
the drug, the method of assessing the results, or some other variable.
This way, the concept has already been milled and all the researcher has
to do is follow the template with new grist.

Neal Barnard, MD, president of the Physicians Committee for Responsible Medicine, once likened animal experimentation to a man searching for his lost keys. After losing the keys on a street without a street light, the man searched there for awhile, but did not find them. He then moved over to the next street, because it had a street light. He found the searching much easier on that street because of the light. Of course, he did not find his keys on that street because he did not lose them there. But it certainly was easier to look. Such is the case with animal experimentation. It is easier than studying humans, but it does not work. The real strides in medicine have not come from the animal laboratory but from clinical research, and other non-animal methods.

Losers seeking keys notwithstanding, at its very core, the education process itself perpetuates animal experimentation. Early on, every student in America is inculcated with the notion that animal models count. Basic science researchers write basic science textbooks for high school, college, and graduate students. Clinicians, who are absorbed in human study, do not. Most of these same researchers are performing experiments on animals; indeed that is how they earn their livelihood. From frogs and fetal pigs forward, all American students are exposed only to the one perspective, and the animal experimenters themselves make more money from writing the textbooks.

Not until later in medical school do textbooks written by clinicians appear. These delineate the actual nuts and bolts of human care—how to treat illness, perform surgery, administer anesthesia, read MRI scans, and so forth. These books contain very little if any, animal data. But by the time the clinical books are in front of them, medical students are too busy absorbing and mastering complex data and procedures to notice, much less question, the largely nonintersecting trajectories of animal and human diagnosis and treatments.

Most medical education is rote memorization. Original thinking is neither required nor welcomed when exhibited. Those who question procedures routinely hear "that's how we do it here." In the early part of the twentieth century, Dr. Walter Hadwen summed up the "inside the box" thinking that still persists:

> No medical man during his student days is taught to think. He is expected to assimilate the thoughts of others and to bow to authority. Throughout the whole of his medical career he must accept the current medical fashions of the day or suffer the loss of prestige and place.[5]

Acceptance is just part of the picture. Participation is the other half, as Dr. E. J. H. Moore concurs, "The pressure on young doctors to publish and the availability of laboratory animals have made professional advancement the main reason for doing animal experiments."

As in most professions, science and medicine do not turn on ingenuity. They are about toeing the line.

Beyond physicians, who may be just too busy to appreciate the lack of connection between basic science instruction and the careers they have undertaken, science majors who go into research have persuasive reasons for overlooking the deception. They are repeatedly reminded who butters their bread, even from the beginning. Graduate students in science fields such as physiology, pharmacology, and psychology learn animal experimentation techniques—and although doing grunt work—get their name on a few of their professors' articles. When they themselves apply for a grant in their new job, they simply rearrange a few details of their previous research and give it a new slant that corresponds to whatever medical concerns are presently pressing enough to fund. As Dr. Julius Hackethal stated, "Today I abhor animal experiments. But there was a time when I performed them, simply because I wanted to become a professor."[6]

In days of yore, most scientists did not expect to get rich from their work. They were smart, curious people who wanted to make a contribution to society. Today is different. Frank Solomon, a biology professor at MIT, commented,

> Good young people and good older people are going without funding, and it creates an environment which is amenable to all sorts of corner-cutting . . . For example, no one ever thought that you could get rich doing biology, and now I am the only biology professor without a Saab . . . The whole tempo has changed. It is possible to become quite well-known doing biology. And our students learn those lessons quickly.[7]

At a conference dedicated to exploring the value of animal experiments in the field of carcinogen testing, Dr. Frederick Coulston of Albany Medical College, noting the absence of reporters, asked for candid views on the relevance of animal-derived data to humans. Coulston himself expressed skepticism and his colleague Dr. Philippe Shubik of the University of Nebraska agreed, stating, "Clearly, right now our animal models are totally and absolutely inadequate to answer all the obvious questions before us." In another quote from the conference proceedings, Dr. William M. Upholt concurred that "extrapolation [from animals to humans] is unscientific."[8]

As noted, researchers are carried forward, both in terms of promotion and in terms of funding, by the number of articles they publish. Not the *value* of research, just the *number*. That in and of itself explains the large amount of garbage in the literature. Many academics list greater than a hundred articles on their *curriculum vitae*. Rest assured, professionals spew out articles to get through their certification process or promoted, not for the sheer thrill of sharing new discoveries. Dr. Edward H. Ahrens, prominent in the field of medicine for decades, wrote in *The Crisis in Clinical Research* in 1992, "The most research-intensive schools employ only one yardstick for measuring the contributions of the entire staff: the number of articles reporting research results. Clearly this is an inappropriate yardstick."[9]

Researchers are paid, but whether or not the knowledge is worth paying for is another question entirely. Their animal study will have no application to humans, but they did not say it would. They only said it would "advance knowledge," not the type of knowledge that will cure or curb disease. Researchers have admitted that most research is of no importance. "Most research is trivial and never cited anyway."[10] So why do it? Because, as Dr. Philippe Shubik put it at the aforementioned conference, "The chief objective here is too keep us all employed."[11]

As the caveat "publish or perish" propels animal experimenters, it also keeps hordes of scientific journals in print. Consider this: In 1665, the first journal devoted to science was founded. Even by 1880, the number of such journals was only 100. In a mere twenty years, by 1900, the number had risen to 10,000 and today there are approximately 100,000. Granted, knowledge has increased in the last 100 years but not enough to constitute this exponential rise in journals.

There are simple reasons for this. If journals were limited in number, then only the important papers would be published. Researchers want tenure, and need to publish to get it. Fewer journals mean more rejected articles. So researchers have demanded that more journals be started, often times with colleagues as editors. It is the "I scratch your back . . ." routine.

A proliferation of journals has diluted even good journals with mediocre or poor articles. Perhaps the most influential critic of the "publish anything" practice has been the deputy editor of the *Journal of the American Medical Association*, Dr. Drummond Rennie. He wrote, "There seems to be no study too fragmented, no hypothesis too trivial . . . no design too warped . . . no methodology too bungled . . . no conclusions too trifling . . . for a paper to end up in print."[12]

Yet, it is nearly impossible for those against the animal model to publish their views in the scientific literature. The editors and scientists who review articles for publication are usually animal experimenters themselves. They have earned a reputation and tenure because they perpetuate the mass delusion. They will do anything to prevent the lack of basis in their research from being exposed. Moreover, many medical journals rely on advertising dollars from pharmaceutical companies and others that make products for experiments on animals.

Recently *Scientific American* (February 1997), a magazine that circulates among scientists as well as nonscientists, published "Animal Research: Wasteful and Misleading," an article by Neal Barnard and

Stephen Kaufman describing the anti-animal experimentation position. This piece brought an avalanche of criticism from subscribers and other science publications such as *The Scientist* and *HMS Beagle*. It struck a nerve.

We should add, though, that there are many excellent journals of clinical medicine, such as *New England Journal of Medicine* and the *Journal of the American Medical Association*, devoted mainly to describing research achievements made on human models. Nevertheless, they are in the minority. The vast majority of scientific journals purporting to advance medical science are predisposed to animal experimentation.

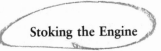

Stoking the Engine

As the animal experimentation status quo is, everyone profits. Money drives education. Money drives research. Money drives industry. Money drives the media. Hence, money is the reason that animal experimentation exists. Whose money is this?

Yours.

We Americans foot the bill for animal experimentation every time we buy a drug, every time we pay our insurance premiums, every time we visit a physician or a hospital or a clinic. We pay exorbitantly. More about these ancillary expenses in a few pages. For now, let us discuss our abundant support of animal models through tax dollars and charitable donations.

The largest single provider of funds to medical research institutions in America is the National Institutes of Health (NIH), located outside Washington DC. It grants approximately one-third of the medical research money in the United States, doling out billions of taxpayer dollars each year. The NIH goal, according to a government publication is:

> to improve the health of our nation by increasing the understanding of processes underlying human health, disability, and disease, advancing knowledge concerning the health effects of interactions between man and the environment, and developing and improving methods of preventing, detecting, diagnosing, and treating disease.[13]

Put more simply, the NIH mission is to do and fund research that will prevent, diagnose and treat disease.

The most frequent NIH grant is for so-called R01 research projects. These are "investigator-initiated," meaning a primary scientist steers the request for funding. Dr. Ahrens' book explains R01 grant allocations:

> No matter how many extramural scientists and other personnel are paid on any one NIH grant, there is only one PI [primary investi-

gator] per grant; and all transfers of funds are made not to PIs personally, but to the *institutions in which they are employed*. All NIH awards consist of direct cost allowances for salaries, permanent equipment, supplies, travel, and publication costs, but also of indirect cost allowances for administration, energy, security, library, and custodial services. Thus, direct costs support the research institution of the PI, while indirect costs are paid to meet the overhead costs of the institution in which the PI works.[14] (Emphasis added.)

So, the traditional R01 grant supports the researcher and the university or institution where he or she works. Universities and institutions are grant guzzlers. Over the last several decades, the cost of electricity, water, security, administrative services, and so on, has risen to more than the amount needed to actually do the research. In some cases the institution receives more money from the grant than the researcher.[15] One can understand why acquisitive institutions frown on rogue researchers who speak out against the tried and true cash cows of animal experimentation. They are usually encouraged to quiet down and are sometimes even dismissed.[16–19]

Donald Barnes, an Air Force researcher, was fired, as have been many others, after speaking out on the futility of animal experimentation. He likens the process of learning to perform animal experiments in graduate school to brainwashing:

When I first left the laboratory, I remained skeptical, stating 'there are some good experiments to be sure, but the majority are worthless,' or words to that effect. Now after years of looking for those 'good' experiments, I have long since concluded that they do not exist. But I had to do the looking for myself. I was simply too conditioned to the 'Party Line' to accept anyone's word for this.[20]

It should be noted that *any* grant adds money to the university budget. Hence, universities often overlook unethical research. A 1991 federal Office of Technical Assessment (OTA) report reinforced this fact by stating:

Since most overhead is brought into the university by a small number of research professors (at Stanford, five percent of the faculty bring in over one-half of the indirect cost dollars), proposals to reduce research output are not looked on with favor by many university administrators.[21]

Even when universities fund beginning researchers with a starter grant out of the university budget it is an investment. The money they give the researcher will come back one hundred times in grant money, alumni donations, and support from pharmaceutical companies if the researcher is at all talented at playing the game.

Before identifying where grants go, it is important to recall our terminology. Remember, a clinical investigator or researcher is a scientist who studies disease and therapies in humans. In 1979, Dr. Wyngaarden, director of the NIH, called clinical investigators an "endangered species."[22] And he was not kidding. Between 1977 and 1987, only 7.4 percent of the NIH's R01 funding went to basic patient-oriented research.[23] The largest percentage of awards went to animal experimentation. In other words, in that decade Americans funded more grants for sick lab animals than for sick humans.

Two reports, straight from the federal government, document the fact that the NIH under-funds patient-oriented clinical research.[24,25] In other words, the NIH intentionally selects for applications that do not include clinical research. Consider the following: "Only one-third of NIH competing research grant applications include *human* subjects."[26] (Emphasis added.)

Naturally, if you are a researcher and only have a one-in-nine chance of acquiring funding, and the funding institution nurtures a fifty percent or greater favoritism toward animal-based studies, and you need that funding so you can keep your job, pay your mortgage, and so on, would you not get busy with lab animals? Congressman Thomas Bliley stated, "It appears that the [medical establishment] system has changed from one of NIH giving grants for scientific research to one of scientific research being done solely to get NIH grants."[27]

In his book, Ahrens does not hesitate to expose the holes in NIH decision making,

By far the largest percentage of NIH support for new R01's . . . is awarded to applicants for studies of animal models of human disease. Yet, most experienced investigators realize that animal models of arteriosclerosis, diabetes, hypertension, and cancer are different in important ways from the human condition they are intended to simulate.[28]

Later in our book, we explain why animals do not get heart disease, and why cancer, diabetes, and other illnesses are not the same from species to species. For now, simply recognize the bias on NIH's part and on the part of researchers and institutions. Throwing money around like this would seem merely capricious if we could already cure the lethal diseases of our time. But we cannot, so it is scandalous.

To its most established researchers, the NIH gives "MERIT" awards. In 1987, only 7.5 percent of the NIH's MERIT awards were patient-oriented basic science research. Only 2.5 percent went to fund research on humans to study disease management. Thus, a vast majority of research was not patient-oriented. If these "top guns" are performing primarily non-clinical research, what does that say about priorities? Studies from the same time period also revealed that more researchers were focusing on animal models of human disease than on humans themselves. We already know that researchers do not really believe we are more like animals than humans; they are just profiting from the convention.

The NIH's predilection for funding non-clinical research is not a new trend.[29] Nor is it necessarily a diminishing trend. According to "Models for Biomedical Research," a report from the Committee on Models for Biomedical Research, *scientists conducting research via animal experimentation received greater than fifty percent of all grant dollars from 1977 to 1983.*[30] From 1988 to 1992, the NIH again gave greater than fifty percent of your money to fund research on animals. The greater than fifty percent figure seems constant from year to year. It is difficult to determine exactly how much greater than fifty percent the actual number is. It could be 51 percent or it could be 85 percent.

In 1986, the president of the Institute of Medicine cautioned that medical research was leaning too heavily on basic animal experiments and not enough toward clinical observation.[31] He called it an "emperor has no clothes" scenario, meaning that no one among the powers could declaim animal experimentation for fear of jeopardizing their own power base.

According to an Institute of Medicine survey, the National Institutes of Health gave only fifteen to seventeen percent of total grant money in 1990 and 1991 to research that could be regarded as human clinical research. That this included research with human cells and tissues, from which so much can be gleaned, is disheartening indeed. Furthermore, only 4.5 percent of grants given the 1990–1991 year went to lab research involving humans. This means, again, that NIH-funded research on animals hugely outdistanced human clinical research.[32]

In 1992, the public, via the NIH, funded approximately $12 billion in grants, a majority of which went to non-human research.[33] In 1993, the National Cancer Advisory Board declared that clinical research was in "crisis."[34] The next year the National Cancer Institute (NCI), a division of NIH, allocated only one percent of its total R01 funds to clinical research. Only one percent![35] If they thought it was in crisis, why did they not fund more?

Although the largest, the NIH is not the only government agency funding grants. So that fifty percent of $12 billion or greater is just a piece of total money exchanged in the animal experimentation industry. Fifteen other government agencies, such as the Department of Defense, also dole out taxpayer money. Together, these fifteen agencies represent approximately twelve percent of all research dollars in the United States. So we can ratchet up that six to eleven billion.

These figures do not include the money spent by private industry to test new medications, therapies, or other products on animals prior to testing them on humans. Americans pay those costs when we purchase them. Nor does this figure include dollars donated to charities that finance animal experimentation. Factor in these expenses along with the sums that the largest government institution representing your interests dispenses to animal studies.[36] Rat-injecting and other lab animal considerations are a colossal enterprise.

What is the process that keeps this enterprise turning? Normally, a scientist will submit a grant proposal to the NIH or other granting institution. A supposedly unbiased board of reviewers then weighs the proposal's merit.[37] Review panels are composed of researchers from universities, pharmaceutical companies, and other institutions. These people are experts; but they also tend to scratch each other's backs as well as the backs of junior scientists who perpetuate research that they themselves began. According to one congressman, the peer review process is "an old boys' system where program managers rely on trusted friends in the academic community to review their proposals. These friends recommend their friends as reviewers . . . It is an incestuous 'buddy system'. . . ."[38]

Everyone is playing the same game. *Don't you veto my project, because then I will be obliged to veto yours. Then the university will fire both of us because it will lose the grant money.* The relationship between researchers and peer review committees is entirely symbiotic.

Grant getting is very competitive. As the OTA stated in the 1991 report,

> There will always be more opportunities than can be funded, more researchers competing than can be sustained, and more institutions seeking to expand than the prime sponsor—the Federal Government—can fund.[39]

As mentioned, only around fifteen percent of all grant applications are funded. So, for every application funded, approximately eight were turned down. That's competition.

Our federal government should, of course, base its allocations on the likelihood of their leading to concrete results in eradicating disease. Since so few projects are funded, would you not hope that those most likely to benefit humankind would get the highest priority?

Agencies like the NIH should take their cue from respected scientists such as Ahrens, who wrote,

> I have gained irrefutable evidence that the study of whole humans is indeed languishing today. But, in addition, that evidence is

strongly persuasive that this kind of research is absolutely essential in furthering the study of human health and disease.[40]

But they do not.

Eradicating disease may be way down the list of the NIH's reasons for being. As the studies in our book will often indicate, sixty to ninety percent of all disease is preventable. Even the Centers for Disease Control and Prevention states that seventy percent of premature deaths are due to lifestyle and environmental factors.[41] Yet, only a very small fraction of the NIH grant money goes to funding preventive medicine, education, and implementing programs that really make a difference.[42,43,44] Could this be because prevention does not keep the economic engine chugging along? It does not employ scientists, nor push scientific frontiers, nor justify research institutions. It just points people toward health.

Few scientists stop to reflect whether consumers are getting their money's worth as long as they themselves are making money. Those who do speak out at their own risk. Still, a rebellious few insist that human lives have been lost needlessly through the delays in treatment and from fallacious results of animal studies.[45-50]

Their peers and the supposedly neutral scientific and medical associations are nearby to squelch their objections, as is the lobbyist machine which we will explain momentarily.[51-55] Information in support of the animal model from the American Medical Association, Stanford University, and the American Veterinary Medical Association—America's most august medical institutions—goes a long way in overturning any dissent.

However, look more carefully at these respected institutions and the professionals within them. Those who decide whether animal lab experiments are meaningful make their livings, directly or indirectly, from the animal lab. Their reliance on the animal experimentation convention has them all but on the dole, hence their enthusiasm for attributing all major medical progress to our furry friends. Crediting our medical acumen to the animal model supports their facade.

This facade cannot suffer any chinks; therefore, they will even resort to the "knowledge for knowledge's sake" rationale. This basic research defense is really the last refuge of the mad scientist. Especially in the field of medicine. We throw inordinate amounts of money at health-care research each year. Yet, millions of people continue to grow feeble and die from diseases that only vaguely resemble those conditions conjured then cured in compromised animals.

If it were true that animals mime human beings, the animal experimentation industry would have numerous examples of the cures the animal model has wrought, or at least an accurate accounting of what our dollars have purchased. As the data in this book will prove, there are few, if any, real examples. And, unfortunately, since so many institutions and researchers and pharmaceutical companies are profiting so immensely, accountability is a non-issue.

In the Grip of Big Business

An idea with as many holes in it as that of using animals for human medical research requires ceaseless vigilance to keep afloat. Realizing this, one of the largest lab animal-breeding facilities in the world, Charles River Laboratories, formed the Association of Biomedical Research to lobby for animal experimenters in 1979. The multinational optics manufacturer, Bausch and Lomb, who purchased Charles River Laboratories in 1984, now controls the lobbying group. (A July 26, 1999 press release stated that Bausch and Lomb was selling Charles River to Global Health Care Partners.) In 1985, the Association of Biomedical Research pooled resources and merged with the National Society of Medical Research, an organization formed after World War II to promote the animal model. This union resulted in a leviathan political lobbying organization, the National Association of Biomedical Research (NABR), complete with an educational arm called the Foundation for Biomedical Research.

NABR claims over 500 members, all corporations and organizations using lab animals, with annual dues ranging from $500 to $12,000. The president of NABR, Frankie Trull, also works independently as a lobbyist, through Policy Directions, Inc., for several companies that sell or use lab animals. These include Charles River Laboratories, Athena Neurosciences, Carnation Nutritional products, Gynecare Inc., and the State University of New York at Albany.

NABR newsletters feature stories about how to controvert the facts we present in this book. Truth is not on their agenda; money is. We invite you to read their claims as published in books like *Animal Research and Human Health*. Examine these against the medical literature we quote and see which is accurate and which is fabrication of data.

The NABR's educational division, the Foundation for Biomedical Research, is a slick PR operation with a penchant for emotional appeal, distortion and prevarication. The unwitting onlooker is easily captivated by their advertisements.

The propaganda machine kept in spin by Foundation for Biomedical Research and other vested organizations and lobbying groups is fierce. All devote as much energy as required to parry those scientists who speak out against animal experimentation. It takes little more than a flick from highly respected institutions such as the AMA or Stanford to discredit these brave few, and no one ever stops to ponder that the plethora of AMA members and Stanford personnel depend, directly or indirectly, on animal experimentation for their very existence.

Vivisectionists waggle all sorts of falsehoods to rally support around their nugatory science. Their propaganda is often just sheer fluff. For instance, Foundation for Biomedical Research produced an ad featuring animal rights protesters with the caption, "Thanks to animal research, they'll be able to protest 20.8 years longer." It is not animal experimentation that has increased life spans. It is sanitation, clean water, decreased poverty, and sound science. Unfortunately, the viewing public does not pause to think claims through to this extent.

One of our favorites is lobbyists' claim that Nazis experimented on Jews because it was illegal to experiment on animals. This assertion would have impressed even the Nazis. As we know, Nazis were masters of propaganda. They frequently stated absolute falsehoods. As the animal experimenter says he cares deeply for the animals he experiments on, Hitler's protégé Eichman said he had many Jewish friends.[56] True, Nazi law forbade animal experiments unless they were "needed."[57] But a perusal of *Pfugers Archiv für die Gesamte Physiologie*, a major science journal of the time, reveals that animal experiments thrived under Nazi leadership. The laws regulating animal experimentation were equivalent to those in England at the time. Nazi Germany records substantiate this. If anything, experimentation on animals led to the Nazis' experimentation on Jews and others.[58-62]

Then there are the skewed studies. Nowhere is the bias for animal experimentation more evident than the Comroe Dripps Report of 1976.[63] This report, touted as disclosing the top ten research contributions to the fields of cardiac and pulmonary medicine from 1945 to 1975, was hoisted as evidence of animal experimentation's merits. Its partiality was so evident that many immediately declared it unscientific.[64]

Drs. Comroe and Dripps were animal testing enthusiasts. They had criticized President Johnson's administration for coming out in favor of clinical, not basic (meaning animal) research. They also criticized the first heart transplant surgeons for failing to publicly state that the operation was only possible secondary to animal experiments.[65]

That heart transplants relied on animal experiments was blatantly false, as you will read in Chapter 9 on cardiovascular disease. There was no mention of the animal model, because it was not true. Many scientists have stressed the clinical discoveries that made the operation possible. Comroe had also written a critique of medical progress stating that all major discoveries had been a result of basic research involving animals.[66,67]

The pair surveyed the "scientific community" to determine which discoveries were important. They sent approximately half of the surveys to scientists performing basic science experiments on animals. Not surprisingly, these scientists concluded that basic science animal studies had been invaluable.[68,69,70] As the assistant editor of the *British Medical Jour-*

nal pointed out, the report entirely left out the clinical discovery of the effects of smoking on heart and lung disease, though this link was the "*most important* therapeutic maneuver for most doctors treating lung and heart disorders." (Emphasis added.)

The Comroe Dripps Report, cited by the animal experimentation lobbyists, was and still is criticized by numerous scientists and clinicians for faults of methodology and bias.

Nonetheless, for the most part, lobbyist efforts such as these pay off. The very government agencies designed to protect citizen health and finances churn out support for their bad grant funding and keep up the deception in the form of policy and propaganda. A U.S. Department of Health and Human Services document called *Animal Research: The Search for Life-Saving Answers* states, "Throughout the last century, medical scientists have depended upon the use of animals for the development of virtually all vaccines, medications, and treatments."

It is easy to get swept up in this message and overlook the way it manipulates the facts. Yes, virtually all medical scientists have used animals; in most cases their education process and even lab experiences required them to use animals. But did their innovations really depend on animals? No. The bulk of this book is devoted to explanations of how animals were not necessary for specific discoveries. Other methods, noninjurious to humans, were available. So yes, they used animals. But when they did they either got misleading results from the animals or when they did not there were other more reliable non-animal methods available. Safe, ethical research on humans and human tissue can always provide better, less flawed results.

The size and force of their propaganda avalanche suggest that animal experimenters are resting on uncertain foundations. If animal experiments are so great, why then protest so much and expensively? They have to, because keeping the truth quiet is costly.

That is incidental, however, because the economic motor supporting the animal experimentation lobby is vast. U.S. Surgical, a manufacturer of surgical equipment, and other companies like it, sponsor the Americans for Medical Progress, a supposedly unbiased consumer group. Founded in 1992 and run by former president Susan Paris, and current president Jacquie Calnan, AMP actively campaigns in support of animal tests. For example, the AMP ran a slanted series of infomercials called *Breakthroughs in Medicine* and a syndicated cartoon called *Heroes of Medicine*. Why? Because U.S. Surgical has a vested interest in the animal experimentation industry. It uses thousands of animals yearly to promote their expensive medical equipment. AMP is sarcastically referred to as "Americans For Medical Profits" because their lobbying efforts are so forceful.

What other businesses profit from animal experimentation and support lobbyists to defend their profits? Beyond the animal breeders and vendors themselves, there are manufacturers and purveyors of cages, isolation cages, syringes and needles, scales, specialized surgical equipment, animal tissues, organs and blood, animal food, watering devices, equipment to kill the animals in a specific fashion, chemicals, microscopes, magnifying devices for microsurgery, scalpels, electrical equipment, blood testing equipment, stereotactic equipment, and so on. The list is almost endless and each item sells at a premium. *Lab Animal* magazine's annual buying guide has over a hundred pages of animals, cages and equipment. Here are just a few:

- Cedar River Laboratories—cages and animals. They specialize in selling cats. Animals less than sixteen weeks old usually sell for $225.00 according to their literature.
- Perlmmune Inc.—chemicals used to analyze rodent blood and tissue.
- ANCARE—cages, bedding, watering equipment and other products needed for animal experimentation.
- ThermoCare Inc.—heated intensive care systems ranging in price from $980.00 to $4,750.00 according to their catalog.
- Therion—DNA analysis of lab animal blood samples.
- Hilltop Lab Animals—numerous animal strains, breeds and species.
- Lab Caster Specialists—casters for lab animal cages and carts.
- Marshall Farms—beagles, a very popular research animal.
- Moulton Chinchilla Ranch—chinchillas.
- Davidson Mill Breeding Labs—supposedly viral free guinea pigs.
- CAMM Research Lab Animals—"high cholesterol" rabbits. (As we point out in Chapter 9, high cholesterol in a rabbit does not mean heart disease like it does in humans.)
- Lomir Biomedical Inc.—animals and biomedical equipment for animal experimentation. Equipment includes jackets for immobilization of animals, pumps for force-feeding and gloves to provide protection from animals that bite when force fed.
- Convance—rabbits, dogs, primates, rodents and pigs.
- Harlan Sprague Dawley—numerous species, strains, and breeds of animals.
- Charles River Laboratories—$14-inbred mice, $56-inbred rats, (It is estimated that up to 100,000,000 rats and mice are used in research each year.) $123 guinea pigs and $720 miniature swine. (1997 catalog) In 1983, Charles River sold at least 22 million animals to researchers.[71]
- Primate Products Inc. of California and Osage Research Primates of Missouri—monkeys and other primates costing in the

thousands and the equipment used to restrain them, which also costs thousands of dollars.
• Hazleton Laboratories—chemical and pharmaceuticals.

The aforementioned companies and many others profit directly from animal experimentation. It is big business! Total money spent on animals and animal support products is difficult to estimate since frequently the companies are private and unwilling to divulge figures. By estimates, the industry grosses between one hundred billion and one trillion dollars per year worldwide. This includes the direct employment of hundreds of thousands of individuals. Indirectly, the industry affects thousands if not millions of people who manufacture steel, plastics, and other materials. Animal experimentation does nothing for your health but it does help keep the economy going.

Pharmaceutical companies and manufacturers of medical equipment benefit indirectly too, and it is not an exaggeration to say that they rely on animal experimentation. For example, let us say a company designs a wonder drug that it wants to sell as a cancer cure. No problem. Just give a university or research institution a few million dollars to "study" the medication. Researchers do tests and more tests on different animal species. Eventually, they either find or create a species that has a cancer and will respond to the drug. Then the drug can proceed to human trials and from there to profits. And in the meantime, the universities and research institutions grow plump.

Same goes for the United States military. In 1994 alone, the Department of Defense funded the following experiments (as extracted from the DOD Biomedical Research Database). All attempted to mimic information already exemplified in humans:

$23,000—Extend previous model of battle fatigue established in hamsters to rats.

$74,942—Test acupuncture and drugs in ferrets that are routinely used to control vomiting in humans.

$17,144—Test the effect of the drug Motilin on dogs that have undergone abdominal surgery.

$395,500—Demonstrate the effects of a chemical warfare agent antidote in non-human primates.

$626,000—Evaluate the potential of vitamin E to reduce nicotine-associated periodontal destruction in rats.

$136,000—Determine if nutrients alleviate stress in rats.

$232,515—Test the efficacy of drugs on dogs and primates that are irradiated until they vomit and bleed.

In 1997 alone the National Center for Research Resources allocated $114,502,974 to seven different institutions for the study of primates. Eighteen thousand two hundred primates were involved. According to some sources, government agencies such as these sometimes encourage biotech lobbyists to discredit the criticism of animal experimentation because they too are vested in maintaining the status quo. Frederick Goodwin, a federal official, was quoted as saying, "We're not allowed to lobby. There's a law against it. [But] all federal agencies have linkages to various advocacy groups interested in the business of that agency."[72]

Many diverse enterprises profit from the animal experimentation industry. Each has an emperor's new clothes-style complicity. The aforementioned Dr. Irwin Bross described the way this "consensus of authorities" agree to overlook the naked truth together for mutual profit of orgiastic proportions.

> It has been historically true in general that "he who pays the piper calls the tune." So what is deemed "officially true" is what is in line with the sponsor's policies, not necessarily what is in line with the facts. Moreover, the "authoritative opinion" nearly always supports the policies of its sponsors. Hence, the decisions in official science are political decisions that only masquerade as scientific ones. Those in official science have the illusion that they are not politically controlled, and at times the public may share this illusion. Whatever may be said, when the time comes to act, the actions are in line with the official policies. . . . Consider, for instance, the fact that the National Cancer Institute has spent billions of dollars on animal experimentation. The myth that such research produced the main chemotherapeutic drugs supports the continuation of this funding. The medical schools and research facilities of the biomedical establishment that share in this bonanza are certainly not going to let mere facts interfere with this lucrative business. So even though the historical facts here show that animal experiments were worse than useless in selecting clinically effective cancer chemotherapies—they were consistently misleading—the "consensus of authorities" will continue to say just the opposite.[73]

The animal experiment convention has become an enabler of unethical business activities of every stripe, a grab bag of lame excuses for every sort of treachery. Government and industry request and buy results from animal experimenters to support any questionable product or situation. If testing one species does not produce the desired result, they prod researchers to find one that does. Bross described the situation thus:

> Whenever government agencies or polluting corporations want to cover up an environmental hazard, they can always find an animal study to "prove" their claim. They can even do a new animal study

which will come out the way they want by choosing the "right" animal model system.[74]

An example is the exhaustive Philip Morris campaign to persuade the public that smoking decreased the aggressive tendencies of humans. Here is a memo from Philip Morris in 1975: "We have had a guiding hand in designing studies of the influence of injected nicotine upon the predatory attack of cats upon mice."[75]

A "guiding hand"? Philip Morris makes it sound as if it had done both mice and us a favor. The Council for Tobacco Research (CTR) awarded over twenty million dollars in grant money per year.[76]

Not until 1997 did the CTR fold up shop, as the multibillion dollar settlement proposed to compensate states for tobacco-related illnesses seemed to suggest that, predatory cats or no, too many feel that tobacco is harmful for it to continue to buy researchers to say otherwise. Their statement: "It seems imprudent to make new grants at this time."

Any big company wanting to prove their product lives up to its claims can probably find an animal "model" to fulfill their expectations. Drug companies and other manufacturers know exactly how to buy "independent" testing for their products. It stands to reason that researchers who receive money from drug companies whose products they study are far more likely to supply a favorable review than those who were not receiving financial support. Of course. Money talks. The *New England Journal of Medicine* examined this conflict of interest in a recently published report.[77] The article pointed out evidence that scientists with financial ties to pharmaceutical companies were much more likely than those without to report favorably on the product being studied. The *Wall Street Journal* reported that in only 0.5 percent of 62,000 articles reviewed had the authors reported their possible financial ties to the institution with a vested interest in the outcome of the research.[78]

Even more unsettling are the perks described in the *Journal of the American Medical Association*. Forty-three percent of more than 2,000 researchers surveyed at the top fifty US research universities stated they had accepted gifts in the past three years. In addition to gifts of trips and equipment, the researchers also accepted cash. Some accepted these gifts even when the giver attached strings such as prior approval of the results of the research being conducted.[79]

So, in addition to contributing little that is positive to medical knowledge and much that resulted in human suffering, white smockers are not always above bribery.

Note this quote from Daniel N. Robinson in *Aping Science*:

... despite the often sentimental humanitarianism of the scientific community, the basis upon which research programs are actually defended are often financial and careerist. For many years scientists engaged in what is called "pure" research regarded it as impertinence to be asked if any actual benefit to mankind or daily life might be forthcoming. As the general population has become more educated and impatient, as the national deficit has taken on galactic proportions, the scientists and their university agents have begun to issue promissory notes in return for their massive subsidies. Meanwhile, as financially strapped universities look to their science (and athletic) departments to underwrite major portions of university expenses, administrators are pushed by their Boards of Directors to secure grants, and individual scientists are spurred by administrators by having their professional status and even income tied to grant application success. George Roche's recent *The Fall of the Ivory Tower*, documents the effect of these grants upon the integrity and independence of the academic world. Thus, beyond the range of problems so precisely addressed in *Aping Science*, the Big Science movement in America has left a trail of broken promises and disasters large and small in its wake . . . The noble goal of relieving suffering and prolonging life prosecuted in a manner that does not strip life of a meaning richer than mere biological survival. It cannot be in the public's interest for its assets to be squandered in support of Big Science peddlers who promise short-cut solutions to societal problems that are at once medical, sociological, political, and in larger sense moral. It cannot be in the public's interest to expend fortunes on oversold "biomedical research" undertakings marred by confusion and occasional fraud.[80]

Becoming a Discerning Citizen and Consumer

The powers that be lull even animal lovers into reluctant support with their claims, perpetrated through the lay media. The media routinely reinforces white coat capers with uplifting articles about mouse cancer cures and rats with lowered cholesterol, and drugs that look like they will alleviate neurologically devastating diseases like multiple sclerosis or Alzheimer's in mice. These are "news." They sell papers and capture public sentiment. As we have pointed out, no one ever seems to get around to confirming when or if *humans* will benefit from these rodent-based revelations.

Further the animal experimenters' public relations engine pounces on any and every opportunity to keep their position in spin. In a recent example, the media quoted Paul McCartney as saying that his wife's cancer medications had to be tested on animals. Taken out of context, this appears to be an endorsement of animal testing by a celebrity whose wife's illness seems to have changed his known aversion to vivisection. In actuality, McCartney's position against lab animal use is stronger than ever. The medications Linda McCartney took had to be tested on animals because *the law required them to be*, not because doing so made

the medications safer for human consumption. The animal experimentation front and the media will always be accurate, as long as regulations
demand animal testing, in saying that drugs were tested on animals. For
reporters and for the public that is uninformed as to the deceptive role
of animal testing, this is too subtle a point. This subtlety works to the
benefit of the vivisectionists and makes the job of outspoken critics such
as McCartney very difficult.

In the area of science and medicine, most reporters, though not all,
are either uninformed or biased or both in their interpretation of the
facts of animal experimentation. To be fair, they too were brought up
and live in a society that perpetuates the animal-model delusion. Very
few have the background and expertise to discern what is meaningful.
Reporters cultivate and mine relationships with their favorite scientists,
ask their opinions and report accordingly. We grant many interviews
from the media and find that most do not understand the problem nor
do they have the time to allow us to explain it. Just as is true in science,
the pace, pressure and money machine of journalism does not allow in-
depth reporting and exposés that may endanger advertising. Sound bites
seldom do justice to science.

Therefore, it is not easy for the layperson to get his or her hands on
comprehensive information. Without voluble public outcry, the animal
testing machine, now large and in perpetual motion, will be difficult to
stop. Anytime animal testing is questioned, there are outcries from many
vested quarters. Scientists. Physicians. Hospitals. Bureaucrats. Pharmaceutical companies. Medical conglomerates. Politicians. Animal farmers
and vendors. Lawyers. News media. All hasten to shore up their posi-
tions and keep clear of litigation.

The interdependency between these various constituencies works like
a finely tuned ruse: The more animal experiments the researcher does,
the more articles get published. The more articles he publishes, the more
grant money he receives. The more grant money he receives, the more
money the university receives. The more money the university receives,
the better its reputation. The better its reputation, the less liable big
business is when the university safely tests its new product and hence
the more products they can sell. The more big business sells the more
money for advertising and hence the more compliant is the media. And
on the other side of this cabal is the unwitting American consumer,
paying through the nose for, at best, nothing and worse, ill health. This
is not a conspiracy, this is simple greed.

Trillions of taxpayer and charity dollars continue to funnel into wasteful experiments which are of no use to the consumer who supports them.
That is why we call animal experimentation "white coat welfare."

We must shake our tacit acceptance of all animal-based medical research! The public who is both benefactor and would-be beneficiary
must demand human solutions to our health dilemmas. Are these pro-

fessionals somehow exempt from the criteria that govern the rest of us? Would your employer allow you to be this unproductive and maintain your job?

We do not have unlimited time, money and scientists. (Even if we did, research on animals would still be bad because of all the misleading data and human suffering it creates.) If the trillions of dollars wasted on the animal model had, instead, gone to human-based alternatives, who knows what could have been accomplished by now?

In this era of budget constraints, science should focus on experiments more likely to yield tangible benefits to humans. We consumers should demand, as Gertrude Elion did, applicable results. Why support animal experimentation when other methods provide real avenues to better health?

chapter 6

Alternatives

The future of biology is really going to be [human] systems
analysis.

—Dr. Leroy Hood, University of Washington

Say we open the cages and let loose the lab animals. Then what? If
we do not experiment on animals, on whom? How will we derive our
discoveries, our cures?

Animal experimenters would have us believe that scientific innovation
would come to a great, grinding halt if animals were let out of the lab,
or as the Foundation for Biomedical Research publication *Animal Research
Fact vs. Myth* puts it: "There are no alternatives to animal research
[for human disease]."

As scientists, we find this insulting and ridiculous. Yes, if we aban-
doned the animal experimentation protocol, many researchers would
have to scramble to learn other, more predictive methodologies; and
certainly there would be major adjustments in publishing and drug approval. However, there are compelling reasons to believe that scientific
innovation would get a big boost if medical research were devoid of
animal models. Other, more rewarding techniques would gather strength
under augmented effort, and maybe we would then find cures for today's
most challenging illnesses.

There is an even more ludicrous scare tactic perpetrated by animal
experimenters and their lobbyists. That is the claim that if there were
no animal experiments we would have to experiment on humans. Human experiments, yes, but not on caged humans, nor prisoners, nor the
mentally disabled, nor lab humans, nor any unwilling experimental humans. We would conduct experiments on human cells and human tissues, examine and document humans at autopsy, tally and analyze the
results of human epidemiology studies, more carefully observe humans
in the clinical setting and spread the word among humans on preven-

tative measures. It is human health that is at risk and human wellness that is our objective. Is it not reasonable to observe the species that needs curing directly?

Everyone agrees that epidemiology makes sense. Same with autopsy. Few intelligent people argue that a clinical condition documented in an actual human never happened. Genetic, *in vitro*, and high tech developments may be inscrutable to the average person. But few question whether it is prudent to study the composition of the very cells and genes that are inflicting or skirting human disease.

These modalities are the research techniques that we should be funding now. Ancient techniques—autopsy, clinical observation, and epidemiology—have worked well in the past; now they are far more sophisticated and accurate. Others are new and incredible, the more so when compared to the atavism of animal-modeled experiments. To date, these alternative methodologies are not anywhere near as well known as animal experimentation. Part of the reason people believe that stopping animal experimentation would put the brakes on medical development is because alternative protocols are not peddled by huge corporations, which have both the money and the incentive to sway public sentiment. Companies with science that works do not need to pay lobbyists and publicists to pave their futures. There is no need to be defensive about effective methodologies. Success speaks for itself.

But success does not yet speak loudly enough. Animal experimentation lobbyist and publicist efforts fall on susceptible ears. Everyone wants to be healthy, but few people can keep abreast of medicine's growing reservoir of complexities. Even many physicians do not have the expertise in comparative biochemistry to make sense of extrapolations from animals to humans. And certainly, lay people are entirely in the dark: justifiably misinformed, since their information comes from slick advertising and reporting of press releases churned out by the animal experimentation industry itself. When they hear that furry little creatures are saving their own lives and those of their children, they do not dare risk disbelieving it.

The animal experimentation lobby is the largest medical research lobby there is. It bathes scientifically illiterate congresspeople and reporters with a steady flow of persuasive half-truths and poignant stories to buoy support for this duplicitous form of science. And while it bathes, taxpayers misspend, consumers misspend, and lives are jeopardized by falsely modeled therapies.

Human-modeled protocols decrease human suffering and increase our medical knowledge base. We define and exemplify each of these following. Subsequent chapters have many more examples. Any one of these modalities described does far more for humankind than animal experimentation, and together they can revolutionize medical research.

Clinical Studies of Patients

The most obvious bellwethers for information about human disease are diseased humans. Careful observations and analyses of patients have always been an important index of medical research. Countless discoveries have occurred at the bedside—the successful treatment of childhood leukemia and thyroid disease, our present level of HIV and AIDS therapy, and the discovery of a number of heart drugs among them.

Clinical observation could be encouraged. Without remuneration, physicians are disinclined to cooperate in studies that could have broad usefulness nationwide. If doctors were compensated, they would eagerly incorporate patients into studies. The information would be far more relevant and valuable than animal studies.

Researchers already rely on healthy human volunteers for studying new treatments and medicines, and strict guidelines control this type of research. Traditionally, volunteers receive tiny, harmless amounts of test drugs. Researchers carefully increase the dosage in the next person, while monitoring effects on breathing, heart rate, blood, urine, and various body functions. In addition to dosages, these tests also indicate how specific drugs are metabolized in the human body, information that cannot be reliably garnered from animal studies since animals metabolize differently than humans.

Called clinical pharmacology, this process is the only way to find out whether a drug will be safe and effective in people, and in what dosage. Studies like this repeat a lot of what drug companies do in animals. However, whereas the animal model tells only about the animal in question, clinical pharmacology produces data that is actually applicable to humans. More often than not, this data is entirely discrepant from that indicated in animal experiments.

In Vitro Research

As other chapters exemplify, *in vitro* research (or *test tube research* as it is also known) has revolutionized medical research, illuminating pathways to discoveries of great importance. Even the federal government acknowledges: "There is virtually no field of biomedical research that has not been affected by *in vitro* technology."[1]

In vitro means, literally, "in glass." *In vitro* research occurs in a flask or another controlled environment, rather than within a living organism or in a natural setting, which would be *in vivo*. To understand illness and therapies better, scientists observe the given culture, and observe the effects of other chemicals on it. When a chemical causes cells to mutate *in vitro*, or if it kills rapidly dividing cells, then it may cause disease in humans. When it interrupts the action of a disease-causing agent, or the disease itself, it may be curative.

For over a hundred years, scientists have refined methods for sustaining somatic cells (cells that make up our bodies, not germ cells). As a result, human cells and tissues, removed during surgery, biopsies or post-mortems, can be grown outside the body in the "test tube." The cells are carefully cultured inside special flasks or dishes, bathed in a nutrient fluid. The fluid is a complex mixture of all the substances essential for the cells' continued survival and contains nutrients, enzymes, hormones and growth factors.

Cell and tissue preservation technology is now so advanced that many different types of cells can be kept alive almost indefinitely. Cell culture is an exciting and rapidly developing field of research that holds enormous potential for improving the quality of medical research. By culturing complex mixtures and layers of cells scientists can create more realistic models of parts of the body, such as skin and capillary vessels. This increases our insight into how they work.

Just as promising as it is controversial is stem-cell research. Stem cells are "master cells" that can grow into virtually any of the body's cell types. Originally harvested from early stage human embryos, it may now be possible for stem cells to be lab-grown. Researchers anticipate that they will be able to grow new cells to replace diseased or damaged cells in patients suffering from Alzheimer's, diabetes, Parkinson's, and other illnesses.

In 1985, the National Academy of Science emphasized the advantages of human studies over animal studies, saying, "Major recent advances in our knowledge of the immune system made possible by cell culture techniques would have been virtually impossible to achieve in intact vertebrates."[2]

Research on human body matter is much more reliable than animal studies since the cells or tissue that are diseased are the same as that you are studying. For instance, let us say you are studying human metastatic cancer. There is no shortage of human cancer tissue. Human tissue, rather than being thrown away after surgery, is now harvested for just such a purpose.[3] No one need observe an animal tumor since human tumor tissue is so abundant.

The leading animal experimentation handbook says that cytotoxicity studies such as the total cellular protein assay and the neutral red uptake assay, the Lowry method, evaluation of cell adhesion, cell proliferation, morphology, membrane damage uptake of radioactive precursors, microcinematography analysis can all be performed *in vitro*.[4] Why then use a rat?

Most illnesses do their work at a microscopic level. Hence, human proteins, ion channels, cells, and cell components such as genes obviously make ideal test beds for determining ways to interrupt the course of human diseases. Even in its early years, *in vitro* science allowed the discovery of antibiotics penicillin and streptomycin, and an understanding of blood types. Human cell and tissue culture observation, in the form of *in vitro* research, has refined the processes of vaccine production, toxicity testing, and selecting new drugs. It is leading to a better understanding of illnesses such as cancer, Parkinson's disease, multiple sclerosis, diabetes, heart disease, viral infections like AIDS, and many more.

On a gross level, surgeons use the human placenta to train to repair tiny vessels and nerves, such as in re-implant procedures. The human placenta can also be used to study reactions to medications and metabolism. Scientists can watch the effects of antibiotics and other medications on cells from specific organs, or on the organs themselves.[5,6,7]

The human placenta has enormous potential for studying metabolic processes without recourse to animal experimentation. Its greatest advantage lies in eliminating the necessity for extrapolating results from animal experiments and trying to interpret them in terms of the human situation.[8]

Scientists have pointed out,

Whenever human material becomes available for research in satisfactory condition and without danger to the patient, it should be preferred to any animal living material.[9]

State-of-the-art *in vitro* technology continues to streamline the medical research process. This demands precise tooling and miniaturization. Further advances in technology have led to the development of extremely sensitive and sophisticated equipment to monitor the cultures and detect minute cellular changes.

To contain human micro-matter, tiny screening plates, now not much bigger than a pager, hold several thousand miniature wells. Scientists can fill them with different cells, then subject these to potential therapies. Fluorescent assay technology then delivers accurate information about the compounds' efficacy fast, as many as 100,000 compounds per day, per screening plate. Moreover, conducting experiments the size of motes economizes what are frequently valuable and limited supplies of human organs, cells, and tissue.

Only the convention for animal testing prevents *in vitro* tests from being used more often. Toxicologist Bjorn Ekwall elucidated,

We should not imitate cell test systems [because] that is an old toxicology; in fact simple cell line tests are much more revealing than people think, but it's difficult to sell the idea because it could be a threat, and the animal testing monopoly would be destroyed.[10]

Drug companies are branching into designing drugs that act specifically along signal transduction pathways. Signal transduction pathways are the "highways" on which many different internal stimuli travel to the cells. Since almost all known diseases make these signals dysfunction, drugs that controvert the dysfunction should inhibit disease. Scientists subject human cells to chosen chemicals *in vitro* and watch ensuing expression. They then record precise data that is far more likely to correlate to that of human clinical trials than data garnered from animals. (More about this in Chapter 7, Real Origins of Medications.)

Many scientists recognize and criticize the limited use of human tissue.[11] Some now state, "Direct extrapolation from animals to humans is frequently invalid . . . recently much interest has focused on use of human autopsy or biopsy tissue as a means of overcoming these limitations."[12]

Autopsies

Autopsies have led to many of the great medical breakthroughs described in this book. They are an essential source of knowledge. If you want to know what caused a failure, investigate the failed entity. Drs. R. B. Hill and R. E. Anderson wrote,

> Virtually the whole field of modern medical knowledge was created through study of autopsies, aided and supported by physiology, physical diagnosis, and microbiology . . . It was above all autopsy study that ushered in the modern era.[13]

Research in diabetes, hepatitis, appendicitis, rheumatic fever, typhoid fever, ulcerative colitis, congenital heart disease, hyperparathyroidism, and many other illnesses has been enriched by autopsies.[14] Autopsies elucidated the mechanisms of shaken baby syndrome, sudden infant death syndrome, and head injuries suffered during car accidents.[15,16,17]

Autopsies also indicate aspects of illness missed in diagnoses. Studies of patients who present for autopsy, performed since 1970, indicate that physicians misdiagnosed approximately ten percent.[18] One study demonstrated that in 64 percent of 2,537 cases, findings at autopsy proved that an undiagnosed disease was present at death. Undiagnosed findings either caused the patients' demise or were an important factor in the patients' health.[19]

In former days, every patient was autopsied, and that is how discoveries were made. Unfortunately, autopsies are not now done with the frequency that they once were. The rate of autopsies has dropped to less than one-quarter of what it was in the 1950s, because no one will pay for them. Once a patient has died, only rarely is anyone on hand willing to go out of pocket to find out why. Pathologists do not routinely perform autopsies unless insurance companies reimburse them, which they usually do not. The NIH funds few research projects that utilize autopsies, therefore few universities perform them. Yet, if just one out of every five patients were autopsied, an immense amount of valuable information would be retrieved. And there were be more organs for research on specific parts of the body. Again, why not divert funds to autopsies from animal experiments?

The infrequency of human autopsy, as contrasted with the bottomless reservoir of experimental zoology, caused Dr. Robert Anderson, a pathologist at the University of New Mexico, to state, "We know more about the causes of death in old mice than we do about the causes of death in old people."

We do not have to kill humans to generate bodies for autopsies. Humans die, and it is not unreasonable, as some European countries have now realized, to use their bodies in order to ease suffering in subsequent patients.

An expert in medication development stated,

No laboratory animal will ever be a completely satisfactory substitute for the human system and the time will come when we shall stop wasting the enormously valuable enzymes and organelles of the dead and instead put these to use to understand the living human being better.[20]

Epidemiology

Epidemiology is another highly rewarding area of medical research. Gathering and analyzing data regarding the incidence and prevalence of specific diseases among populations presents very valuable information about why and how the illness occurs. Scientists use this data as a point of departure for examining which genes confer either to disease or immunity. They can also draw conclusions about environmental or lifestyle factors that influence susceptible people positively or negatively. These insights suggest preventative measures that can mitigate the frequency of illness.

Epidemiology today is greatly facilitated by computer-accessible medical records that track thousands of patients at multiple institutions. Though now vastly more sophisticated, epidemiology is not a new field. Accumulated data about patients brought an end to the practice of blood-letting centuries ago.[21] In 1747, James Lind noticed that sailors came down with scurvy during long voyages. This epidemiological observation resulted in preventative action. The Royal Navy began to take limes and other citrus fruits on voyages; thus sailors were referred to as "limeys."[22]

Epidemiology uncovered innumerable occupation-induced diseases. One of the first to discover the association between industrial chemicals and disease was Alice Hamilton. Though hindered by gender bias at the turn of the century, Hamilton persisted. Her first observations revealed that lead was harmful. She went on to diagnose phosphorous poisoning in munitions workers, silicosis in sandblasters, mercury poisoning in felt workers, and carbon monoxide poisoning in steel workers. Hamilton's clinical observations and subsequent epidemiological studies laid the groundwork for many reforms in industrial health.[23] For example, wearing protective masks to filter out the silica particles now prevents silicosis.[24]

Building-related illnesses such as Legionnaires' disease, Pontiac fever, flu- and cold-like illnesses such as irritation of the upper airway, headache and difficulty focusing on the tasks at hand, allergic reactions, and immune system problems have all been discovered through epidemiology.[25] Causes include exposure to cigarette smoke, viruses, building materials, fungi, mites, and many other negative influences.

Epidemiological studies discovered the link between folic acid deficiency and spina bifida. They also showed the cause/effect relationship between smoking and cancer, heart disease and cholesterol, high blood pressure and stroke, high blood pressure and heart disease, repetitive motion and carpal tunnel syndrome, smoking and heart disease, coal dust and black lung disease, cotton dust and byssinosis, dietary fat and cancers of the colon and prostate, laundry and dry cleaning industries and cancers, and so on. Through epidemiology we learned how AIDS is transmitted.[26,27] The examples go on and on, as this book's later data indicate. As long ago as 1980, the U.S. Congress Office of Technological Assessment Report stated that epidemiological studies were more reliable than animal studies.[28]

Epidemiology gives us the opportunity to prevent disease but issues little profit to industry. This is probably why there is not a multimillion dollar political action committee called Americans for Epidemiology.

Mathematical Modeling and Computer-Assisted Research

Mathematical modeling is a relatively new area of research, as is computer-assisted research. Yet, computers are as commonplace in the laboratory as they are elsewhere, and they are broadening the scope of information that can be accurately recorded and analyzed.

When computers simulate parts of the human body as mathematical equations, it is called *mathematical modeling*. Although this process requires the enormous simplification of various body systems, it is producing some surprisingly accurate results. For example, an American computer model of 10,000 brain cells produced signals similar to those given out by a real brain. In another example, scientists use a model of a "slice" of brain to investigate how people think and remember, as well as to shed light on disorders such as epilepsy. A computer model analyzing the body's response to cancer at the National Cancer Institute in Maryland was able to show that the immune system could both fight cancer and stimulate it. Researcher Dr. DeLisi said, "It comes up with things you might otherwise miss."

Breast cancer is another area illuminated by mathematical models. We describe others elsewhere. Mathematical modeling pointed out differences between breast tumors that looked identical under the microscope. This provided clinicians the basis for different therapies for what had, at first glance, appeared to be the same tumor.[29,30]

Using computer graphics, programs can create the three-dimensional structure of molecules on screen. By studying the shape, structure, and active sites of molecules known to be medically useful, scientists can then attempt to design similar or improved structures. Already some drugs, such as the high blood pressure medication, Captopril, have been designed this way.

Similarly, chemical structures known to be toxic can be analyzed to predict toxicity of new substances without resorting to animal tests. One program called COMPACT, at Surrey University predicts chemical toxicity based on likely interaction with body enzymes. The system has already been tested on more than one hundred chemicals and so far has an accuracy of 82 percent. That is far greater than the average accuracy of animal testing. COMPACT could have predicted the toxicity of Opren, an anti-rheumatic, anti-arthritis drug withdrawn after causing liver damage.

The Electric Cell Substrate Impedance Sensing (ECIS) device uses electricity to study complex cell behavior. This non-invasive technique for testing cell cultures follows a cell's behavior at quarter-second intervals. Imagine continuing the animal testing convention in an epoch when this kind of observation is possible. Some call the people who work in these computer-driven biotech industries "robochemists."

Medical students now use interactive computer models that mimic various body systems to learn physiology. Students can prescribe drugs, monitor changes in heart rate, blood pressure, urine output, and so forth, and investigate the effects of altering certain variables. This software saves staff time, money, and space compared with animal experiments.

Instead of repeating previously conducted experiments, students, scientists, and physicians can access comprehensive medical databases to glean information, then devote valuable time and dollars to fresh explorations.

Genetic Research

Genetic research, such as the technologies created in the government-funded Human Genome Project and parallel pursuits funded by private enterprise, are changing the face of medicine. They have produced high-throughput DNA sequencing, gene mapping, and bioinformatics—fancy words for discovering what genes do. Scientists hope to identify the hundreds of thousands of genes that make up the genetic map by 2010.

The genetic variability that is so apparent in such features as height, skin and hair color, as well as temperament, extends to our health. Different genes alter susceptibility to disease, drug metabolism, and drug response. In other words, genes not only determine how we look, they also govern whether we will contract certain diseases, and how we will react to therapies. We do not yet understand even a small percentage of the total gene map and the Human Genome Project and private efforts will not answer all these questions. It may be a century before we know what all genes do and how they cooperate. But it goes without saying that the more research dollars devoted to this effort, the more expediently useful knowledge will reveal itself.

By inserting new or different genes into existing DNA strands, scientists can already correct or alter some genetic traits. They use a restriction enzyme as a sort of genetic scissors to cut a gene from a donor organism. Then they insert it into a viral DNA or plasmid (segment of DNA independent of chromosomes) that will carry it into the host cell. Scientists now use this recombinant DNA technology, as it is called, for the questionable purpose of attempting to create human diseases and human characteristics in lab animals. Instead we should be funding research that will allow the information to be used to cure human disease. It has the potential to correct birth defects and cancer susceptibility, *in utero.*

This research has already yielded insulin from humans instead of animals, decreasing the side effects of animal-derived insulin. (Many patients were unable to tolerate insulin injections or developed allergies to cow or pig proteins, after years of injecting it.) Vaccines, enzymes, antibody fragments, and growth hormones have also come from recombinant-DNA research. Using recombinant DNA in combination with microorganic hosts such as bacteria, instead of animal tissue, decreases the risk of side effects and cross-species contamination as has occurred with SV40 and the TSEs, the most notable being bovine spongiform encephalopathy or Mad Cow disease. It also allows a more pure medication, vaccine, or other product to be marketed.

Gene insertion or DNA insertion could replace the altered gene thus preventing the child from ever experiencing the birth defect. We could prevent the diseases affecting twenty million children.

Pharmacogenetics determines how genetic factors sway response to drugs. Pharmacogenomics is applied pharmacogenetics, a "gene-to-drug" strategy. It predicts a person's response to a given drug before exposure to the drug. Though still in development, pharmacogenomics will be able to customize therapies to meet explicit genetic criteria, as described in more detail later.

John Bellenson of Pangea Systems Inc., says this about technology's contribution to studies of the human genome:

> Robotics, automated sequencing, and data compilation software have enabled the sequencing of thousands of genes and gene fragments . . . Making sense of this information, and understanding how these DNA sequences and sequence fragments correlate to specific genes and molecular targets has required the development of new analytic and visualization tools and the ability to think about biology in new ways.[31]

"New ways," as he describes them, are essentially more sensible ways. Watching the basic components of our human systems to see how they respond to medications and our environment makes sense. The old way—working exhaustively to give animals diseases that only vaguely resemble human diseases then trying to cure them—does not.

Dr. David Valle of Johns Hopkins University emphasized that the informational biology that is emerging from human systems analysis is synonymous with transferring the focus on treatment to a focus on prevention. "There's no question that if you can find a way to prevent disease onset, you're way ahead of the game."[32]

Diagnostic Imaging

Why should researchers plumb animals when state-of-the-art diagnostic imaging technology lets physicians peer into afflicted and non-inflicted patients without invasive dangers or discomforts? The most commonly used scanning tests are ultrasound, positron electron tomography (PET), computed tomography or computer-aided tomography (CT or CAT), and magnetic resonance imaging (MRI). A new imaging technique called the Fly-Through uses software to assemble slices of CAT or MRI imagery into a 3-D image of a patient's interior. Physicians can use this to simulate the operation before touching the patient.

Postmarketing Drug Surveillance

After drugs make it through clinical trials and are approved, pharmaceutical companies release them to the public. Postmarketing drug surveillance (PMDS) is the reporting of any side effect of a medication after its release. Since no surveillance systems are presently required, and only infrequently do doctors volunteer to report side effects, it is impossible to keep comprehensive data on any given drug's potential for negative reactions. Moreover, there is often confusion as to what caused a side effect. Without reporting systems and methods of analyzing input, the key postmarketing drug surveillance component is almost nonexistent.

Nevertheless, were PMDS in place, it could prevent many disasters. Thalidomide might have affected a few children, but not 10,000. The methodology would also increase the odds of finding new uses for old drugs. As you will read, many of the medications used today were intended for other illnesses. Only serendipity allowed us to discover their real potential.

Scientists have this to say regarding post marketing drug surveillance:

Another objective of PMDS is to discover beneficial drug effects (anticipated or unanticipated) after a drug has been marketed. Although it is not possible to systematize serendipitous discoveries, it is desirable to approach the discovery of new indications for drugs more systematically. For example, careful follow-up of published reports of new effects of marketed drugs . . . or the monitoring of trends in medical events (e.g., cardiovascular deaths) in our population may provide useful clues about unanticipated beneficial effects of drugs. This objective is by no means a trivial one, as many additional benefits of drugs have been discovered after the drugs have been approved for marketing. Such discovery is not only beneficial for populations having a disease treatable by the new use of the approved drug, but also represents an improvement in safety and economy in drug development, since many new uses may reduce the cost of development and simultaneously prevent unnecessary exposure of subjects to potentially toxic and/or ineffective experimental drugs.[33]

The sheer bulk of these viable alternatives knocks the legs out from under the animal experimentation community's position, yet government, research institutions, and corporations continue to insist that animals are necessary to "validate" human findings. You will read throughout this book how ludicrous the insistence is. Scientists have gone on record supporting the fact that laboratory tests on animals ". . . cannot provide reliable risk assessment." and that, ". . . for the great majority of disease entities, the animal models either do not exist or are really very poor."[34,35]

Many of the causes of disease in humans cannot even be reproduced in animals. Even if animals could model the actual diseases exactly, which they cannot, the influence of human genetics, emotions, and lifestyle is essentially irreproducible.

In conclusion, it is becoming increasingly difficult to marginalize these outstanding alternative modalities, given their overwhelming superiority. Plus, scientists who recognize the inefficacy of extrapolating animal data to humans, as well as the efforts of biotech firms that wish to replace animals with their superior technologies, are making some inroads into change. As Stephen Sullivan, chairman of the board of biotechnology company Xenometrix, Inc., said,

> I'm going to guess it could be ten or twenty years, but eventually, gene expression and protein expression testing will probably replace animal testing . . . It's going to be an evolutionary process, not a revolutionary process.[36]

Many people and conventions thwart a rapid conversion of animal studies to these sophisticated alternatives. But it will happen. Why wait in the dark ages when the *Star Trek* sick bay is at hand?

chapter 7

Real Origins of New Medications

And How to Test Their Safety

Animal tests conducted to establish the effect of medicaments for humans are nonsense.

—Dr. Herdegg, animal experimenter presenting at Conference on Laboratory Animals, Hanover, Germany, as quoted in *1,000 Doctors against Vivisection*[1]

The alternatives to animal experimentation are elegant. They are forward thinking. They save lives. But the public is still mired in the atavistic mindset that medicine will not progress without cages full of furry quadrupeds. They keep asking, "Where will medications come from if we do not test them on animals?" The truth is that new medications do not spring from lab rat to bottle.

Lab animals are only an unnecessary intermediary step between the design phase and clinical trials. Before the animal-testing stage, other factors suggest a given substance's usefulness and deploy scientists to verify their hypothesis. Great new medications are not hiding in mouse urine or chimp spit. There are four tried and true methods for finding fresh drugs:

- Discover new substances from nature.
- Uncover a different curative value in an existing medication.
- Modify the chemical structure of a similar medication.
- Design a new medication from scratch based on what you want the medication to do.

Once researchers have theorized about a substance's usefulness and tested it in test tubes, they administer it to animals to see whether or not it works on them. They obtain plenty of feedback about its effectiveness in the species tested, and if it is positive we will find out about it in the media. Nevertheless, just because it cures mice does not mean it will do the same for humans. As demonstrated in previous chapters, this animal testing often works at cross-purposes to discovery.

From prehistory forward, humans have gathered information about human cures only from trying them out on humans. Everything we know about drugs relates back to this data. The truth is, even now with the prevalence of the animal-model, real developments always arise from a human-modeled foundation.

Natural Legacy

Prior to the 1900s, all medications resulted from astute observation and skillful application. Though certainly pharmaceutical development has accelerated enormously since the mid-nineteenth century—a pill for every ill—many, indeed most therapies have their foundation in curative ingredients passed from generation to generation throughout time. To say otherwise is deceptive. Of these, the following are but a few examples:

- Curare, a substance the Incas used to paralyze their prey, is now used to relax muscles during surgery. The drug is extracted from the wourali root.
- Vincristine, an anticancer drug is derived from the rose periwinkle plant. It is a frequently used chemotherapeutic.
- Yohimbine, a medication used to reduce high blood pressure in humans came from the bark of the African Rubacae tree.[2] (Yohimbine is used for the opposite purpose in dogs, in which it increases blood pressure following certain types of anesthesia.)
- Digoxin is also a botanical extract, from the foxglove plant, digitalis. William Withering, an English physician interested in botany, heard of this folk-remedy for "dropsy" from his patients. Unlike many physicians, he listened. He found foxglove in 1775, extracted digitalis from the plant, and gave it to patients suffering from the condition. It worked. Today "dropsy" is known to be a symptom of heart failure, and is treated with the modern version of digitalis, digoxin. Doctors also prescribe the medication for irregular heartbeats. In 1905, Dr. James Mackenzie gave the drug to patients suffering from rapid heart rates. It improved their condition and has been used ever since. This was discovered clinically as well.[3,4]
- Morphine is a potent painkiller extracted from poppy flowers.
- Quinine, a medication to treat malaria comes from cinchona bark. Serendipitously, a famous physician discovered that quinidine, also derived from cinchona bark, could treat irregular heartbeats.[5] In 1914, a patient of the now legendary Dr. K. F. Wen-

kebach was diagnosed with atrial fibrillation, which then had no treatment. The patient told the great doctor that he would just take care of it himself. The next day the patient returned, apparently cured. Wenkebach reportedly locked the door and told the patient that neither of them was leaving until the patient had explained how this miracle occurred. The patient was a businessman whose travel required him to take quinine for malaria protection. He had noticed that this sometimes helped his atrial fibrillation. Wenkebach took this information and published it. He noticed that quinine did, in fact, work, but not all the time. He, and others, therefore studied quinine, quinidine, and cinchonine and compared their ability to inhibit atrial fibrillation. Quinidine was the most effective and is still used today.[6,7]

- Artemether, a new antimalarial medication, was derived from the Chinese shrub wormwood plant. Physicians use artemether to treat cerebral malaria and forms of malaria that are resistant to more commonly used medications for malaria such as quinine.[8,9]

- Atanine, a drug derived from the plant Evodia rutaecarpa, kills the parasite responsible for schistosomiasis, a debilitating disease.[10]

- Aspirin was first prescribed by Hippocrates, around 400 B.C.E., in the form of willow bark. In 1853, a German scientist refined the active ingredient from willow bark. Bayer began commercially producing aspirin on August 10, 1897, making it the first mass-produced drug. The most commonly used medication in the world, it owes nothing to animal experimentation.

Weighing the whole of modern pharmaceutical progress, it is impossible to disagree with the following assessment by Dr. Anthony Dayan of Wellcome Research Laboratories:

The weakness and intellectual poverty of a nave trust in animal tests may be shown in several ways, e.g. the humiliatingly large number of medicines discovered only by serendipitous observation in man (ranging from diuretics to antidepressants), or by astute analysis of deliberate or accidental poisoning, the notorious examples of valuable medicines which have seemingly "unacceptable" toxicity in animals, e.g. griseofulvin producing tumors and furosemide causing hepatic necrosis in mice, the stimulant action of morphine in cats, and such instances of unpredicted toxicity in man, such as the production of pulmonary hypertension by Aminorex and SMON. The rapidly increasing interest in clinical pharmacology, and the drive to better means of measurements in man, also reflect the uncertainty of animal experimentation and realization that the study of man alone can ever prove entirely valid for other men.[11]

Modifying Chance Cures

Consider what actually raises scientists' awareness of a compound's therapeutic potential for a particular condition. Look back over the history of drug development. Trace the antecedents of drugs like protease inhibitors. They were developed by rearranging chemical structures already known to produce specific effects. You will find that each has, at its origins, one aspect, and one aspect alone that directed recognition of the drugs' applicability to specific purposes. That aspect is chance.[12–15]

Some scientists take credit for discoveries which, in fact, were brought about by observing unexpected results. True, they had to notice the results and that demanded attentiveness, but the truth is they were just lucky. *Chance favors the prepared mind.* It is time that science and society stop crediting new drugs to animal experimentation and instead credit serendipity when appropriate.

We have already described what is possibly the most serendipitous occasion in medical history—the discovery of penicillin. Many other fortuitous discoveries, made without use of the animal model, or despite the use of the animal model, are described throughout this book. Examples are the use of nitrogen mustard, prednisone, and actinomycin D as cancer treatments, as noted in Chapter 8, Cancer, Our Modern-Day Plague.[16,17,18] Potassium bromide was introduced as an epilepsy treatment when in 1853 it prevented a young woman from having further seizures.[19] The bulk of curative compounds, accidentally discovered throughout history and acting as the foundation for present-day pharmaceutical development, is persuasive.

You have read how animal testing frequently attributes properties to compounds that ultimately prove incorrect when they reach the clinical trial phase. The effects that these compounds demonstrate during human testing sometimes suggest other uses. Or as one authority described,

Perhaps a look into the past can give a glimpse of the future. In this regard, the potential of serendipity cannot be overlooked when evaluating treatment strategies. Throughout the history of medicine, there are examples of significant advances coming about as a result of careful clinical monitoring of a drug that was supposed to do something but had an effect in an unpredicted direction.[20]

Hence, humans now use the same drugs for entirely different purposes. Some are as follows:

- Catapres (Clonidine) is a drug originally intended to control headaches and sinus congestion. Allegedly, animal experiments suggested clonidine's effectiveness for these symptoms, though this does beg the question, how does one know when a rat no longer has a headache? It was tested and FDA-approved as a headache remedy. In point of fact, clonidine proved more useful as an anti-hypertensive agent, a use discovered clinically by physicians.[21,22] One unfortunate side effect of this drug is a withdrawal phenomenon. Patients must taper off the medication over a prolonged period of time, lest they suffer severe withdrawal symptoms. After the fact, scientists were unable to reproduce this withdrawal in rats, cats, or dogs.[23,24] Ironically, physicians discovered that clonidine aids humans in withdrawing from other drugs, a purpose for which it is now routinely administered.
- Another drug category, antidepressants, issued from clinical observation, not animal experimentation. Doctors administered iproniazid to tuberculosis patients to control secretions. The euphoria it caused suggested a new class of antidepressants. In 1983, N. Sitaram and E. S. Gershon noted iproniazid was effective in relieving depression in humans, and found that the drug induced hypothermia in mice. They conjectured that any other drug that could induce hypothermia in mice might also act as a human antidepressant. However, it turned out that this effect was unique to iproniazid. Iproniazid provided the basis for monoamine oxidase inhibitors. Another example of drugs conceived for other purposes are the tricyclic antidepressants originally developed as antipsychotics.[25,26]
- Antabuse developers designed the drug as an antiparasitic agent. They took it themselves, then had a cocktail and became violently nauseous. Antabuse is now used to discourage alcoholics from imbibing.[27]
- Non-steroidal anti-inflammatory drugs introduced as arthritis treatments are now used for dysmenorrhea, pain, and other orthopedic conditions.
- Selective serotonin-reuptake inhibitors such as floxetine (Prozac) and sertraline (Zoloft), first prescribed for depression, are now used for bulimia, anxiety, obsessive-compulsive disorder, alcoholism and other psychiatric conditions.
- Insulin has been found effective for lowering potassium as well as for treating diabetes.
- Calcium channel blockers, introduced for treating angina, now help patients with high blood pressure, headaches, coronary vasospasm, and dysrhythmias.

- Lidocaine is a commonly used medication for ventricular dysrhythmias. Its use was discovered accidentally during a heart
  catheterization.[28,29] Another medication used for irregular
  heartbeats is phenytoin. It was originally designed for use in
  epilepsy and is still used for that. However, during clinical trials
  it affected the irregular heartbeats of some patients.[30]
- Beta-blockers were originally used for irregular heartbeats, and
  still are, but during clinical use scientists noticed that the medication lowers blood pressure and relieves angina and headaches.[31]
- Grapefruit has an enzyme-suppressing ingredient that, should it
  be added to certain drugs, will reduce the needed dose. This
  was discovered accidentally by a doctor with a preference for
  grapefruit juice.[32]

These are but a few random examples. The point is this: Nature, experience, and human observation have always provided us with abundant direction. They continue to do so, and the directions benefit from
all that modern biotechnology has to offer. This reservoir of indicators
is more than sufficient, used in tandem with human-modeled assays, for
drug development and testing. Any processes that employ nonhumans
are senseless and dangerous.

Finessing New Medications through the Human Element

According to the Pharmaceutical Research and Manufacturers of America, it takes an average of fifteen years to bring a medication from con-
ception to human patients. The organization estimates that only one
percent of new medications tested in labs go on to human trials, and the
Food and Drug Administration eventually approves only five percent of
these.[33] Typically, it takes around $350,000,000 to get a drug from the
idea-phase to the shelf.

Prior to granting an IND (Investigational New Drug) number, the
FDA presently requires data in regard to a new drug's toxicity, teratogenicity and carcinogenicity, its actions on the molecular and cellular
levels, and on animal organ systems—the central-nervous system, cardiovascular system, blood, lungs and reproductive system among them.

Animal tests are not needed to explore the efficacy of a drug's target
action. *In vitro* biochemical assays (such as those described in Chapter
6 on alternatives) can determine whether the drug does what it is designed to do. The strength and superiority of biotechnological substitutes
for animals is best reflected in AIDS medications, since demand for the

drugs has hastened them to market without protracted animal testing. (See Chapter 10 on AIDS.)

As regarding toxicity, Clark Heath, the vice president for epidemiology and surveillance research at the American Cancer Society, stated,

> With respect to how we judge the toxicity of potential biologic activity of a given compound, animal tests are not necessarily the final word. They're probably misleading. High doses of a particular compound given over a period of time may suggest carcinogenicity not so much from their innate carcinogenicity but the fact that they have caused so much tissue damage and tissue [proliferation] that the risk of cancer increases.

Most tests are conducted on animals, leading to inapplicable results. Animal testing does provide controlled outcomes and the illusion of predictable results, as counseled by one researcher,

> Finally, surrogate end points are often developed in animal models of disease, since changes in a specific variable can be measured under controlled conditions in a well defined population. However, extrapolation of these findings to human disease is likely to be invalid.[34]

Note this from the *Federal Register*, August 21, 1996:

> The current regulatory requirements for the assessment of carcinogenic potential of pharmaceuticals . . . provide for the conduct of long term carcinogenicity studies in two rodent species . . . Since the early 1970s, many investigations have shown that it is possible to provoke a carcinogenic response in rodents by a diversity of experimental procedures, some of which are now considered to have little or no relevance for human risk assessment.

The *Federal Register* of only a few days later, August 26, 1996, continues, "Acute toxicity studies in animals are usually necessary for any pharmaceutical intended for human use."

In spite of confessing that animal testing does not work, the government goes on to reinforce the requisite for it. Why? We have already exposed the vested-interest groups who are making money off this process, members of the AMA among them. Certainly government ambivalence does not motivate these groups to make changes so desperately required.

The White Paper, the American Medical Association's pro-animal experimentation document, admits, "They [alternative methods to animal experimentation] cannot reproduce exactly the intact biological system

provided by live animals. Each method suffers from at least some inherent deficiency."[35]

In truth, no method—animal, human, or test tube—can reproduce the
reactions of every patient with one hundred percent accuracy. Reactions
to diseases and medications often differ, even dramatically, between men
and women, between races, between age groups, even between family
members. Even the best drugs work in less than one hundred percent of
patients. Many work in as few as twenty percent.[36]

For example, since women are more responsive to drugs that bind to
kappa receptors than men are, some drugs are effective on women and
ineffective on men. Black patients suffering from high blood pressure are
more affected by sodium restriction than whites.[37] People of Asian descent metabolize the anti-tuberculosis medication isoniazid rapidly, while
whites do so slowly.[38] One-in-three-hundred whites possesses two copies
of an otherwise harmless genetic variation that renders prescribed
lymphoblastic leukemia drugs fatal.[39]

We are all different, but not as different from each other as we are
from animals. There, the differences are so enormous as to render animal
testing meaningless.

As we have already pointed out in previous chapters, the inability to
extrapolate data even between species of animals exaggerates this meaninglessness. A recent article in the *Journal of the Veterinary Medical
Association* reinforced this with examples: the LD50 of digitoxin is 670
times greater in the rat than in the cat. The anticancer medication azaur-
idine is tolerated by people but causes lethal bone marrow suppression
in dogs. Serotonin raises blood pressure in dogs and people, but lowers
it in cats. To examine other incongruities, how about diphenhydramine,
marketed most commonly as Benadryl? Benadryl works well in humans
and dogs, but at widely discrepant dosages. If humans take more than
one-fourth the dose recommended for their Labrador retriever, they sleep
for two days. The female mouse microsome metabolizes chloroform ten
times slower than the male. Male mice are more susceptible to kidney
damage from chloroform than are females.[40] Mice, rabbits, and horses
cannot vomit, while dogs and cats can. As the journal author concluded,
"It is unwise to extrapolate information concerning drugs from one species to another."[41] And this from the journal *Bio/Technology* in 1992:
"One fundamental deficiency of animal tissue is that it contains *animal
receptors*—a boon in the development of drugs for rats, cats, and dogs
but of dubious value in human health care."[42] (Emphasis added.) Since
animals cannot predict the reactions of other animals to a drug, it is not
surprising that they fail to predict human reactions.

No matter how exhaustive the animal testing, problems can still develop. Fenclozic acid, a potential new anti-inflammatory drug, showed
no side effects in mice, rats, dogs, rhesus monkeys, patas monkeys, rabbits, guinea pigs, ferrets, cats, pigs, cows, or horses. But the drug caused

acute cholestatic jaundice, a type of liver failure, in humans.[43] Tragedies
like these happen all the time.

Animal models for human reactions to medications simply do not
exist. A renowned pharmacologist, Dr. B. B. Brodie, while accepting a
prize for pharmacology, said this to a room full of scientists who make
their living testing drugs for toxicity on animals, it is "a matter of pure
luck that animal experiments lead to clinically useful drugs."[44] Relying
on luck to prove efficacy is neither scientific nor safe.

Non-animal methods are not comprehensive, but they certainly offer
more security than animal tests. And eliminating animal tests would free
up funds for more comprehensive non-animal methods.

One important point glossed over by the animal-experimentation
lobby is this: new medications must still go through clinical trials prior
to being released to the public. This stage alone has the potential to
predict adverse reactions accurately. Unfortunately, clinical trials are
usually way too brief, both in scope and duration.

These human trials are known as phases I, II, and III. Phase I is conducted on healthy volunteers, phase II on a small number of patients
who hope to benefit from the drug, and phase III on large numbers of
patients as it was designed to be used. Not surprisingly, since drugs were
animal-modeled not human-modeled, only one-in-twelve even survives
phase I—a scintilla of a success rate, much more microscopic than the
fifty-fifty chance discussed previously.[45] If these phases progress without
a hitch, the medication may be released for the general public.

Finally, with human consumption of new medications, scientists can
accurately assess the side effects. Still, many pro-vivisectionists insist that
animal testing is necessary because these clinical phases still fail to reveal
all the dangers. Well, yes, we agree. The clinical phases fail to reveal
dangers, but not because humans are bad predictors for humans, but
because *they are much too condensed both in terms of duration and
variety of recipients.*

Even with three phases, far too few people receive any given drug in
clinical trials prior to its being released. The people who do take the
medication are usually healthy and are rarely taking other medications.
Characteristically, clinical trials exclude children, pregnant or lactating
women, and the elderly. Also excluded are individuals not likely to benefit from the intended use of the medication. In addition to being narrow
subject-wise, the brevity of clinical testing works at counter purposes to
consumer health. Many adverse side effects will not be noticed in the
short time frame.[46]

The three-phase process only predicts what will happen when some
people take the drug. Other individuals may still have an allergic reaction or an idiosyncratic reaction. Occasionally, side effects do not
manifest until after drugs are used by thousands of people over an extended period of time. Just look at the examples in the earlier chapter.

Remember, all went through animal tests. Clearly, the side effects are not found in animal experiments. Only human use revealed the side effects. It hardly matters if a drug has sailed through animal tests if it subsequently kills and injures people taking it.

Many, if not most new drugs are ultimately administered for illnesses other than those for which they were originally designed, as described in a previous chapter. This means that a patient population different from that tested in clinical trials winds up taking the drug, therefore diminishing the worthiness of the clinical trials. Also, since children, lactating and pregnant women, and the elderly do not usually participate in the clinical testing phase, their reaction to the drugs is unknown. The duration and scope of clinical testing plainly needs expansion.

In addition, humans frequently use combinations of drugs, and animal testing fails to predict how those drugs will interact. These interactions sometimes create severe and life threatening reactions, not evidenced until humans take the medications.[47]

Obviously, the protocol demanding animal testing is absurd since only human-based testing offers relevant data. Bypassing the misleading animal phase of medication testing would greatly improve the quality of the process, and leave more funds to support broader clinical testing and more extensive *in vitro* testing. New medications would not be withheld from patients for years because of fallacious animal data, and bad medications would be picked up in the extended clinical human trials.

It is important to emphasize, as we do again in Chapter 8 on cancer, the critical need for extending clinical trials. To summarize, present clinical trials are ineffective for three reasons. They are too short in duration. They do not test enough people. And they do not test a broad enough range of people (different ages, ethnic groups, and sexes). Moreover, too often side effects that conflict with animal data are disregarded because there exists a strong predilection in favor of the animal model.

Without the animal model, common side effects would be, as they now are, routinely identified during pre-clinical *in vitro* analysis and human trials. Rare ones would not emerge until large numbers of patients take the drug, just as they do today.

The only way to identify side effects that occur in low numbers is via postmarketing drug surveillance. This data can be difficult to acquire because surveillance systems are not presently in place or are not enforced. Researchers cannot keep humans under observation in cages, injecting them until they become sick and die. They must rely on humans—either patients or physicians—to report reactions to drugs.

There is a considerable chasm in communication. The critical phase of drug testing is left too much to volunteerism from people who already have too little time. Presently, people do not report adverse drug reactions because they are busy or because they are not completely sure that symptoms are due to the drug. For example, heart attacks in Viagra users might have been naturally occurring or brought about by the drug. When physicians administer pharmaceuticals, they may see one or two reactions in their patients. Those may not seem significant until they learn that other physicians have seen the same one or two also. And the only way to learn about these others is if their peers report them. Plus, filling out forms is time-consuming and distracts from their remunerative task of giving therapy. There exists the added drawback that any interaction with the government is unlikely to be efficient. Clearly, some serviceable reporting system, together with incentives, is required to streamline and assure comprehensive postmarketing drug surveillance.

Importantly, circumventing the animal testing phase would not increase the peril to humans. Actually, tragedies would decrease if the FDA changed the way medications are evaluated prior to releasing the drug on the unsuspecting public. By ceasing animal testing of drugs, we forfeit only expense and a very false sense of security.

As an editorial in *Nature* pointed out in January 2, 1997: ". . . judgments have to be made at many stages, even in supposedly objective studies. Extrapolation from animal models to human impacts of drugs carries uncertainties; apparently reasonable assumptions can turn out to be disastrously wrong." In short, only by observing humans and testing on human tissue we will be able to prevent the next thalidomide, the next Opren, the next clioquinol, and the next Eraldin.[48]

A Plea for Much Overdue Reform

Nonanimal dependent science and technology have evolved at an inconceivable pace since the Kefauver-Harris Act passed in 1961. Now, hightech nonanimal testing procedures create a vast and increasing repertory of alternatives to animal experimentation. The nonanimal procedures are actually predictive, whereas the animal tests never were and still are not. They would make a joke of the existing protocol, were animal-testing not so tragic and expensive.

Biochemistry is now sophisticated enough that researchers can even design new medications from scratch, based on what they want them to do at the cellular level. To create cures, scientists analyze how cell structure functions to facilitate or thwart the disease process. And they examine the genetic makeup that predisposes us to diseases.

We now know that our cells await instructions from a wide array of bodily signals, including hormones, growth factors, neurotransmitters, and cytokines (protein hormones secreted by T-cells that stimulate inflammatory response). In response to these signals, cells may divide, express genetic attributes, or die. Healthy functioning cells respond to messages from these different internal stimuli. Since almost all known

diseases produce dysfunction in these signals, drugs designed to controvert the dysfunction often inhibit disease.

Scientists subject human cells to chosen chemicals *in vitro* and watch
ensuing expression. They then record precise data that is far more likely
to correlate to that of human clinical trials than data garnered from
animals. Dr. Dennis Parke writes,

> there are indeed more appropriate alternatives to experimental an-
> imal studies and, for the safety evaluation of new drugs, these com-
> prise short-term *in vitro* tests with microorganisms, cells and tissues,
> followed by sophisticated pharmacokinetic studies in human vol-
> unteers and patients.[49]

In part, Dr. Parke is writing about "custom" drugs, drugs tailored to
the human who requires them, and an exciting new field called pharmacogenetics illustrates just how far we have traveled. This new modality examines how the genetic makeup of specific individuals prede-
termines reactions to given medications. Researchers have, to date,
identified more than 6,000 genes involved in drug pathways. Pharmacogenetics illustrates what those genes do in response to certain chemicals. It predicts which drugs produce which side effects and which will
work best in which patients. It identifies subsets of people in whom
specific drugs work and do not work. Indeed, leaders in the industry
anticipate that as much as twenty percent of drug development costs
could be reduced through pharmacogenetics.[50]

Pharmacogenetics is far more precise science than pumping Mickeys
and Plutos full of chemicals, then waiting for them either to recover from
diseases (diseases they would never contract naturally) or fall over dead.
Yet, scientists still test medications on animals and fallaciously assume
that the results are predictive. Despite the fact that animal studies are so
unreliable, they continue to cost drug companies and hence patients,
insurance companies and government billions of dollars. Vested interest
groups have sold us a billion dollar whopper by forcing the pharmaceutical industry to test on animals. To repeat, the only reason this practice
continues is for the legal protection of pharmaceutical companies.

Instead of unreliable animal studies, why not utilize more extensive
computer modeling; pre-clinical testing on human tissue; larger, longer
clinical trials with a more diverse population of individuals; and mandatory postmarketing drug surveillance? These procedures would offer
the general public vastly safer medications. They would go a long way
to preventing the problems we see today. When the FDA shifts its emphasis to predict drug-drug interactions and predict how tissues will respond to the medication using now-available biotechnology, we will finally pay for and have highly useful human data.

chapter 8

Cancer, Our Modern-Day Plague

Everyone should know that most cancer research is largely a fraud, and that the major cancer research organizations are derelict in their duties to the people who support them.

—Linus Pauling, PhD, two-time Nobel Prize–winner

Cancer is our grim reaper, a dark and terrible health threat and destroyer of lives. Every one of us knows its pervasive countenance, either personally, or through loved ones and acquaintances. Projections indicate that one of every five Americans will die of cancer. Forty percent of us will have a diagnosis of cancer at some time in our lives. Ominously, cancer's shadow pervades everything. We read about it, hear about it, and fear it more deeply than any other present disease. It sways decisions about the way we work, eat, parent, travel, and spend our time and our money. Cancer is the harbinger of death, but its threat defines life.

This, our greatest common paranoia, first went political in 1971 when the Nixon Administration declared the "War on Cancer." The medical establishment then shouldered their research muskets, not just as healers, but as mercenaries. Sensing inexhaustible revenue sources, scientists began serving up grant proposals. The government's call-to-arms has received allocations unprecedented in history.

We all know the battle is not yet won, even with billions poured into the war per year. In fact, cancer deaths have increased steadily. From 1973 until 1992, the death rate from cancer actually increased by 6.3 percent.

The obstacles to winning against cancer are immense, complicated, and multifold. However, the failure is in large part due to our proclivity for animal experimentation. Here we address this major aspect of the flawed "War on Cancer" strategy.

Although the battle is waged on human behalf, it is animals who have been the foot soldiers—and humans who have suffered as a consequence. In hopes of identifying which substances can induce cancer and which can cure it, thousands of substances have been fed to, painted on, and injected in hundreds of millions of animals. If this had made the world a safer place, perhaps the experiments would have had some arguable merit. But it has not. In many cases it has actually led to more life loss and introduced new dangers. We will prove this and show that animal testing for cancer is, at its foundation, misconceived. Even as long ago as 1976, only five years into the "war," scientists confessed, "Unfortunately, extrapolations from animal results to man remains largely problematic and no amount of mathematical sophistication can render such extrapolation more certain."[1]

It is not just about entirely bogus science. The fact that animal-model cancer experimentation fails, again and again, to make meaningful contributions to cancer research, and billions of grant dollars continue to be funneled into these projects yearly is criminal. These assets, which could go to any other anticancer venue, are totally wasted. And of course, we cannot put figures to the human costs.

What Is the Beast We Call "Cancer"?

To comprehend the insanity of animal-modeled cancer research, one must understand the nature of cancer itself. Cancer is an umbrella term applied to a great number of diseases. There are over 200 different forms of human cancer alone. Simply put, all cancers share one characteristic—untrammeled reproduction of genetically flawed cells.

In a healthy organism, cells die off in a systematic order, and another cell of the same type replaces each dying cell. When this one-for-one replacement system becomes unregulated, a single cell, with distinct genetic characteristics, "goes onco." It begins wildly reproducing itself without regard to function or system needs. It becomes a malignant neoplasm.

This results in an aggregation of millions of replicates of the one flawed cell. The location and type of cells that go berserk define the type of cancer—breast cancer from breast cells, leukemia from certain blood cells, and so on.

According to present understanding, exposures and genetic predisposition bring about most cancer. We now know that some genes leave some people more vulnerable to cancer, leading to cancer if stimulated by certain chemicals. Exposure to carcinogens, stress, poor diet, and unhealthy work and living environments may introduce these chemicals, thus weakening our bodies' ability to fix themselves. Over a period of time, these variables interact in our systems, in degrees both subtle and potent, to compromise our healthful cell reproduction. As we age, we eventually manifest cancer or we do not. But cancer, in whatever of its 200–some guises, takes a long time to replicate into a visible tumor.

Again, these 200 cancers are only human cancers. Some of them have counterparts in some animals, but the nature of these counterparts—in terms of cause, effect, treatment, and prognosis—differs greatly from that in human cancer. Why? Because, as we have explained in earlier chapters, animals are not proto-humans.

The discrepancies between cancer in different species are glaring in every case. A physician and pet owner heard that a small tumor on his Dalmatian's leg was a histiocytoma. His knowledge of human medicine led him to the worst possible conclusion. He immediately burst into tears. In humans histiocytoma is highly malignant and carries a grave prognosis. What he did not know is that, in dogs, this is not the case. Dogs recover without treatment. Though the condition has the same name in both species, its properties are different. Humans can die from histiocytoma. Canines do not.

So, in the case of histiocytoma, and in every other instance, the cancers are specific to the species. Their molecular, immunological, and genetic differences always subvert comparisons. Each creature has different physiologic and pharmacological responses. As Nobel laureate Renato Dulbecco said: "If we wish to understand human cancer, the [research] effort should be made in humans because the genetic control seems to be different in different species . . ."[2]

Humans and chimpanzees, though hardly a close match in terms of disease susceptibility, have more in common than humans and rodents. Yet, it is rodent study that pervades cancer research. Obviously, experimentation on rodents poses fewer objections and is much cheaper than experimentation on chimpanzees or humans. The cheapest lab mouse costs five dollars. Chimpanzees cost thousands to hundreds of thousands of dollars to obtain, house, and maintain. Everyone on both sides of the lab animal commerce knows how to economize on materials costs. The economics of animal vending and buying is its own ghastly story, but what bears repeating here is this: Though we find malignant neoplasms in both humans and lab animals, the cancers are very different.

As Animal Experimentation Metastasizes

When you think of the abundance of flawed animal-model experiments reproducing themselves one after another without any regard for the overall health of humans, standard cancer research seems like its own rampant malignancy.

Half a century ago, there was already plenty of doubt about the efficacy of using animals in human cancer research. In 1952, *The Lancet* cautioned against it, "Warning is given not to carry over, without reservation, to man, the conclusions based on animal experiments. In monkeys none of the powerful carcinogens [of man] has been shown to produce cancers."[3]

Nevertheless, by the time the War on Cancer was declared, research facilities in the United States were already years into "weapon" development. An analogy with the defense industry, fat with newly-developed munitions and looking for a war, is not far off. Both animal-model concepts and creatures were rife and ready to deploy by the Nixon years, because earlier legislation had catalyzed animal purveyors and the animal experimentation industry.

Despite many doubts, the belief that animal testing could resolve every quandary was at its apogee in the late 1950s, though ironically, the only known carcinogens were those found by studying actual humans epidemiologically. For example, it was already known that exposure to arsenic led to skin cancer and chimney sweeps exposed to tar developed scrotal cancer.[4] The chimney sweep data led researchers to apply tar to rabbits' ears and to mice, in order to "validate" what they already knew. The rabbits got cancer; the mice did not.[5] What could researchers deduce from this? That mice and chimney-sweeps are the same? That rabbits and chimney-sweeps are not? Already decision-making based on animal-models was wildly ludicrous.

Yet, we will see this illogical chain of events again and again. Once epidemiological evidence of carcinogenicity appears, scientists then attempt to validate the findings in the lab with animals, sometimes succeeding, though usually not.

Clinical evidence of human carcinogens was not, for some reason, proof. Instead, human cancer victims were regarded as fodder for more and more ghoulish animal experimentation. For example, study of dye workers showed a high incidence of bladder cancer. Droves of dyed lab animals failed to prove the rule. Chromium was shown to be carcinogenic in humans but not in animals. The link between radiation and cancer was also reported from clinical studies by that time. In 1956, British doctors warned of carcinogenic effects of X rays in pregnancy resulting in childhood cancers. But no amount of irradiated pregnant quadrupeds necessarily produced the same effect.

In these instances and many others, the inability to validate carcinogenicity in animals kept cancer-causing agents legal for a much longer time. Scientists were more convinced by animal experiments which "disproved" carcinogenicity than they were humans with cancer. People were completely bamboozled into accepting that the laboratory was, as Bernard had written, the "true sanctuary" of medicine.[6–10]

Without any evidence that the same substances could cause cancer in humans and animals, Congress busied itself with legislation that legitimized and promoted chemical testing on animals. Legislators passed first the Federal Food, Drug, and Cosmetic Act of 1958 (though critics claimed that it would do nothing to enhance food safety[11]), then the Delaney Clause, which stated that "no additive shall be deemed safe if it is found to induce cancer when ingested by man or animal." This Delaney Clause became the basis for testing of everything from new foods to drugs on animals.

Delaney received one of its first applications in asbestos testing. This episode's untidy tragedy introduced a syndrome that has repetitively dogged anticancer initiatives: While scientists try unsuccessfully to give animals cancer with a specific known human carcinogen, squandering inordinate sums of money and time, people continue to get cancer from that carcinogen. The link between asbestos and human cancer was described based on clinical studies as long ago as 1907. After Delaney, eager to "prove" asbestos' toxicity in non-humans, scientists were unrelenting in their efforts to induce cancer in animals through asbestos exposure. Although painful lesions did occur on animals, they disappeared as the asbestos was withdrawn. In animals, the disease was not permanent. The New York Academy of Sciences assured people in 1965 that,

> ... a large literature on experimental studies has failed to furnish any definitive evidence for induction of malignant tumors in animals exposed to various varieties and preparations of asbestos by inhalation or intratracheal injection [a needle is inserted into the windpipe directly depositing chemicals to the lungs bypassing the mouth and pharynx].[12]

 Not so in humans. People who inhaled asbestos fibers and dust continued to contract asbestosis, and later lung cancer and mesotheliomas (inoperable cancer of the chest and abdominal lining). But resistance from the asbestos lobby was fierce. It took nearly thirty years before the sheer bulk of human-model evidence against asbestos became irrefutable.

Not until 1986 did the Environmental Protection Agency recommend an immediate ban on asbestos' major uses and products. However blatantly wrong this expensive attempt to coerce a match between human and animal physiology was, it did not, in any way, slow the forward motion of animal-model cancer research.

No amount of caution could contain the macabre enthusiasm for animal-model experimentation. First Delaney and then almost twenty years later the declaration of a war that could not, inexplicably, be waged without lab animals? Between 1970 and 1985, fervent researchers subjected animals to over half a million compounds for anticancer effects. 500,000. Based on these animal experiments, only eighty compounds progressed to clinical trials. A mere twenty-four proved to have any anticancer activity in humans. Of the twenty-four, twelve went on to have a substantial role in chemotherapy.

Twelve new anticancer medications sounds pretty good until we learn that all twelve of these were analogues or chemical variations of previously-known chemotherapeutic agents. The fact that these chemicals could be used to fight cancer had *already been predicted by their chemical structure*. Animal experimentation proved nothing new.[13,14,15] This was entirely expected, as it had long been known that cancer in animals did not mimic human disease. What an alarmingly poor return on the investment of fifteen years and billions of dollars. A poor return that is unless you were one of the researchers, universities, or university presidents whose salary was paid by the funding.

Of Mice and Men

Every few months the media announces a groundbreaking offensive in the War on Cancer. Almost all of these developments have concerned our War on Cancer frontline soldiers, mice.

In a recent example, Dr. Judah Folkman discovered that naturally occurring proteins, endostatin and angiostatin shrank tumors in mice. Although this was announced in November 1997, not until May 1998 did the media seize on it: Front page news. An avalanche of detailed scientific explanations. A groundswell of praise raised hopes in cancer-afflicted humans.

More circumspect were the responses of knowledgeable doctors and scientists. Nobel Prize–winner James Crick threatened to sue the *New York Times* for claiming he had said that the discovery would lead to a cure for cancer in the near future. G. Timothy Johnson, MD, medical editor for ABC News and WCVB-TV news in Boston, wrote this in a letter to the editor of the *Boston Globe*, published on May 22, 1998,

> My own medical perspective is that animal cancer research should be regarded as the scientific equivalent of gossip—with about the same chance of turning out to be true, i.e., truly effective in humans. Some gossip turns out to be true, but most of it does not . . . and gossip can cause great anguish for those affected, in this case millions of desperate cancer patients worldwide.

In response to Folkman's discovery, Dr. Richard Klausner of the National Cancer Institute summed up the mice's life in the trenches:

The history of cancer research has been a history of curing cancer
in the mouse. We have cured mice of cancer for decades, and it
simply didn't work in humans.[16]

Why would scientists be so skeptical about so great an achievement?
Because Folkman's brand of chemistry is not new. After promising results in animals, nine other medications with a similar mechanism of
action had already been tested in humans. The results were not news-
worthy. Dr. Philip DiScaia, deputy director of University of California,
Irvine's Chao Family Comprehensive Cancer Center, admonished, "I get
very concerned for the patients who have a false sense of hope that
something can come of this immediately, when that is just not the
case."[17]

Interestingly, the initial discovery preceding Folkman's was a combination of serendipity and *in vitro* research. Like any cell, cancerous cells
require the growth of new blood vessels so they can continue to proliferate. By accident, a yeast, *Aspergillus fumigatus*, contaminated a cell
culture that was growing red blood cells. It stopped the cells from growing, a process called angiogenesis inhibition, but did not kill them
(shades of Alexander Fleming's experience described in Chapter 2).[18]
Later, Folkman isolated the chemical in the yeast responsible for growth
inhibition and went on to manufacture similar chemicals.[19] The chemicals worked well in mice. But as Klausner said, "The mouse versions
don't work in humans."[20]

The Maryland–based company that Folkman is working with, Entre-
med, has been unsuccessful in producing a human form of the proteins
thus far.

Researchers have found many chemicals that inhibit the blood supply
needed for newly forming cancers in animals. However, they have not
yet found a chemical that works in humans. Recently, human-based evidence indicated that the reason for this may be that human cancers
actually grow their own blood vessels. One of the discoverers, Dr. Andy
Maniotis of the University of Iowa, commented, "People are very complacent with their animals models. But this begs the question of whether
there exists a good model of cancer."[21]

Past years are filled with other hope-inspiring developments—such as
interferon, interleukin, and taxol—that worked well in animals, mostly
mice. They were hyped to the public, but when actually given to humans
they did not live up to expectation. Dr. LaMar McGinnis, an oncologist
and medical consultant to the American Cancer Society, stated, "We
thought interferon was 'chicken soup' in the early '80s. I remember how
excited everyone was; it seemed to work miracles in animals, but it didn't
work in humans." Johanna Dwyer of Tufts University agreed, "The major problems of animal studies are the validity of cross species comparisons and relevance to the human disease."[22]

This cross-species problem can be illustrated by the following lack of parity. Of twenty compounds known *not* to cause cancer in humans, nineteen *caused* cancer in animals.[23] On the other hand, of nineteen compounds known *to cause* oral cancer in humans only seven caused cancer in mice and rats using the standard National Cancer Institute protocol.[24] For example, the industrial chemical, benzene, causes cancer in humans, but not in mice.

Science editor Philip Abelson has asked, "Are humans to be regarded as behaving biochemically like huge, obese, inbred, cancer-prone rodents?"[25] Yes, if weighing the standard cancer research protocol. Careless conclusions that overlook or ignore crucial distinctions between species are the backbone of animal experimentation.

At first glance, we find that mice are highly susceptible to tumors of the mammary glands, liver, pituitary, thyroid, lung, and lymph systems. This suggests their suitability for studies of those cancers in humans, and has, of course, been used to justify murine (mouse) experimentation. However, closer scrutiny of these tumors reveals huge discrepancies between human and murine variations. Even though they are located in the same regions, they are not the same cancers. Plus, the natural incidence of these cancers in mice is so high that it is difficult, if not impossible to determine if a chemical given to induce cancer caused the tumor, or if the tumor was "spontaneous."[26,27] (Naturally occurring cancer is called "spontaneous" cancer.) In a specific incidence, one research group concluded that the use of mice and dieldrin-aldrin, a cancer-inducing chemical, to study liver cancer was not indicative of human risk.[28]

Some common human tumors such as prostate, colon, and rectal cancer are rare in rodents.[29] David Rose of the American Health Foundation stated, "Indeed, there continues to be a lack of a universally accepted animal model for the human disease [prostate cancer]."[30]

Hence, researchers have to toil long to inflict prostate, colon, and rectal cancer on their lab animals. And when these cancers are forced upon rodents by induction, they are deviant, behaving very differently than they do in humans. Note this: Rat colon tumors kill by obstructing the colon. Human colon cancer kills by metastasizing to other places in the body. The tumors of the rat bowel do not usually spread. In rats, it is most often the small bowel that is affected; in humans it is the large bowel or colon.

Despite these dramatic differences between species, we call both diseases "colon cancer" and proceed with millions of dollars-worth of tests on rodents to obtain information, information that cannot be extrapolated to humans. Is a cancer the same cancer, no matter where and in which species? No.

Intuitively, one would suspect that mice and rats, as tiny quadrupeds with big round ears and long tails, would share more similarities than either species shares with people. Yet, tellingly, rats and mice cannot agree on their cancers either, making the effort to mime human medicine in rodents even more of a folly. Studies conducted on mice and rats found that forty-six percent of chemicals found to be cancer-causing in rats were not cancer-causing in mice.[31] Furthermore, mice do produce tumors in response to chemicals that do not cause cancer in rats.[32] Liver tumors, for example, can be induced via chemicals in mice, but the same chemicals will not induce cancer in rats or hamsters.[33]

In one test, rats and mice gave the same results, at most only seventy percent of the time.[34] Another study revealed that only fifty-four percent of chemicals found to be carcinogenic in one species were carcinogenic in the other. Differences also exist between sexes. Of thirty-three chemicals that caused cancer in both rats and mice, only thirteen caused cancer in both males and females.[35] These sorts of tests cost upwards of two hundred fifty million dollars annually in the United States.

 Take a syringe and inject almost any chemical into humans, then into different rodents and you will get widely varied results. There is a gulf of discrepancy between species. Benzedrine, for example, causes bladder tumors in humans, liver tumors in hamsters, and acoustic (middle ear) tumors in rats. Another cancer researcher resolved, "It is painfully clear that carcinogenesis in the mouse cannot now be predicted from positive data obtained from the rat and vice versa."[36]

Yet one more naysayer stated that,

> As a researcher I am involved with mutagenesis and cancerogenesis, two areas in which experimentation is fundamentally indispensable. I therefore know what I am talking about. And I say "no" to vivisection . . . above all on scientific grounds. It has been proved that the results of research with animals are in no case valid for man. There is a law of Nature in relation to metabolism, according to which a biochemical reaction that one has established in one species only applies to that species, and not to any other. Two closely related species, like the mouse and the rat, often react entirely differently . . . [37]

The bottom line is, again, this: Rodents are not small furry humans. Scientists who conduct cancer experiments on mice and rats have concluded that, ". . . The lifetime feeding study in mice and rats appears to have less than a fifty percent probability of finding known human carcinogens . . . We would have been better off to toss a coin."[38]

Better off in terms of evidence gathering perhaps, but not in terms of funding labs and scientists. As historical ledgers indicate, getting paid to toss coins has been remarkably good business during the cancer offensive. Do we really want to foot the bill for extravagant speculation, at huge human expense? This crapshoot is the reality of our national cancer inquiry.

The Disease-Making Enterprise and Its Consequences

Another situation disturbs efforts to gather useful data in the lab. Think: How do we acquire cancer? Slowly. Weighing what we currently know about the way naturally occurring or "spontaneous" cancer transpires, it does not appear to be "instant" as it is when induced in lab animals.

Dr. R. L. Carter explained the conditions that determine broad discrepancies in naturally occurring cancers, "Spontaneous tumors in rats and mice . . . [vary] widely according to sex, strain, diet, conditions of maintenance, hormonal status, immunological status and latent virus infections."[39]

So, many influences may or may not lead to cancers that are themselves different. Of course, the same is true of spontaneous tumors in humans. But cancer researchers cannot wait for spontaneity. Keeping those labs financed and papers published demands immediacy.

As quoted in *Business Review Weekly,* the director of the Center for Toxicological Research in Arkansas said this about lab tests for cancer on rats:

> Our risk models are based on at least fifty assumptions, none of which has been scientifically demonstrated. For example, we assume there is no difference between continuous [as in induced animal exposures] or intermittent [as in naturally occurring human experience] dosages. But that ignores our growing knowledge of the way in which DNA repairs the human system.[40]

In animal experimentation, researchers are interested in *turbo*-cancer. They want immediate disease, so they induce cancer artificially. How? By exposing animals to as much of any given chemical as they can tolerate without dying. This amount is called the maximum tolerated dose or MTD. As you might imagine, the consequences of an intermittent drip from a chemical over a period of years differ greatly from those of a complete immersion as frequently as an animal can bear.[41]

A 1997 edition of the journal *Regulatory Toxicology and Pharmacology* explains the scientific ineptitude of MTD-induced cancer testing by pointing out that the chronic wounding that MTD delivers so radically diminishes overall health that it in no way mirrors the results of lower doses.[41]

The authors compared epidemiological evidence of cancer risk to cooked-up cancer tests performed on animals and found epidemiology a much more persuasive indicator of risk. They concluded that animal tests for carcinogenicity "have limited predictive value for the human situation."[42]

As one oncologist stated in *Clinical Oncology,* "It is in fact hard to find a single, common solid neoplasm [cancer] where management and expectation of cure has been markedly affected by animal research. Most human cancers differ from the artificially produced animal model . . ."[43]

In addition to the physiologic gulf between humans and other species, and results skewed by artificially inflicted cancer, another aspect torques animal studies—stress.

It cannot yet be said that accelerated breeding programs have rearranged the course of evolution and made the laboratory environment a natural one for mice. As a result of living in this netherworld, the animals experience unquantifiable stress. This stress causes numerous conditions that interfere with scientific accuracy, including susceptibility to infections, susceptibility to certain tumors, and disruption of hormonal regulation.

Moreover, discrepant conditions between labs skew results. Diane Birt of the Eppley Institute for research in Cancer and Allied Diseases explained,

> One difficulty with animal investigations is the different results observed when comparing a series of studies. Depending on design aspects, including dietary variables, the results of tumorigenesis studies can differ even when the same experimental model is used . . . different models of cancer at a site can give entirely different results.[41b]

Hence, when substances are forced upon animals, they may cause cancer in some, but not in all. The same substances may not adversely affect humans in any way. The converse is also true, as illustrated with asbestos experimentation on animals. All this proves that there is not parity between species. Worse, continued animal-model studies confound efforts to make real progress toward preventing human cancer.

Moreover, our zeal to flush out every carcinogen as it affects rodents has actually served unwarranted setbacks to other types of human medicine. Many may remember when artificial sweeteners containing cyclamates were removed from the market. Studies indicated that they caused a type of bladder cancer . . . in rats and male rats only . . . a type of bladder cancer that does not even occur in people. Why do humans not contract bladder cancer when exposed to cyclamates? Because, unlike male rats, we do not have the protein alpha-2u-globulin, a high urine pH, and a high sodium concentration in the urine that combine with cyclamates to induce cancer.

The chemical solvent used in manufacturing, butadiene, is carcinogenic in the B6C3F1 strain of mice. In humans however, it is not. Likewise, there was a big commotion when it developed that the acne medication benzoyl peroxide causes cancer in certain rats. Happily for teenagers, the makers of one acne medication fought back, dismissing the findings thus: "Available scientific evidence does not allow the results of [the rodent studies] to be meaningfully applied to human safety assessments."[44] Dr. Tony Chu of Hammersmith Hospital in London stated, "If you paint these products onto mice . . . you can induce skin cancers. But how that relates to the human system, nobody actually knows."[45]

Remember when the media exposed that large quantities of the anticonstipation medicine Ex-Lax (active ingredient phenolphthalein) caused cancer in rats? Once again we were told that a medicine used for years without complications in humans is bad, based on studies in animals. Whether about diet, food, or medications, these deductions proved grossly erroneous when extrapolated to humans. And they cost taxpayers and consumers billions of dollars.

Dr. Albert Sabin, developer of the polio vaccine, concurs:

> The cancer research bodies cause pain and suffering to hundreds of thousands of animals every year by inducing in the animals, through chemicals or irradiation, larger cancerous growth in their bodies and in their limbs. Giving cancer to laboratory animals has not and will not help us to understand the disease or to treat those persons suffering from it . . . Laboratory cancers have nothing in common with natural human cancers. Tumorous cells are not unrelated to the organism that produced them. Human cancers are greatly different from artificial tumors caused by the experimenters in the laboratories.[46]

Repetitively, Sabin and other outspoken authorities—respected, vested scientists—have insisted that assuming similarities in physiologic and pharmacological response in different species is fallacious and irresponsible. Nevertheless, testing chemicals for carcinogenicity in animals drunkenly persists. And we continue giving money to those trying out new anticancer medications on animals.

Giving Whole New Creatures Cancer, an Accomplished Task

How to overcome the differences between human and rodent cancer? Researchers lit on the obvious: Why not make men of mice? Visited by the kind of vision we associate with Mary Shelley, scientists genetically engineered a creature they call the "oncomouse." They insert human cancer genes into embryonic mice, who can at that point reproduce the genes. One can almost imagine the back patting and test-tube clinking that accompanied this idea. But after spending billions of dollars in development, scientists acknowledged failure: ". . . in the course of tumor progression, it has been known for many years that mice and men are totally different . . . tumor suppressor genes and oncogenes behave very differently in mouse and man." [47b]

Oops. Other mad-science confections, the so-called xenograft mice, are mice that have cancer from human tumors inserted into them. These man-mice have not panned out as predictors of the human effects of anticancer drugs either. Of xenograft mice and oncomice experiments Edward Sausville, associate director of the division of cancer treatment and diagnosis for the developmental therapeutics program at the National Cancer Institute (NCI), was quoted in *Science* as saying, "We had basically discovered compounds that were good mouse drugs rather than good human drugs."[48]

The NCI treated mice that were growing forty-eight different kinds of *human* cancers with twelve anticancer drugs currently and effectively used in humans. In thirty out of the forty-eight, the drugs did not work. Sixty-three percent of the time the mouse model collapsed when applied to human tumors. Oncomice, who had the gene causing the cancer inserted, did not predict human drug response much better. Mice who have the genes for colon cancer, retinoblastoma, and other cancers just do not replicate the human condition. Dr. Tyler Jacks of the Massachusetts Institute of Technology stated,

> One might expect that these animals would mimic human symptoms, not just the genetic mutations. In fact, that is usually the exception, not the rule . . . the genetic wiring for growth control [cancer growth] in mice and humans is subtly different . . . Animals apparently do not handle the drugs in exactly the same way the human body does.[49]

The *Science* article goes on to state that, according to the NCI, animal models may miss effective chemotherapeutic medications and do not predict the successful ones. So the NCI may have discarded perfectly good anticancer drugs just because they did not work on mice and rats.

The executive director for cancer research at Merck Research Laboratory cautioned, "The fundamental problem in drug discovery for cancer is that the [animal] model systems are not predictive at all."[50]

To reiterate, whereas efforts to solve the human cancer mystery have been thwarted, the causes and cures for murine cancer are an expanding volume.

Primate testing is dicey too. Dr. Dzhemali Beniashvili is a specialist in primate experimentation, and as such, a proponent of the primate model. In his book, *Experimental Tumors in Monkeys,* however he writes, "Many researchers believe that monkeys have an inherent specific resistance to malignant tumors. The low incidence of spontaneous tumors in monkeys has been associated with difficulties in experimental induction of tumors in these animals."

When, through exposure to radiation or toxic chemicals, researchers succeed in producing tumors in primates, the tumors are not the same as those that develop spontaneously in humans.[51] Remember, those two hundred forms of human cancer are *strictly human.*

Getting out of the "Mouse Trap"

Many would say that we must rely on laboratory animal testing in cancer research, even with all its flaws, because it is the best option available. This thinking is woefully misguided.

Recall, it was Claude Bernard who led medicine away from the human bedside and into the animal-lined lab. This unsound diversion has rendered scientists more and more myopic and less responsive to dire contemporary health issues. Stuck in a paradigm that did not even benefit the epoch in which it was conceived, they overlook the enormous opportunities technology has brought to tried and true human-model research. They are out of touch.

Almost ten years ago *Science* editor Philip Abelson, announced that, "the standard carcinogen tests that use rodents are an obsolescent relic of the ignorance of past decades."[52]

He knew that animal experimentation has always resulted in fallacies and that science and technology now proffer better human-model research, described as follows. By employing it we can leave off curing mice and pick up the more pressing business of eradicating cancer in humans.

Clinical Observation

Whereas the animal model continues to misguide science, the bedside still offers tangible, useful facts about the nature of cancer. Plus, there have been remarkable advances in our knowledge of diagnosing, curing, and preventing cancer.

Throughout the "War on Cancer," acknowledged experts in the cancer research field have repetitively spoken out against animal experimentation and in favor of clinical observation. Again, as described in Chapter 6 on Alternatives, the word *clinical* means actual observation and treatment of diseased patients rather than conjecture or experiment.

The first really successful medicines to treat cancer were discovered on the battlefield. During World War I, physicians noticed that soldiers exposed to mustard-nerve gas experienced low white blood cell counts. They wondered if something similar would counteract leukemia and lymphomas, cancers where the white blood cells are over produced.[53,54] Based on this, mustard gas derivatives became effective chemotherapeutics.

Other medications were also discovered by astute clinical observation, sometimes in spite of erred forays precipitated by animal experimentation. For example, animal experiments had suggested that cancer patients would benefit from folic acid. Unfortunately, in humans the results were disastrous, making the cancer worse. Scientists, therefore, decided to try medication that would inhibit folic acid, methotrexate. They skipped the animal trials and instead gave the medication to actual humans, children suffering from leukemia. Today, methotrexate is a widely used chemotherapeutic.[55]

Chemotherapeutic agents that met with success, most markedly in childhood cancers, have all come from nonanimal means. Dr. Irwin Bross, formerly of the Roswell Park Memorial Institute for Cancer Research, in testimony before the U.S. Congress stated in 1981,

> the discovery of chemotherapeutic agents for the treatment of human cancer is widely heralded as a triumph due to the use of animal models . . . However, there is little, if any, factual evidence that would support these claims . . . Indeed, while conflicting animal results have often delayed and hampered advances in the war on cancer, they have never produced a single substantial advance in either the prevention or treatment of human cancer.

Not a single one.

The *Journal of Clinical Oncology* credited clinical research for radically modernizing treatment in several types of cancer: Breast cancer management was revolutionized by clinical trials that spared the breast and used systemic treatment. The use of tamoxifen as a breast cancer preventative was not conceived in the laboratory. Rather it developed through follow-up of patients on adjuvant trials of tamoxifen. This finding has lead to a new generation of prevention studies. While the jury is still out as to the ultimate role of tamoxifen in preventing breast cancer, it can be said with certainty that any true knowledge did come and will come from studying humans.

Lance Armstrong might never have won the Tour de France in 1999 had it not been for clinical trials. Armstrong took a less toxic chemotherapy, developed based on human observation, for testicular cancer.[56,57] Organ-sparing therapy for patients with carcinoma of the bladder and carcinoma of the rectum is currently under investigation in clinical trials. Larynx preservation has become commonplace in the treatment of laryngeal cancers, thanks to the results of clinical research. Improvements in esophageal, lung, and colon cancer therapy have been carefully documented by clinical investigation, and this research has changed how we manage these malignancies.[58]

The use of radiation to treat cancers was first undertaken in the early-twentieth century. But it was not until physicians gave radiation in incremental doses that it began to be effective without killing the patient.[59]

As Dr. Richard C. Lewontin reported,

Most cures for cancer involve either removing the growing tumor or destroying it with powerful radiation or chemicals. Virtually none of this progress in cancer therapy has occurred because of a deep understanding of the elementary processes of cell growth and development, although nearly all research, above the purely clinical level, is devoted precisely to understanding the most intimate details of cell biology. Medicine remains, despite all the talk of scientific medicine, essentially an empirical process in which one does what works.[60]

Today, National Cancer Institute-designated cancer centers, such as the University of Rochester Cancer Center, credit clinical trials for helping cancer patients "beat the odds." In their publications they state, "The most important breakthroughs in cancer treatment have been made in clinical trials."[61]

The testimonials to clinical research's merit go on and on. Steroids have been used to treat cancer. Their use was based on clinical observation of human patients suffering from an over-production of natural steroids, Cushing's syndrome. They were found to have tissue destruction. This prompted scientists to try corticosteroids on cancer patients to see if it would destroy the cancer tissue. Despite the failure of other steroids on animals (steroids inhibit some animals' response to chemotherapeutics), they were developed and given to cancer patients with success.[62,63]

On the diagnostic side, every major cancer was first observed in human patients and described on that basis. As Dr. Alexander Haddow points out in regard to leukemia,

The characteristic effects in leukemia were detected solely as a result of clinical observation. The various leukemias in the mouse and rat were relatively refractory to the influence of urethane, and the remarkable effect in the human might have eluded discovery if attention had been directed to the animal alone. That illustrates the hazards of such work.[64]

In vitro *Research*

Although many pharmaceutical companies and the NCI continue to use animals, the best methods for screening chemicals for carcinogenicity and curative potential lie with *in vitro* or test-tube technology, also described in Chapter 6.

The Ames test, which utilizes the common bacteria *Salmonella typhimurium* to test for mutagenicity, is faster, less expensive, and more reliable than animal tests.[65,66] The Williams DNA repair test utilizes liver cells, which can be human. Using a combination of these two plus the p-post-labeling technique provides very accurate carcinogenicity testing.

Scientists in other countries, less encumbered by the animal experimentation machine, have been able to move ahead without their use, as in Umberto Veronesi's (of the Italian National Cancer Institute) advocacy of *in vitro* methods.[67] A combination of *in vitro* techniques and epidemiology is ideal for testing chemicals already in the market place. *In vitro* tests identified or confirmed benzene, vinyl chloride, arsenic, and chromium as carcinogens.[68]

Curatively, scientists now grow a patient's own tumor in a culture and test various compounds against the tumor cells. This allows for the development of very specific treatment plans.

In vitro testing has also revolutionized diagnostic science. Cervical cancer detection is one of the oldest and most successful forms of *in vitro* testing. The Pap smear, invented in the 1920s by Aurel Babés and developed by George Papanicolaou, is now used in ninety-seven percent of all cervical cancer diagnoses.[69]

The idea to use human cells to test for human disease, though balked at by institutions that prefer to watch animals get cancer, is not new. The Linus Pauling Institute, in the vanguard of non-animal testing research, has been using them since at least 1985. John Leavitt of the Institute stated,

> The Pauling Institute decided to explore the mechanism of carcinogenesis with an emphasis on human cells rather than on the cells of animals. Only recently have we begun to realize the significance of this intuitive premise that human cancer, while fundamentally the same as rodent cancer, may have critical mechanistic differences which may in turn require different, uniquely human approaches to cancer eradication.[70]

In vitro testing using human cells is far more predictive of human response than animal tests ever were.

Epidemiology

Immense progress in cancer research has come through studying populations of people and linking lifestyle to disease. This straightforward branch of science can be understood as "who gets cancer and why." Tracking all kinds of carcinogenic materials and environments, epidemiology issues valuable information about the nature of the disease itself, and preventive and curative strategies. Since epidemiology does not claim to "fix" cancer, it is more difficult to sensationalize than lab science. Nevertheless, it is hard to refute the accurate evidence that epidemiology reveals about cancer's causes and plausible preventative measures. When it comes to cancer, an ounce of prevention equals much, much more than a pound of cure.

In the United States, the Centers for Disease Control and Prevention (CDC) tabulates information provided by physicians from all over the world to identify newly emerging diseases and track changes in existing ones. This type of tracking provided the evidence that smoking, alcohol, radiation, poor diet, and lack of exercise are all not just bad but potentially cancerous. It illustrated the association between pipe smokers and lip cancer, radiologists and skin cancer, dye workers and bladder cancer, and coal workers and lung cancer.[71] For example, a plant in New Jersey employed individuals to paint watches with radium, so the watch faces would glow in the dark. The employees started coming down with a rare form of cancer. It was found that the radium was causing the cancer.[72] This was solid, dependable data.

The results of epidemiology are regularly refuted by animal-experimentation results, as described with the asbestos debacle. In another example, tests using rats, hamsters, guinea pigs, mice, monkeys, and baboons revealed no link between glass fibers and cancer. In 1991, due to clinical studies, OSHA labeled glass fibers carcinogenic.[73,74,75] An Office of Technology Assessment (OTA) report (*The Causes of Cancer,* Oxford University Press, 1981) stated that epidemiological studies were more reliable than animal studies because animal tests "cannot provide reliable risk assessments."[76] To say the least!

Time again, epidemiology has confirmed simple but unpopular truths, such as the association between diet and cancer. We now know that fat and meat in the diet can lead to cancer.[77] Scientists in Great Britain have stated that as much as one-third of all cancers could be prevented by changing diet, specifically by decreasing the amount of meat in the diet. The World Cancer Research Fund took a more definitive position, suggesting that people should avoid all red meat.[78] Epidemiology also linked obesity to cancer of the stomach and esophagus.[79]

In other examples, a diet high in fiber and vegetables was shown to protect against colon cancer.[80] Italian scientists found that about one-third of breast cancer cases could have been prevented by reducing alcohol intake, increasing the amount of fruits and vegetables, and engaging in more physical activity.[81]

Using epidemiological studies, scientists found that a sexually transmitted virus probably causes some anal cancers and that using a condom could prevent them.[82] That women who gain weight after reaching adulthood are at an increased risk for breast cancer was also discovered epidemiologically.[83] The list of epidemiological data that support prevention is long.

Over the last three decades faster cancer detection has improved the prognosis for some cancers. None of these—colonoscopy, breast examination, or prostate exam among them—have benefited from animal experimentation. Instead, these methods emerged out of data com-pounded by physicians working with human patients, in other words, epidemiology. Women with lumps in their breasts may now avoid biopsy by benefiting from a T-Scan 2000 machine. By passing electrical current through the body it registers a different signal for cancerous and non-cancerous tissue.[84]

Gene Therapy

"God knows we've cured mice of all sorts of tumors. But that isn't medical research,"[85] So remarked Thomas E. Wagner, a molecular bi-ologist and long-time cancer researcher, as he left his position in 1998 as senior scientist at Ohio University's Edison Biotechnology Institute. Wagner now heads a program in gene therapy research, the most excit-ing area of cancer intervention today.

By observing humans suffering from cancer, not animals, researchers have been able to determine that some genes activate and deactivate the uncontrolled proliferation of malignant cells. The most high profile among these is the *p53* gene. Scientists believe that its loss of control contributes to at least fifty percent of all cancers. Clinical observation, epidemiology, and *in vitro* research have all contributed to these discov-eries. And *in vitro* research is now designing treatments aimed at these genes.

The Human Genome Project, an international effort, is attempting to map all human genes, as described previously. All one hundred thousand plus of them. Research of this type has revealed protective genes, such as those that helped some people resist toxification from sarin, the poison gas released on a Japanese subway in 1995. Other genes pre-dispose to disease. These genes are called *environmental susceptible gene variants*. They are the culprits that convert environmental sub-stances such as cigarette smoke, pesticides, and alcohol into disease-causing chemicals.

Consider the skin cancer, melanoma. The first English report of this disease, in 1820, was an epidemiological study. The authors reported on a family prone to skin lesions. By the 1970s, scientists began to study the human gene responsible for the cancer. They found that the presence of a type of mole, a dysplastic nevus, might lead to malignant melanoma. Having identified those at risk, the researchers then studied the genes. They found that the gene *CMM1* on chromosome 1p36, *CDK4* on chro-mosome 12q14 and *CMM2* on chromosome 9p21 were markers for the disease. (All genes have alphabet-number combination names such as these that describe locations.) Epidemiology and *in vitro* research iden-tified people at risk for malignant melanoma, then urged them to look for skin changes and seek medical advice much earlier than people with-out those genes.[86]

The gene causing Peutz-Jeghere syndrome (melanomic polyps in the stomach, small bowel and colon) was isolated via clinical studies and *in vitro* research.[87] Researchers drew blood from patients suffering from the disease and used the blood to look for differences in the genetic composition. Other stomach cancers have been linked to certain genes as well.[88]

Some cancers do not stem from inherited genetic predispositions but occur due to genetic mutations. Twenty different cancers have already been linked to mutation. Acute lymphoblastic leukemia, for example, is a cancer affecting children with a particular gene defect. Rather than being inherited, the gene is damaged during pregnancy. Since damage appears related to the mothers' alcohol consumption during pregnancy, the disease may be entirely preventable.[89]

Previous human studies had linked breast cancer to eating high fat foods and radiation. A combination of human clinical studies and test tube research led to the discovery that cigarette smoking combined with mutations at sites on *NAT2* increase the risk of breast cancer.[90] The importance of this finding is underscored by the fact that the researchers estimate one out of two white women are born with these genetic mutations. The incidence decreases with other races; thirty-five percent of African-American women, and twenty percent of Chinese women. Recently, a mutation in another gene, *BRCA1*, was linked to breast cancer via clinical and *in vitro* research. The fact that women with this mutation have more severe forms of breast cancer will influence the type of treatment they receive.[91]

Knowledge of these genes will revolutionize our lifestyles.[92] By uncovering our vulnerabilities to specific kinds of cancer, we can avoid unnecessary risks and receive a focused exam more frequently. Patients will have the option of knowing what to look for, and researchers can study cancer with the advantage of knowing the outcome.[93]

Physicians will some day prescribe medication based on a patient's genetic profile. Already, chemotherapy tailored to the patient's genetic makeup—as in the dosages administered to children suffering from acute lymphoblastic leukemia—produces better results than standardized therapy.[94]

Tobaccogate

Nowhere is the evidence favoring human research over animal experimentation so compelling as in the study of smoking and lung cancer. Of all cancers, lung cancer claims the highest mortality, almost half a million people a year in the US alone.[95] The volume of these figures has motivated our nation's health agencies, but to do what? Yes, they have invested in an apparent struggle against cancer. Helped along by campaign contributions from pharmaceutical companies, research animal vendors, medical associations, and tobacco companies alike, politicians got elected and stayed in office by directing allocations toward lung cancer research through the National Cancer Institute, the Centers for Disease Control and Prevention, National Institutes of Health, and other cancer-concerned pockets of the federal government to the tune of approximately five billion dollars a year, according to the CDC. However, consider that smoking itself cost the American people fifty billion dollars in direct medical costs in 1993. The accumulated cost of lung cancer is actually greater by a factor of ten.[96]

Private citizens also make charitable contributions to the above agencies and others. Scientists, who need money to continue being scientists (publish papers, and so on), have tapped these resources by configuring their grant applications in a way that seems to address the lung cancer problem. However, as we will demonstrate, research is not the same as prevention or cure.

Agencies have invested billions to prove what we already know—that smoking is hazardous to your health. For centuries, people had only to watch smokers to deduce that tobacco might lead to illness. As long ago as the 1600s, the English introduced a tax on cigarettes for health purposes. In 1761, human studies associating tobacco with cancer of the nose and in 1795 to lip cancer. Many years ago, controlled population studies confirmed the link between smoking and lung cancer. Twenty-seven controlled studies on humans had been done before 1963.[97]

Animal-model-obsessed scientists began their grand experiment—trying to give animals cancer with tobacco smoke. Why is smoking-related cancer difficult to reproduce in lab animals? Logic dictates that creating nicotine-addicted animals might be problematic. Animals do not smoke. In one study, lab rats even used their feces to block a pipe that pumped cigarette smoke into their enclosures. Animal experiments failed notoriously to demonstrate a smoking-cancer connection for over a half a century.[98]

Yet, epidemiology linked lung cancer to smoking.[99,100,101] Many continued to dismiss this science of "epidemiology" as impure science. Note, for example, Jesse P. Greenstein's statement in his *Biochemistry of Cancer,* 1954:

> Morbidity data on cancer of the respiratory tract have shown an increase in incidence during the past thirty years, particularly in regard to pulmonary neoplasms, and the possible etiological [causal] relation of this fact to the smoking of tobacco has been advanced. This emphasis on the predominance of a single etiologic environmental factor has been a matter of some controversy, which is not yet settled. The essential weakness in the arguments pro is due to the lack of any sound experimental [meaning lab animal] evidence that tobacco is carcinogenic. The best that epidemiology

can do under the circumstances is to draw some correlation between an increase in cancer incidence and a parallel increase in some suspected etiologic factor.[102]

In other words, since animals do not get cancer from tobacco, there is no proof that tobacco causes cancer.

Hence, the tobacco industry used this lack of animal model to their advantage for years, claiming that smoking absolutely did not cause lung cancer. It even paid physicians to advertise cigarettes in the fifties and sixties. In large part, these wily tactics delayed the mandatory health warnings on cigarette packaging. One researcher stated in 1957 that,

> The failure of many investigators . . . to induce experimental cancers [in animals], except in a handful of cases, during fifty years of trying, casts serious doubt on the validity of the cigarette-lung cancer theory.[103]

Other scientists, not on the dole from tobacco companies, were more forthcoming about the inadequacies of using animal models for cigarette-induced cancers, as the publication *Human Epidemiology and Animal Laboratory Correlations in Chemical Carcinogenesis* warned, "Clearly, we still do not have a good animal model for the most important and well established hazard to man."

The authors went on to describe dosage differences of cancer-causing chemicals that,

> seem to require only minute levels to induce cancer in man [but] it seems very large doses are required to induce bladder cancers in dogs and hamsters . . . Here again, it seems to me, we have a discrepancy between animal data and human data . . . Clearly, right now our animal models are totally and absolutely inadequate to answer all the obvious questions before us.[104]

Nevertheless, consumers and the Surgeon General bought the tobacco companies' "smoke screen" for three reasons. The established protocol favored the animal model over the human. The tobacco lobby was simply too powerful. Plus, smokers wanted to believe that they could keep smoking and remain healthy, just like the rats. The tobacco industry got away with this, and hundreds of thousands more smokers died. This data alone should refute any possible arguments for continuing animal experimentation.

If the greatest killer of our time was promoted by physicians based on animal experiments, there is obviously something terminally wrong with the system. The epidemiological and clinical evidence against smoking was overwhelming.

The connection between second-hand smoke and smoking-related diseases was proved in human studies that isolated the chemicals responsible for cancer in patients exposed to second-hand smoke.[105] Epidemiology showed that women who do not smoke, but who live with men who do smoke, have a fifty percent greater incidence of lung cancer than women who live with non-smokers.[106] Using *in vitro* analysis, the cancer-causing chemical in tobacco was isolated. A derivative of benzo(a)pyrene actually activates the genes that cause malignancy. Another cancer-causing chemical in smoke is an amine.

If you take the number of packs smoked per day and multiply it by the number of years a person has been smoking, you get a statistic term called a "pack-year." Human and *in vitro* research combined to reveal why people who smoke a certain number of pack-years are more likely to suffer from cancer. Researchers found a certain molecule receptor, GRP (gastrin-releasing peptide), activated in smokers with twenty-five pack-years; it is seldom activated in people who smoke much less. The activation of this receptor may stimulate cancer growth.[107]

As the tobacco industry's culpability was revealed, tobacco companies hastily introduced new types of cigarettes. Manufacturers touted filtered, low-tar cigarettes as reducing the risk of cancer and lung disease. Just the opposite proved true for certain types of cancer. Researchers found that because of the filters, people had to inhale deeper thus forcing the smoke farther into the lungs. Epidemiology and human observation were responsible for this new knowledge. Obviously, it would have been impossible to analyze such breathing patterns in rats.[108] Scientists publishing in the *Journal of the American Medical Association* acquiesced,

> The Council's consultants agree that to identify carcinogenicity in animal tests does not per se predict either risk or outcome in human experience . . . the Council is concerned about the hundreds of millions of dollars that are spent each year (both in the public and private sectors) for the carcinogenicity testing of chemical substances. The concern is particularly grave in view of the questionable scientific value of the tests when used to predict human experience.[109]

Finally, clinical research, not research on animals, linked smoking to a litany of heinous diseases—bladder cancer, lung cancer, lip cancer, tongue cancer, pancreatic cancer, stomach cancer, mouth cancer, esophageal cancer, larynx cancer, liver cancer, kidney cancer, salivary gland cancer, heart disease, peripheral vascular disease, cataracts, respiratory disease, bone fractures, periodontal disease, and many others.[110]

Everyone knows smoking is a death sentence. However, federal agencies still give taxpayer money to scientists studying the effects of tobacco smoke on animals because tobacco lobbyists compel them to do so. In

1996, the National Cancer Institute awarded over $123.3 million to lung-cancer research.[111] The same year, the National Institutes of Health awarded over $28 million to 123 tobacco researchers. At least forty percent of the grants went to animal experiments.

The experiments read like a deranged 4-H project. The government and charities continue to fund rat experiments that are designed to induce bladder cancer via cigarettes.[112] Rats are studied for smoking-induced cardiovascular disease.[113] Rabbits are studied to reproduce the human data concerning bone fracture healing time.[114] If we already know it happens in humans, why do we have to "validate" the data in rabbits? Rats were also studied to duplicate and "validate" human data that showed that it takes longer for ulcers to heal in smokers than in non-smokers.[115] Human studies had confirmed this twenty-three years earlier![116]

Moreover, but beside the point: we do not need these animal experiments. If there still exists any doubt about the ill effect of smoking, we can study the effects of smoking on human lung tissue *in vitro* by using human cells harvested during bronchial washings or from surgeries.[117] Certainly, there is no shortage of lung tissue from smokers at autopsy. Nevertheless, the illogical and corrupt roller coaster of animal experimentation continues to carry our money away on its wasteful rampage.

No matter what, it is still difficult, if not impossible, to reproduce cancer from smoking in animals.[118] In 1988, in the book *Perspectives in Basic and Applied Toxicology*, Dr. M. Utidjian stated,

> Surely not even the most zealous toxicologist would deny that epidemiology, and epidemiology alone, has indicted and incriminated the cigarette as a potent carcinogenic agent, or would claim that experimental animal toxicology could ever have done the job with the same definition.[119]

Despite everything, multiple animal studies looking at addiction to nicotine persist. Epidemiological studies in humans in 1972 scientifically validated that fetal abnormalities result from smoking. Even with all this human data, researchers still received money to demonstrate the same thing in mice.[120] Nicotine withdrawal symptoms were scientifically confirmed in humans in the 1970s.[121] Nevertheless, rats were still being studied for signs of nicotine withdrawal in 1994.[122] And the practice continues today.

One of the more contrived animal studies on smoking was performed on dogs in 1987. Dogs with erections were forced to inhale cigarette smoke! Most of the dogs failed to maintain an erection after the smoke was inhaled. The researchers said this observation lent support to the human observation that smoking interfered with a man's ability to maintain an erection.[123] Who dreams this stuff up? Why are we forced to give our tax dollars to them? Why does the government continue funding animal experiment in spite of its proven inability to prevent or cure cancer?

In 1995, 419,000 Americans died from smoking. At what point will the researchers be satisfied that smoking is unhealthy?

Personal Choice: Passive Suicide or Prevention

As we have shown, animal experimentation cannot cure or prevent cancer. But *personal responsibility* can—people taking control of their destiny through prevention. Prevention is not glamorous, and is not even viewed by some as scientific. People prefer to continue their less healthful habits knowing that "science" is at work on a cure for their dissipated systems. Plus, it must be said that prevention does not finance labs the way animal experimentation does.

Smoking causes thirty percent of all cancer deaths. Another thirty percent is attributed to diet and lifestyle factors.[124] Saturated fats and animal fats have been linked to prostate, breast, colon, and rectal cancer.[125] Other scientists estimate eighty to ninety percent of all cancers is related to diet, tobacco, environment, and lifestyle.[126] All things over which we have control.

On November 19, 1996, researchers from Harvard published a study, which was reviewed in the *Boston Globe*, simply stating that, "Cancer is a mostly preventable disease that can be avoided through shunning smoking, eating well and exercising regularly." Dr. Dimitrios Trichopoulos reinforced this sound counsel by saying that, "prevention has much more potential than treatment" for curbing cancer.

Even if we lower that ninety percent to a more conservative sixty percent, the potential for eradicating cancer through prevention is phenomenal. Stop the presses and call out the networks! However, people are lazy and resistant to change. Most could give up Brussels sprouts, but actual preventative measures such as forgoing tobacco, alcohol, meat, and meat by-products is too much to ask. So is getting regular exercise. Driving the message home would require that the federal government spend money on the historically less attractive areas of education and prevention, irrespective of the powerful tobacco, alcohol, meat and dairy lobbies. No one profits from prevention—just the patient.

The Deception Machine

In addition to spending billions on utterly useless and misleading animal experiments, our government and other vested associations also have propaganda machines that churn out booklets in support of their animal-cancer studies. Those cost money too. Even within the government, some find this appalling. In 1987, the General Accounting Office reported that the National Cancer Institute, the government's leading cancer research facility had, "artificially inflate[d] the amount of true progress made in the area of cancer research."[127]

How? The NCI merely counted as "cured" any cancer patient who died at least five years after the diagnosis. Die of cancer four years and eleven months after diagnosis and you are a NCI fatality; die after five years and one day and you are "cured."

Although adjusted death rates since 1970 have not changed, early detection has raised the way survival rates look on paper. Twenty-five years ago, most cancers were detected only three years prior to death, on the average. Today they are detected six years prior to death. So, the number of patients still alive five years after diagnosis is now greater. Cancer patients' lives are in no way extended, just the number of years they survive after the earlier diagnosis. Nonetheless, the natural history of the cancer has not changed. It still kills the patients exactly when it would have.

Those citing progress, the NCI among them, refer to this "five-year rule." Additionally, this "five-year rule" ignores quality-of-life issues. You can be hospitalized, on a respirator, and fed through a tube. As long as you pass your fifth anniversary of diagnosis, the system calls you "cured."

In actuality, the only statistic with meaning is the adjusted death rate from cancer. ("Adjusted" means people who die of cancer only, not those who die of other causes secondary to a cancer diagnosis.) The truth is that small improvements in prevention, early detection and treatments have not put a dent in this overall mortality rate.[128]

According to Dr. J. C. Bailar III, chief administrator of Richard Nixon's War on Cancer, "Age-adjusted mortality rates [from cancer] have shown a slow and steady increase over several decades and there is no evidence of a recent downward trend . . . Some 25 years of intense effort focused largely on improving treatment must be judged a qualified failure."[129]

Again, the reason there has been no change in adjusted mortality, that no cures for human cancer have been found, is that we have been curing mice of cancer, not humans. With all the money relegated to animal-based research, we have starved human-based research—such as clinical studies, epidemiology and *in vitro* testing—of resources. Cancer is just as big a killer now as it was in 1971.

Many informed people saw this coming years and years ago. Only a few years into the "war," in 1979, Dr. Heinz Oeser stated, "As a cancer specialist engaged in clinical practice, I can't agree with the researchers who believe that results obtained with laboratory animals are applicable to human beings."[130]

We have not won the war because we have been looking at animals, not humans. The system makes it difficult for scientists to speak out against animal experimentation. But nonetheless many are truthful about the impossibility of determining carcinogenicity based on animal tests: "Available methods for estimating the risk to humans of exposure to mutagens are still so full of uncertainties that for the time being no method can be recommended."[131]

Contrast this with the following statement from the American Medical Association's White Paper (in response to criticism of animal experimentation), which claims, "Animal research holds the key for solutions to AIDS, cancer, heart disease, aging, and congenital defects."[132]

Thousands of times over the last 150 years, scientists have used the animal model to refute clinical knowledge about cancer. Fantastically, our governing agencies that distribute research dollars supported these pseudoscientific experiments. The reservoir of egregious examples is inexhaustible. Over a twenty-five year time period, in hopes of developing new treatments, the NCI screened 40,000 plant species for antitumor activity on animals. Regardless of the results from animal studies, all the chemicals tested were either too toxic or ineffective in humans.[133] Forty thousand! *The Handbook of Laboratory Animal Science* reports: "This means despite 25 years of intensive research and positive results in animal models, *not a single anti-tumor drug emerged* from this work."[134] (Emphasis added.)

At least they gave animal testing a very ample opportunity to work. One wonders when they first spotted the trend? After five thousand failures? Ten thousand?

The same 1987 report from the General Accounting Office that called the NCI to task for artificially inflating research progress, added that the NCI had discouraged preventative measures. Where are the *LA Times* and *60 Minutes* when you need them? This and the countless animal experimentation fiascoes, prompted the prestigious journal, *Science*, to publish an article in the early nineties stating, ". . . with trillions of dollars, loss of competitiveness, and jobs at stake, searching review of the risk assessment methodology of the regulatory agencies is overdue."[135]

As long ago as 1986, Dr. J. C. Bailar said, "[We] are losing the war against cancer . . . A shift in research emphasis, from research on treatment to research on prevention, seems necessary if substantial progress against cancer is to be forthcoming."[136]

In 1997 he intensified his position,

Now, with 12 more years of data and experience, we see little reason to change that conclusion . . . The war against cancer is far from over. Observed changes in mortality due to cancer primarily reflect changing incidence or early detection. The effect of new treatments for cancer on mortality has been largely disappointing. The most

promising approach to the control of cancer is a national commitment to prevention, with a concomitant rebalancing of the focus
and funding of research.[137]

There has been some shift in the direction of Dr. Bailar's suggestions,
by individuals, and indeed at least smoking-related cancers are now beginning to decline. But as Bailar remarked in 1998, "The government
has had little role in directing the recent improvements, which reflect
decisions made by millions of individuals to improve their lifestyles."[138]

Learning from the Past—the Future of Cancer Research

The use of human cells to study human disease, one would think, would
have been a no-brainer. Unfortunately, acceptance of this "revolutionary" idea has been hard won, regardless of the logic and enormity of
evidence in its favor. After three decades of exploiting, deluding, and
effectively killing American citizens by depriving them of sound science,
agencies have begun at last to alter their strategy in the War on Cancer.
    In the journal *Science*, in 1997, a group of doctors wrote about the
changeover.[139] The NCI now uses a screen of about 100 *in vitro* tests
with human cells to test cytotoxins (cancer-causing agents and medications).[140] Finally. However, the NCI still directs many millions of dollars
into animal experimentation.
    The American Cancer Society (ACS), another big bankroller of ani-
mal-model research, has the temerity to sponsor a fundraiser called
"Dogs Walk against Cancer" wherein fortunate pooches, which have
not been subjected to carcinogenicity testing, parade about with their
owners. Some of the money collected, the ACS claims, goes toward finding a cure for cancer in man's best friend. The truth is that the ACS
provides money to institutions to develop new anticancer drugs and to
study the effects of radiation on dogs in order to extrapolate it to humans. It also supports gene therapy, surgical training and other cancer-
related experimentation on the luckless creatures. But if a cure for dog
cancer emerges, the ACS can claim that it was looking for this all along.
    Though the "Dogs Walk Against Cancer" persists, American Cancer
Society's former president, Marvin Pollard admits: "We have relied too
heavily on animal testing, and we believed in it too strongly. Now, I
think we are commencing to realize that what goes on in an animal may
not necessarily be applicable to humans."[141]
    In acknowledgment of the futility of searching for a cure for human
cancer in animals, other federal agencies such as the Environmental Protection Agency are beginning to use better methods based on human
tissues, cell preparations, and *in vitro* experiments. The EPA has, in fact,
pioneered the way to more reliable, less archaic, non-animal techniques.

In contrast to similar agencies, the EPA has never relied solely on animal tests. Although the EPA has not completely dispensed with animal tests, as of 1997 they no longer use them routinely.[142]

In 1993, the Department of Transportation (DOT), which is charged with testing certain corrosiveness of certain substances, began *in vitro* tests using artificial or human skin instead of animals. Not until 1995 did the Department of Health and Human Services change the criteria for determining carcinogenicity. It now sometimes uses cell cultures instead of testing mice and rats routinely. This policy is similar to the EPA policy.

As explained in previous chapters, the United States, though enjoying the highest regard worldwide for its medical achievement, has shackled its science to the Dark Ages through preference for animal experimentation. This predilection continues to permeate our fight against cancer. Unfortunately, even the most substantial progress we have yet made toward overcoming our "modern plague"—the development of monoclonal antibodies—has been stalled by reliance on animal sources. Preposterously but tellingly, other western countries without the same resistance from powerful lobbying groups, are moving more quickly toward real solutions.

An antibody is a naturally produced Y-shaped protein molecule that disables disease molecules and signals the immune system. Ron Levy of Stanford University discovered that customized antibodies cured cancer in a single human patient. Thrilled to champion a "miracle cure," Levy founded his own company and stock prices soared. Then subsequent research with mice led to new breakthroughs and medications. Mice again. The unfortunate patients who used the mouse-derived miracle cures did not benefit at all. In fact, some even died from the medications. *Science* stated, "Although Levy's antibody worked, the effects of other antibodies in humans did not match those in mice, and unexpected toxicity even killed patients, bringing clinical trials to an abrupt halt."[143]

The only promising medication to come out of Levy's original research is a structurally very similar chemical now undergoing trials—monoclonal antibodies. These identical antibodies are derived from a single cell; they are monoclones.

In the United States, monoclonal antibodies are brewed in the bodies of our ubiquitous test-species—mice. Contamination and allergic reactions have made the product dangerous, not to mention inefficient and expensive. "Despite their enormous potential as therapeutic agents, monoclonal antibodies of non-human origin have performed poorly in clinical trials as a result of immunogenicity, poor pharmacokinetic properties, and inefficiency in recruiting effector function."[144]

When are we going to get the message? In Europe by contrast, *in vitro* methods are more commonly used. Switzerland and the Netherlands no longer use animal-produced monoclonals, and England may actually outlaw production soon. Cesar Milstein, who won the Nobel Prize in 1984 for monoclonal-antibody production, reported that his lab uses only the *in vitro* method.[145] In addition to being more cost effective, it is safer. Animals can carry viruses that can be transmitted to humans. (See Chapters 10 and 11 on AIDS and xenotransplantation.)

Whereas transplanting antibodies from animals to humans is potentially very dangerous, vegetables may be even better for us than always touted. Scientists working with plants, in lieu of mice and other lab animals, are revolutionizing medicine. Through genetic engineering, they can now grow corn that makes antibodies. By implanting a human gene that produces antibodies in corn, the corn becomes an incubator for the much-needed monoclonal antibody. These antibodies possess no contaminants, like retroviruses, which could be present in antibodies made from animals. Attaching radioisotopes to tumor-specific antibodies, then injecting them into cancer patients will kill the tumors. It is anticipated that this technology will be cheaper than traditional methods. Potentially, enough antibodies to treat all cancer patients in the United States could be made from corn grown on only thirty acres of land. Scientists call these antibodies "plantibodies."[146]

These achievements and the myriad developments in biotechnology reflect a state-of-the-art mindset. This science is solutions-oriented. Continued cancer research on animals is archaic and profligate. The following quote from Dr. Irwin Bross summarizes our indictment of animal experimentation as it pertains to cancer:

> From a scientific standpoint, what is pertinent is that . . . "animal model systems" in cancer research have been a total failure . . . not a single essential new drug for the treatment of human cancer was first picked up by an animal model system. All of the drugs in wide current clinical use were only put into animal model systems after finding clinical clues to their therapeutic possibility. The money was spent . . . for two main reasons. First, it was a highly profitable undertaking for certain medical schools and research institutions that were incapable of doing any genuine cancer research. Second, it was sustained by a superstitious belief in a grossly unscientific notion: Mice are miniature men . . . In sum, from the standpoint of current scientific theory of cancer, the whole mystique of the animal model systems is hardly more than superstitious nonsense . . . The moral is that animal model systems not only kill animals, they also kill humans. There is no good factual evidence to show the use of animals in cancer research has led to the prevention or cure of a single human cancer.[147]

As we have quoted, many, many respected scientists have come to the same conclusions throughout the "War on Cancer" and even before.

Finally, the 104th Congress recognized the problem of testing animals for human cancer and repealed the Delaney Clause. On August 3, 1996, President Clinton signed this into law. This act would seem a cause for great jubilation if it did, in fact as well as philosophy, cease the use of animal-models. However, many other laws passed since Delaney, specifically those governing medication approval, are still on the books. Our institutions, organizations, and agencies continue animal experimentation, and that is, as we have said, its own corrupt sickness.

The momentum of nonhuman experimentation has such thrust, such habit and so many dollars behind it that it will die hard. Legislation banning animal testing may be required to halt its havoc. Perhaps only prevention, *legislated prevention of animal experiments*, has the force to contain the animal experimentation contagion.

chapter 9

Diseases of the Cardiovascular System

Biomedical research does not need animals any more, but should use computers. It is pointless and even dangerous to continue following the traditional paths, for the difference between man and animals is so great that it mostly leads us into error.

—Dr. Luigi Sprovieri, contributor to the invention of the cardiopulmonary bypass machine in *La Nazione,* Florence, Italy, October 5, 1980

H*omo sapiens* is the only species that naturally acquires coronary artery disease, and indeed more Americans succumb to diseases of the heart and great vessels than to all other diseases combined. Nevertheless, no small vat of fat has gone into trying to explain and treat cardiovascular disease through lab animals. Try as researchers might, animal experimentation in this field has but befuddled our understanding and delayed treatments.

No successful medications have derived from animal models. Nor has animal experimentation accurately predicted the effects and side effects of the drugs. Even knife and scalpel techniques successfully performed on animals needed modification because they killed humans. Though this was not always so, it happened frequently enough to prove that animals are not reliable predictors of human response.

There are simple reasons for this. Animals do not, under natural circumstances, suffer from most cardiovascular diseases. When they do, the anatomical and physiologic differences between species negate the similarities. And when researchers try to reproduce human-like diseases in lab animals the same problem occurs, as we will explain in a few paragraphs.

Hence, we can credit only epidemiology, autopsies, *in vitro* research, clinical observation and techniques perfected on cadavers for the great advances in the field of cardiovascular disease—in other words, human-based research alone. Likewise, these same methods have suggested life-styles and diets that could mitigate cardiovascular disease's incidence.

Revelations from Yesteryear

Modern feats of surgical derring-do—transplants, angioplasty, by-passes—while deft and fabulous, obscure the issue of where cardiovascular disease comes from to begin with. Before celebrating the contributing factors to the contemporary field, let us credit those medical sleuths who uncovered true knowledge of heart and vessel mechanics.

Not until the Renaissance did real understanding of our cardiovascular system overcome falsehoods brought about by Galen's second century animal investigations. When scientists overrode the Church's bias against autopsies, at last concrete information began to link anatomical causes to physiological effects.

As discussed in Chapter 2, based on human observation Hieronymus Fabricius of Aquapendente and William Harvey established the truth about blood circulation around 1622. In 1783, Edward Jenner conducted autopsies that indicated coronary arteries were "bony canals." Bony canals filled with what would later be identified as plaque.[1]

Chest pain, or angina as it is called, is an early warning of heart disease. No one over the centuries needed animal experiments to explain that people who ate and drank without restraint might ultimately suffer chest pain. Though this has been evident forever, in the eighteenth century William Heberden described the sensation to the Western world in writing after watching his (human) patients—an example of clinical observation, plain, simple, and on the mark.

In autopsies of the early 1800s, Dr. Jean Nicholas Corvisart identified abnormalities that cause what we now know as congestive heart failure. Austin Flint, considered by some the greatest physician of the nineteenth century, acquired more information on the human heart the old fashioned way. He simply listened to his patients' hearts with a stethoscope, thus diagnosing conditions such as mitral valve stenosis, a complication of rheumatic heart disease.

Edward Jenner of vaccination fame discovered via autopsy that obstruction of coronary arteries led to chest pain and death. Despite Jenner's findings, however, it was not until 1910 that scientists ceased to believe that inflammation of the heart led to death. They refused to believe that blood flow was obstructed. Physicians made meticulous autopsies of patients who had died with chest pain. Discovering, as Jenner had, that arteries going to the heart were clogged, they postulated—

accurately—that the decreased blood flow to the heart provoked chest pain. When the heart muscle does not receive enough blood and therefore oxygen, it reacts by complaining or causing pain. The concept of *myocardial infarction*, or heart attack, arose from these observations and was described by Sir Thomas Lewis in 1934, "It has been established beyond reasonable doubt by *clinical observation* that pain is produced [in the heart] by occlusion of coronary vessels, and that this pain is indistinguishable from that of spasmodic angina pectoris in situation, radiation, and character."[2] (Emphasis added.)

Autopsies further revealed that positive pressure from blood or fluid in the pericardial sac, a condition called *pericardial tamponade*, could stop the heart from beating. Théophile Bonet, in 1679, autopsied patients who had died with pericardial tamponade. He concluded that the positive pressure had stopped the heart. Many others then began to look for tamponade on autopsy. Again through autopsy, cardiologist Arbour Stephens found there was normally negative pressure in the pericardial sac.[3] Eventually surgeons punctured the pericardium to relieve the pressure.[4] Subsequent autopsies supplemented knowledge and treatment of many other diseases of the heart and aorta. Arteriograms conducted on corpses ascertained the amount of blood the heart could contain, as well as how disease decreased the blood flow.[5]

As early as the sixteenth century, doctors associated a slow heartbeat with fainting and sometimes death, as many times the heartbeat will slow down on its way to stopping completely. In 1774 in London, a man named Squires used faradic current to resuscitate a child who had been declared dead.[6] In 1798, M. F. Xavier Bichat examined the hearts of men who had been decapitated in France and noted that they still responded to electrical activity. Attempts to resuscitate animals addled the concept for over a hundred years.[7] Even afterward there was no success in extrapolating to humans. Only after a period of trial and error did physicians realize how to perform cardiopulmonary resuscitation on humans.[8]

Heart Disease

Heart disease is the number-one killer in the United States. The list of heart diseases is long and includes congestive heart failure, congenital heart disease, aneurysms of the heart wall, mitral valve disease, aortic valve disease, tricuspid valve disease, cardiomyopathy, and idiopathic hypertrophic subaortic stenosis, among others. However, the most common, present-day heart disease is coronary artery disease (CAD), caused when arteries that supply blood to the heart become clogged.

CAD seems a relatively new event because not until recently did many humans live long enough to develop symptoms. But today 500,000 Americans die of CAD per year and twelve million suffer its effects.[9] A large number suffer unwittingly. As many as thirty percent of our population do not even know they have this potentially fatal disease.[10] Roughly one third do not survive their first heart attack—twenty percent dying before ever reaching the hospital.

CAD is characterized by atherosclerosis—accumulations of fat, cholesterol, calcium, and fibrin (a substance that causes blood to clot) called plaque. Over time, these plaques silently narrow arteries. Heart attacks may follow, occurring in two ways—when these "clogs" or plaques break off, or when they obstruct blood flow. Either way, heart muscles are deprived of oxygen and a condition called *ischemia* results. (Ischemia occurs when tissue is deprived of oxygen, in this case due to constricted or blocked vessels.)

The link between cholesterol and heart disease had suggested itself by the early-twentieth century, however animal experiments, for instance those of a Russian named Nikolai Anichkov, repressed aggressive steps to change diets, because animals did not acquire atherosclerosis through a high cholesterol diet.[11]

The first prospective research on cholesterol and heart disease was called the Seven Counties Study and was initiated by cholesterol pioneer Ancel Keys. Keys compared cardiovascular disease in typical American businessmen and Europeans after World War II. The European population ate barely enough to survive. To Key's surprise, he found that well-fed Americans had a much higher incidence of CAD than near-starving Europeans.[12]

For purposes of assessing heart disease risk factors in humans, scientists began looking at lifestyles in residents of Framingham, Massachusetts beginning in 1948. The study proved groundbreaking. It established beyond doubt the relationship between CAD and hypertension, smoking, and high fat diets. The Framingham experience still constitutes one of the most significant epiphanies in medicine. Among other watershed discoveries, it would lead to the identification of HDL (high density lipoproteins) as good cholesterol and LDL (low density lipoproteins) as bad.

Attempts to Induce CAD in Animals

Given the bulk of human-based information, there certainly was not any point in waiting for animals to lament over severe tightening of the chest and the accompanying shortness of breath. Nevertheless, researchers tried. Efforts to reproduce Framingham in animals, to "validate" these findings, consistently failed. Researchers have tested a Noah's Ark worth of species including rabbits, bears, dogs, cats, rats, kangaroos, seals, sea lions, pelicans, monkeys, chimpanzees, baboons, gorillas, pigs, horses, parrots, ducks, and chickens. In none of them did atherosclerotic plaques form as they do in humans.[13] Since atherosclerosis is a condition that develops with aging, and animals are not long-lived, this is not surprising. There were and are always major differences in induced versions of this uniquely human problem. As Thomas M. A. Bocan of Parke-Davis Pharmaceuticals recently stated, "There is no one perfect animal model that commonly replicates the stages of human atherosclerosis."[14]

Rabbits are popularly employed in CAD research. First and most importantly, no rabbit would come down with heart disease on its own. Researchers artificially induce the disease in the rabbit by forcing the arteries to clog. But rabbits' artificial plaques do not ulcerate and break off as plaques can in humans and this is a huge difference.[15]

Treated thus, rabbits will eventually develop atherosclerosis, but not in the right place for heart disease. It usually occurs in the thoracic aorta and aortic arch, not in the coronary arteries as it appears in humans. The fatty lesions are also different from those naturally occurring in humans. The same is true of guinea pigs and mice.[16] Furthermore, some rabbits differ in their response to diet. Since diabetic humans are predisposed to coronary artery disease, researchers induced diabetes in rabbits, then fed them a high cholesterol diet. The rabbits developed *less* CAD.[17]

Other common lab animals, rats and mice, are not suitable models either since they metabolize fats, also known as lipids, differently from humans. A high-fat content in rats and mice diet does not elevate cholesterol levels as it does in humans because lipoprotein metabolism differs between species. Plus, rat hearts derive blood supply from coronary arteries, the subclavian and internal mammary arteries.[18] These notable differences led researchers to state, "The rat is not an appropriate human model for studies involving lipids."[19] Other scientists emphasized, "It is not possible to extrapolate directly from rat to human studies because of differences in plasma lipoprotein [cholesterol and triglycerides] metabolism between the species."[20]

Through genetic manipulation, researchers have fashioned ever-newer mouse models for studies of CAD, each incarnation touted as more humanlike in their acquisition of cardiovascular disease than the one before. But even with the disease, these mice still do not have strokes or heart attacks. As scientists writing in *Nature* state, "Perhaps neither [of two new recently developed animal models] completely resembles the most common form of human hyperlipidemia [high cholesterol]."[21] In 1970, the *Medical News Tribune* said, "Much of the experimental animal work on atheroma [the atherosclerosis of CAD] has held back our progress rather than advancing it."[22]

This, of course, did not stop the government from funding animal-based research to reanswer the questions already addressed in the human-based research. Billions have been wasted over the last thirty years subjecting animals to all manner of weird trials while the scientists chasing their tails try to advance knowledge concerning CAD.

Well, humans are not that much like rabbits or dogs or guinea pigs. How about the great apes and pigs? Pigs and some nonhuman primates will develop lesions in the coronary arteries, but they do not respond to medications and other interventions the same way as humans. This limits their usefulness.[23] Baboons, another favorite of researchers, have CAD induced over a course of hours, not years as in humans. Since baboons do not get CAD naturally, researchers have to work with healthy baboon vessels that bear little in common with the diseased human vessels they are trying to emulate. This protocol becomes even less efficacious as scientists are now suggesting that underlying problems with the vessels are just as much of an issue as plaque. There is another blemish in the baboon model. Whereas human plaque is composed of blood, fat, and other substances, baboon clogs have little if any fat or cholesterol. Human plaques cause further changes in the artery, which blood, alone, will not. When chimpanzees receive a high fat diet, only one type of fat in their heart increases. In humans both alpha and beta lipoproteins increase. This invalidates any research on chimpanzees regarding heart disease.[24] So much for our closest relatives.

Evidently, bypassing the clogged vessel would overcome the acute problem of lack of oxygen. We now bypass the clogged vessel with a vein, but animal studies suggested an entirely different approach.

Animal studies in the 1930s, 1940s, and 1950s indicated that tying off an artery in the chest, named the internal mammary artery, would divert more blood through occluded coronary arteries. The detoured circulation worked great in dogs . . . but not so in humans.[25-28] This was just one of many failures in humans that worked well in dogs.[29] More later on how surgery to improve blood flow to the heart developed.

Medications

Pharmaceutical companies have approached CAD therapies from several angles over the years, the animal model consistently flummoxing the outcome. Too bad they did not stick to the known winner, the human model. As early as 1867, a physician named Sir Lauder Brunton, who was experiencing angina, helped himself to a little nitroglycerin. Brunton was amazed to find his symptoms relieved. The rest is history.[30,31] Nitroglycerin is still the most commonly used medication for controlling angina. Small pills can be placed under the tongue or the medication can be given directly into a vessel. This serendipitous clinical discovery has saved millions of lives and is used daily.

Aspirin, developed before insistence on animal models, is one of the most effective treatments for CAD. By inhibiting the aggregation of platelets, which lead to blood clots and subsequently to heart attacks and strokes, aspirin reduces the risk of heart disease by half. As you remember, aspirin causes birth defects in some animals and blood abnormalities in cats; it would never have been approved if it had been introduced after Kefauver-Harris. (See chapter 3, Legislated Ineptitude.) Not exactly a prime example of parity between species.

Many other examples point to the same disparity. There was a stir when researchers discovered that a common chemical, acetylcholine, dilated coronary arteries in dogs. Physicians gave acetylcholine to humans, but it had the opposite effect. Constricting human arteries, it caused subjects to suffer heart attacks. Bradykinin, another common chemical, behaves diametrically, constricting cerebral arteries in dogs but dilating them in humans.[32,33] The leukotrienes, LTC4 and LTD4 constrict blood vessels in guinea pigs but dilate them in humans and pigs.[34]

Milrinone, a medication designed to aid failing hearts actually *increased* mortality when administered to humans. It worked well on animals. Human use indicated that it was effective but only when taken for a shorter period of time, so it was relabeled.[35] Pimobendan, flosequinan, and vesrinone did likewise.[36,37] As these examples indicate, developing heart disease drugs through the animal model has been a complete boondoggle.

The first drug to counter high cholesterol, a risk factor for CAD, was triparanol. It was recalled because it produced cataracts in those who took it. Prior animal tests had showed no vestige of this. Even once the effect was recognized in humans, scientists faced insurmountable obstacles in trying to reproduce it in animals. Finally they found some rats that, when given enough of the drug at the right time, developed cataracts. What did this putative validation show? Nothing. One scientist stated:

> There are only a few proven causes of induced cataracts in human patients, yet the literature is replete with discourses on experimental cataracts in animals. Some drug will produce cataracts in humans as well as in a few species of animals. Others will produce cataracts in some species of animals but not in others. The naïve reader may become misled by trying to apply experimental findings [on animals] to his patients.[38]

Since then, cataract formation in animals has been a persistent finding in drugs designed to diminish cholesterol. The recent anticholesterol drugs cause cataracts in some animals, but not humans.

"Statins" are the new wonder drugs for reducing cholesterol and triglycerides. Including lovastatin, pravastatin, simvastatin, mevastatin, fluvastatin, and pravastatin, the statin family arrests the enzyme that allows the body to make cholesterol. Researchers happened upon the statins' cholesterol-inhibiting properties while looking for an antifungal agent. They confirmed its action *in vitro*. The first marketed statin, lovastatin, is a metabolite of fungus, isolated from cultures of *Monascus ruber* and

Aspergillus terreus, obtained from soil samples. Others, with the exception of fluvastatin, are variations on the chemical theme of lovastatin. Fluvastatin is chemically unique. Pravastatin was first found in the urine of dogs who were being forced to take mevastatin. Alternatively, it could have been found in the urine of humans taking mevastatin.

When they administered these drugs to animals, they decided not to pursue development. Lovastatin caused a twelve-fold increase in triglycerides and a 2.4–fold increase in cholesterol in hamsters.[39] Simvastatin caused optic nerve degeneration in dogs and cataracts in dogs and rats. Other statins caused cataracts in dogs too. Even rats, which can be made to mimic humans in their response to fibrate-type drugs do not respond like humans to statins. Many drug companies ignored the statins because of misinformation from rat studies. Humans could have benefited from these drugs sooner. Pharmaceutical researchers, Drs. B. R. Krause and H. M. Princen stated, "Therefore, the rodent species thought to resemble humans with regard to regulation of LDL (low density lipoprotein) metabolism has contributed little to our understanding of statin pharmacology."[40]

On the other hand, scientists learned retrospectively that rabbits respond similarly to humans with statins. True, they suffer profound liver, gall bladder, and kidney changes with simvastatin, as do other animals, but they react to nicotinic acid and fibrates entirely differently than humans.[41] Note what one clinical pharmacologist says about the stunted pace of heart medication development,

> Few would dispute that the most significant advance in the last hundred years in the treatment of angina pectoris was the introduction of the nitrate drugs by Lauder Brunton in 1867. This advance was the result of observing the anginal patient and did not depend on any experimental model at all. Departure from this approach may be largely to blame for much of the unprofitable effort expended in the search for better agents in the subsequent 99 years.[42]

Authorities acknowledge that "any *in vitro* method using human tissue gives a degree of reassurance not provided . . . by animal experiments."[43]

For new cholesterol-lowering drugs, researchers are turning not to animals but to genetics.[44,45] They have compared the genes of people with normal to elevated cholesterol levels and those who have very low cholesterol due to an inherited disease that impedes the conversion of dietary fats into cell-nourishing forms. After identifying the gene that leads to excess cholesterol in otherwise healthy individuals, they then developed a substance *in vitro* that interrupts the gene's action. Though not yet on the market, these drugs augur a different and very much more effective technique for countering high cholesterol.[46] Someday the good gene may even be inserted into those who do not have it, thus offering protection.[47]

Prevention

In the late 1950s, scientists stated in government testimony,

> The indications of current research findings that this [atherosclerosis] may be essentially a nutritional disease raise questions that cannot be satisfactorily answered in the laboratory. In fact, atherosclerosis is one of several areas in which research has reached the practical limits of laboratory investigation with the present state of our knowledge and techniques. The road to further progress now seems to lie in large-scale and long-range epidemiological studies utilizing large population groups as the basic unit of study.[48]

And indeed, looking back over that long, costly interlude between the 1950s and today, that is what has happened. Legitimate heart disease data has derived entirely from epidemiology, clinical, *in vitro* research, and autopsies. Framingham and other epidemiological studies provided more information about CAD than any other modality. By now everyone knows high cholesterol is a ticket to a heart attack.

Over time, clinical studies, not animal data, reinforced the correlation between CAD and cholesterol levels. And epidemiology gradually exposed other risk factors, such as hypertension, cigarette smoking, diabetes, family history of the disease, lack of exercise, obesity, and stress. Recent clinical studies have revealed precise data, for example, about exercise's favorable influence on immune cell function among individuals at risk of ischemic heart disease.[49] Epidemiological studies of autopsy data also tracked patients who died of CAD. A review of their medical records augmented our current knowledge of CAD risk factors even further.[50]

CAD can be prevented or kept in abeyance by diet.[51] One epidemiological study, commonly called the "Grand Prix," examined the diets of people from sixty-five countries and concluded that a diet high in fat and meat was a major cause of disease.[52,53] Asian people who consume a low fat, low meat diet are healthier, and suffer less cancer and heart disease. Interestingly, when Asian people switch to a Western diet, they boost their risk of suffering from these diseases—the point being that though genetics can determine susceptibility to CAD, it does not prevent heart attack, but lifestyle can.[54] Since meat contains a type of fat called stearic acid that encourages blood to clot, a non-meat high fiber diet prevents inappropriate clotting.[55]

Though information about the hazards of high cholesterol is everywhere, unfortunately, the cholesterol levels of many Americans are not decreasing. Recent autopsy studies found that CAD was present in seventy-eight percent of people under the age of thirty-five.[56]

As Dr. David Nash of SUNY in Syracuse states,

> While it may be dramatic to demonstrate our technical skill in replacing blocked arteries, or even with a mechanical device, risk factor reduction is a far more realistic, cost-effective and humane approach to resolving this serious health problem.[57]

Epidemiology also suggested that low estrogen levels and high levels of C-reactive protein in the blood may bring on CAD.[58,59] Other studies of populations and autopsies revealed that quantities of a naturally occurring bodily chemical—homocysteine—elevate in people who are vulnerable to cardiovascular disease and may augment susceptibility to cardiovascular disease.[60] The American Heart Association now recommends increased dietary intake of vitamins B6, B12, and folic acid to reduce homocysteine levels and the risk of heart attack or stroke.[61,62]

Using a combination of epidemiology and *in vitro* research, researchers have located one of the genes responsible for familial *hypertrophic cardiomyopathy*, which occurs when there is a defect in the gene coding for myosin and troponin.[63] Why researchers needed to attempt to introduce this defect into the mouse family in order to validate it is anyone's guess.[64,65,66] Likewise, scientists are seeking the gene responsible for the lethal cardiac dysrhythmia ventricular fibrillation. They have already found the gene responsible for idiopathic ventricular fibrillation by studying six families who suffered from the illness.[67] Correspondingly, they have pinpointed two genetic mutations that lead to Holt-Oram syndrome and atrial septal defect, and severe heartbeat abnormalities.[68] Scientists can use this increased knowledge of genetics to study heart disease prevention and closely monitor people with these genes for manifestations of the disease.

The more information we garner about the causes of heart disease—whether they issue from genes or lifestyle or both—the better equipped we are to alter our habits so as to lessen its effect. The good news is that mortalities from CAD are decreasing, not due to animal experimentation, but thanks to prevention and technology.[69]

From 1990 to 1999, deaths from heart disease decreased in the United States due mainly to prevention. More and more Americans understand that changing diet and lifestyle can be more productive for good health than anything else they can do. Stopping smoking, monitoring blood pressure, decreasing cholesterol levels, and changing diet have been the main reasons for the decline.[70]

Technology

We cannot overemphasize the contributions technology has made. If those suffering from heart attacks make it to hospitals with coronary care units in time, doctors can restore flow to coronary arteries, administer medications, and evaluate risks using many contemporary innovations, none of which depended on animals for development.

During cardiac arrest, the ability to deliver medication directly to the heart is aided by insertion of a pulmonary artery catheter (PAC). The PAC also allows physicians to measure the pressure inside the heart and determine which medication to prescribe as well as the amount and rate of blood being pumped out of the heart, a very important concept during surgery and critical illnesses.

For the development of cardiac catheterization, we have a German urologist, Werner Theodor Otto Forssmann, to thank. From very early in his career, Forssmann entertained the possibility of cardiac catheterization. He tried catheterizing rabbits but they died of dysrhythmias as soon as the catheter touched the heart.[71] In 1929, he successfully experimented on himself, placing the catheter into his arm, threading it through to his own heart, and inventing the PAC. As he described the process,

> After the success of the experiments on *cadavers*, I undertook the first investigation in living humans through self-experimentation. First of all, in a preliminary experiment, I allowed myself to be punctured in the right elbow vein using a large bore needle. One of my surgical colleagues kindly placed himself at my disposal for this purpose. I then introduced, as in the experiments on cadavers, a well-oiled ureteral catheter through the cannula into the vein. The catheter was then easily introduced for a distance of 35 cm of height. Because further catheterization appeared to my colleague to be too risky, we interrupted the experiment, although I felt completely well. After one week I undertook alone further experimentation . . . and introduced the catheter 65 cm . . . The position of the catheter was proven by x-ray and indeed I observed the tip of the catheter itself in a mirror held in front of the illuminated screen by a nurse. (Emphasis added.)[72]

Forssmann continued his experiments, becoming the first person to inject contrast dye into a human heart, his own. His brave and self-confident proofs provided the basis for modern day cardiology. Typical of a scientific climate that refuted all but animal-based evidence, no one was convinced of his newfound catheter technique and refused to fund continued experiments until other scientists "validated" them on animals.

Today, we realize how much we owe to Forssmann, including our basic knowledge of the physiology of the heart and lungs. Without his determined efforts, the diagnosis and treatment of many heart diseases and birth defects of the heart would be impossible. The PAC paved the way for the specialty of cardiology, leading to technological therapies such as angioplasty, stents, pacemaker insertion, and heart surgery, as well as an avenue for evaluating and treating the severely ill.

A research team composed of Drs. Swan and Ganz improved the PAC. The problem with the catheter was getting it to go in the proper direction; the way the blood is flowing. One day while observing sailboats, Dr. Swan had the idea of attaching a sail onto their catheter and letting it float into the heart with the blood. Since a sail seemed impractical, he used a tiny inflatable balloon to carry the catheter to the correct location.

Various tests can now diagnose heart disease or quantify how bad the disease is, so a patient can get proper medication or undergo surgery. Ultrafast CT scanning ascertains calcium levels in the coronary arteries and catches CAD in its very earliest stages.[73] Stress tests evaluate symptoms such as chest pain or shortness of breath during exertion. These are either treadmills or pharmacologic tests for people who cannot exercise. Pharmacologic tests mimic the effects of exercise by raising the heart rate. There are even studies underway to perfect a new blood test that indicates susceptibility to cardiovascular disease by quantifying levels of the aforementioned C-reactive protein.

Imaging of the heart, using radioactive tracer chemicals (radionuclides) such as thallium or sestamibi, with or without stress testing, evaluates if and how much CAD is compromising blood flow to the heart. These methods also quantify the degree of damage after a heart attack, assessing the quality of the left ventricle, or monitor for damage that certain chemotherapeutic medications may cause to the heart.

PET scans, CAT scans, and other devices evaluate the arteries and heart. A common method of assessing ventricular function is a multiple-gated acquisition analysis (MUGA). This technique efficiently appraises the heart's ability to pump blood without catheterization or other invasive procedures. Technical innovations such as defibrillators, angiography, and ultrasound have also improved diagnoses and treatment of heart disease.[74]

Another great step in the diagnosis and treatment of heart disease is trans-esophageal echocardiography (TEE), a type of ultrasound. Prior to its development, cardiologists viewed the heart through the chest wall. They were limited in their observations of the heart by skin, tissue, and bone. Inserted into a patient's esophagus, the TEE provides a better viewing since there is less distance to the heart and therefore much less interference to the sound waves. This has allowed many advances. For example, most thoracic aortic aneurysms can be diagnosed in time for effective therapies, or surgery if medications do not decrease the risk of rupture.[75]

All these technological advances relied on hard work, savvy scientists, and a fundamental understanding of engineering, physiology, and anatomy, not animal experimentation. Combined with better health regimes, technology continues to go a long way toward decreasing the fatality of this prevalent disease.

High Blood Pressure and Strokes

Approximately fifty million Americans have high blood pressure or hypertension (HTN). As our population ages, the condition has become more prevalent, with approximately fifty percent of Americans over sixty-five affected. But it is not just a disease of the elderly. Nearly thirty percent of black Americans and twenty percent of whites over the age of eighteen years have hypertension.

Untreated hypertension can lead to eye damage as well as life-threatening conditions such as stroke, CAD, and kidney failure. Thanks first to clinical studies, improved detection, and treatment of hypertension have diminished the inevitability of these sequelae over the past twenty years.[76,77]

One of the first treatments for hypertension was a restricted-salt, high-fiber diet and rest. Dr. Kempner, in 1944, recommended this and it worked. Knowledge of the impact of salt on blood pressure, subsequently confirmed by epidemiological research in Great Britain, led people to restrict their salt intake, allowing many to decrease or even discontinue medications.[78] Simply modifying diet and lifestyle is remedial.

Accumulated clinical evidence about the influence of diet and lifestyle on our blood pressure notwithstanding, researchers have labored hard and long to produce hypertension in animals then cure it. But there is nothing about animal models that can reliably be applied to human hypertension. Again, we have spent a fortune milking bad models.

As even a book supporting the use of animal experimentation stated:

> The fact that there are so many [animal] models for hypertension and atherosclerosis indicates that none of them is completely satisfactory . . . Identical observations can be made for the other severe cardiovascular pathologies: coronary ischemia, cerebral ischemia, cardiac insufficiency and rhythm disorders.[79]

Medications

Dr. Franz Gross, an HTN researcher remarked,

It has to be admitted that the antihypertensive effect of some drugs such as the diuretics, clonidine or the beta-adrenergic blockers was first observed in man, and only later studied in animal experiments with respect to their blood pressure-lowering activity.[80]

Dr. B. Pritchard was a physician who was administering a beta-blocker to a human patient suffering chest pain when he noticed the blood pressure decrease. His observation led to anti-angina medications such as propranolol, metoprolol, atenolol, and others being used for hypertension. Animal studies had predicted previously that they would not lower blood pressure.[81,82,83] "Nothing in our work [on animals] predicted the slowly developing antihypertensive action of pronethalol which Pritchard and Gilliam have described."[84]

Dr. B. Fitzgerald comments on Dr. Pritchard's clinical observation, "Pritchard's tenacious studies on the hypotensive action of propranolol eventually paved the way for the extensive use of beta-blockers in hypertension, even though this therapeutic application was not predicted from animal studies."[85]

Today, millions of people use beta-blockers as treatment for HTN. Even animal experimenters admitted the failure of animal models of hypertension in this regard. Many other anti-HTN medications such as alpha-methyldopa, calcium channel blockers, and clonidine were not predicted based on animal studies.

Conversely, once researchers attempted to "validate" the usefulness of beta-blockers, these animal tests did not foretell beta-blocker side effects such as heart failure, bronchospasm, fatigue, and others.

> Unwanted effects such as bradycardia [slowing of the heart rate], hypotension, heart failure, bronchial spasm, cold extremities and easy fatiguability are attributable to known actions of beta antagonists. With the exception of bradycardia, *none of these was predicted from the initial animal studies.*[86] (Emphasis added.)

We can also credit the diuretic treatment of HTN entirely to clinical experience.[87] As long ago as 1937, doctors noticed that patients who took medications to increase urine output began to breathe better. As a patient's heart fails, fluid fills the lungs and he or she essentially drowns. Diuresis allowed the congested lungs to get rid of excess fluid; thus patients could breathe easier. The scientists then modified the medication's chemical structure to isolate the diuretic effect and the thiazide diuretics were born. Lasix is one commonly used example. The substances were never tested on animals. Ray Gifford, MD, a major contributor, acknowledged, "We had no protocols, no informed signed consents, no statistical consultation. We just gave the drugs in any combination we thought would reduce blood pressure and minimize side effects."[88] Dr.

Karl Beyer stated, "We did not assess the activity of chlorothiazide in hypertensive animals prior to clinical trial."[89] Dr. Gifford added, "I can't help but wonder how long it would take to get hydralazine or chlorothiazide on the market today?"

Although those who earn their living by experimenting on animals will try to convince you that all medical miracles arose from calculated experiments on animals in controlled laboratory environments, clinical initiative is how discoveries actually emerge. Many more such examples abound, more than the vested interest groups would like to reveal. The development of the anti-hypertensive medications not only was not dependent upon using animals, it would have been impossible using them. Dr. F. Gross states in the textbook *The Scientific Basis of Official Regulation of Drug Research and Development,*

> The antihypertensive effect of diuretics does not occur in normotensive animals and is difficult to obtain in hypertensive rats or dogs. Similar problems have to be faced with respect to the antihypertensive action of beta-adrenoreceptor blocking drugs. The beneficial effect of phentolamine, of prazosin, or of hydralazine in the treatment of heart failure is hardly demonstrable in experimental animal models . . . The predictive value of the results of numerous preclinical [animal] tests or experimental models for the therapeutic use of a drug is at best uncertain, and the predictability will not be improved by simply increasing the number of tests . . . One of the most widely studied examples of a disease model is experimental hypertension, but for the development of new drugs for the treatment of high blood pressure the various types of experimental hypertension are dispensable tools.[90]

Strokes

Strokes, a sometimes consequence of hypertension, are the leading cause of disability in adults and the third greatest cause of death in the United States. They occur when occluded blood vessels in the brain inhibit the delivery of oxygen to brain cells or when a plaque breaks off also resulting in ischemia. As with heart attacks, damage from a stroke continues to spread the longer the region of the brain is deprived of oxygen. Some label strokes "brain attacks" because the action is a sort of siege, similar to a heart attack.

Approximately 500,000 people suffer a stroke each year. Many stroke victims live with damage from the devastating attack: paralysis, loss of the ability to speak or understand speech, to walk or feel sensations, loss of memory, and other terrible consequences.

Clinical observation and epidemiology have revealed all the known causes of stroke including hypertension, high cholesterol, diabetes, heredity, and smoking. Only rarely does one find patients for surgery of the heart or great vessels who did not smoke or eat a high fat diet. What is certain is that although we cannot stop aging, we can dramatically lower the inevitability of stroke just by taking care of our bodies, as is the case for heart disease.

Naturally, aging and other factors can contribute to diseases of the circulatory system. Atrial fibrillation, a type of irregular heartbeat, can also lead to stroke. Another stroke risk factor, found through clinical observation, is atherosclerotic plaque, deposits in the carotid arteries (the blood vessels in the neck that supply blood and oxygen to the brain). When the deposits dislodge into the brain circulation, they occlude blood flow.[91] Physicians can observe atherosclerotic plaque through angiography; a radiographic technique invented based on clinical research.

Attempts to Induce Stroke in Animals

Vivisectors have attempted to identify these factors again and develop techniques to mitigate the effects of stroke. This would make sense, maybe, if animal's cerebral blood supply was the same as humans. But most animals have greater cerebral circulatory *reserve*, which confuses the implications of any research findings. Moreover, naturally occurring strokes are extraordinarily rare in animals. Cats can become hypertensive but usually suffer only eye problems, not strokes. Dogs do not become hypertensive, but will on occasion have strokes. Usually, this occurs when they receive steroids or have a disease causing them to over-produce steroids. Steroid use hardly ever causes strokes in humans. Again, the nonparallel. J. P. Whisnant said of animal studies in 1958:

> For the most part, these studies have tended to lag behind clinical and pathologic-anatomic investigation and too frequently have served as confirmatory work after clinical impressions have been virtually accepted . . . "It is obvious at the outset, that investigations with laboratory animals can not be directly related to human disease. No experimental animal has an entirely comparable cerebrovascular supply to that of man[92]

This was echoed by a Dr. S. Neff at New England Medical Center in a 1989 issue of the journal, *Stroke*: "The repeated failures of laboratory proven stroke therapies in humans can be due only to the inapplicability of animal models to human cerebral vascular disease."[93]

Researchers have been entirely fruitless in their efforts to reproduce human stroke in animals for over 150 years.[94] It would seem they should have wised up. Instead they defend animal models of stroke because:

- Rats are consistent with each other in their anatomy and physiology. In other words, a rat is a rat is a rat.
- The stroke area can be controlled in rats.

- If a stroke is induced by a consistent technique, the outcome in the rat will be predictable.[95]

This rationalization is daft because its very consistency limits the relevance of the information to the rats in question. Consistency in rats has nothing to do with humans. The defense of rat models may be convenient for the researchers and make for tidy data on scientific papers, but it reflects nothing about what will happen in humans.

To repeat, animals are different from humans in their cerebral blood supply, in the way their brains respond to stroke, and in the treatments that are effective in decreasing the severity of the stroke. This is well known and documented in the medical literature.[96-99] Between 1978 and 1988, twenty-five drugs proved effective in treating stroke in animals. None worked in humans.[100] Animal experiments predicted that barbiturates would protect against stroke. In humans they did not. MK801 protected some animals but not others, including humans. And so on. Twenty-five failures. As is typical of scientists whose livelihoods depend upon animal experiments, Drs. J. A. Zivin and J. C. Grotta offer the excuse that "our drug studies in animal models have not yet translated into effective therapy in humans." However they stated that animal models should not be done away with because someday they might yield results.[101] That is like saying lend me a dollar today and even though I have never paid you back, I promise I will pay you back tomorrow.

Dr. David Wiebers et al., of the Mayo Clinic, summarized the contribution of animal experimentation to our knowledge of strokes as follows:

> A large proportion of patients with ischemic stroke have underlying multifocal atherosclerosis which has developed over many years or decades. Such individuals may have numerous associated risk factors which predispose to this disease process . . . Some attempts have been made to model atherosclerosis in some animal species and to account for hypertension and increasing age, but it is clear that these circumstances do not reproduce the human situation. In fact, most models of ischemic stroke are derived from young animals with no underlying chronic disease or any genetic predisposition to such diseases . . . Many variations, both within and between species, have been recognized not only in the vascular anatomy, but also in histopathologic response to identical ischemic insults and treatment responses to cerebral ischemia . . . While the use of these experimental [animal] models has provided much information about the methods of producing and potentially treating cerebral ischemia and infarction in specific animal species and experimental circumstances, the relevance of most of these data to human conditions remains dubious . . . although animal models of cerebral ischemia have been used extensively to test new therapies in human stroke, their record for identifying clinically effective drugs has been

disappointing . . . Among those compounds subjected to clinical trials, none has proven efficacious, nor have any of these agents come into general clinical use. Ultimately, however, the answers to many of our questions regarding the underlying pathophysiology and treatment of stroke do not lie with continued attempts to model the human situation more perfectly in animals, but rather with the development of techniques to enable the study of more basic metabolism, pathophysiology, and anatomical imaging detail in living humans.[102]

Everything in this book exemplifies that animals and humans are far from clones in their responses to disease and medications. As we have commented earlier, very often different races, different genders and different ages are widely incongruous in their susceptibilities and reactions.[103] These incongruities are called heterogenicity. Hypertension is a great example of heterogenicity of response.[104]

Epidemiology, not animal studies, indicated that the risk for a stroke can be inherited through a gene mutation.[105,106] Blacks are most vulnerable, with twice the risk of HTN and twice as many deaths as whites. It is now evident that some possess a certain gene variant that renders them highly salt-sensitive and that contributes to this susceptibility to HTN.[107,108,109] White women show a higher incidence of death from coronary heart disease due to hypertension than do white men.[110] Response to hypertension medication also varies.[111]

As we have said before, how can animals be expected to be good predictors, if we cannot even rely on humans of the same race but of different genders to produce consistent results?

Treatment for Stroke

The quicker patients receive treatment for stroke, the higher the probability of limiting the stroke's effects. Biotechnology has responded with ever more sophisticated mechanisms for hastening response. Using a functional MRI scanner with diffusion-weighted imaging speeds up diagnosis to as little as six minutes. Researchers have begun using biochemical markers to locate brain injuries. By identifying the location, scientists can design treatments to halt or slow the progression of cell damage.[112]

Since both heart attacks and brain attacks are caused by insufficient blood delivery to cells, scientists deduced that heart attack protocol would work for strokes. Effective stroke treatment demands prompt administration of anti-clotting medications, preferably during the stroke or as soon afterwards as is feasible. If a clot is responsible for the blockage, administering medications such as streptokinase and recombinant tissue plasminogen activators will dissolve the clot, restoring blood and oxygen to the cells. Once again, clinical observation of clot-dissolving medications advanced treatment while animal experiments did not.

Of course prevention is more valuable than cures. To begin with, by eating better, exercising, and refraining from cigarettes, alcoholic beverages and cocaine-related drugs people may avoid strokes entirely.[113] With early detection of susceptibility, improved habits and proper medication (antiplatelet agents such as aspirin, and cholesterol-lowering drugs such as statins) for conditions such as hypertension that may lead to strokes, the incidence of strokes decreases as does the need for surgeries.[114]

Results of *in vitro* research suggested that patients prone to stroke could decrease the risk of stroke just by taking aspirin prophylactically.[115] We mentioned this mechanism earlier in this chapter in reference to heart disease. Again, aspirin is not healthful for all animals.

Perhaps the money misallocated to animal experiments on hypertension should be redirected toward preventative measures, and early detection. The outcome would diminish the prevalence of this disease in our country.

Cardiovascular Surgery

The number of animals who have undergone experimental cardiovascular surgery surely numbers in the millions. If these experiments have contributed, as pro-vivisectionists claim, just what were those precise contributions? Our research unveiled details about the experiments that those in favor of them leave out. Not surprisingly, many of these details worked against humans rather than for them.

Granted, animals are not so dissimilar to humans that techniques used in one can never be used in the other. However, since non-humans are not *consistently predictive* models, the first humans to undergo procedures are every bit the guinea pig, no matter how much animal practice occurred prior. Using animals has been a convention, but an unnecessary and unreliable one.

Post-mortem experiments on cadavers yield better information without exposing patients to the risk that all the differences between humans and animals imply. This is true throughout the history of cardiovascular surgery.

Vascular Surgery

Consider the fundamental technique of blood-vessel repair, a landmark surgical innovation. Sometimes a surgeon can simply stitch the original vessel back together after an injury, but other times the original needs replacing. The replacement may be a manmade vessel, one of the patient's own vessels, or one harvested from another person. All operations involving the vascular system use this technique—called a vascular anastomosis—including heart-bypass operations, organ transplants, and aneurysm procedures.

Early surgeries for aneurysms augured the development of vascular anastomosis. In 1785, based on human observation, John Hunter tied off a femoral artery. The femoral supplies blood to the popliteal artery, which in this case contained an aneurysm.[116] Hunter's operation was not entirely successful but he proved that operating on vessels was possible, which indicated the way to successful anastomosis surgery. Other surgeons would go on to perfect the aneurysm procedure without animal studies.[117-21]

As a result of human autopsies, late-nineteenth century pathologist Ernst Ziegler observed that the inner lining of vessels has the capacity to form scar tissue after being cut.[122] Just as skin heals after a cut, vessels do too. This was the first indication that one vessel might be successfully attached to another. Clinical observation too, in the battlefield and elsewhere, indicated that veins might be sewn to each other or that sewing the end of a vein to an artery might be accomplished.[123]

As you can deduce, scrutiny of human vessels suggested the actual anastomosis technique, but its timely innovation floundered around animal evidence. Some surgeons tried to perform a vascular anastomosis on rabbits, but the procedure failed.[124] Fortunately, optimism persisted, despite the animal fiascos. In 1897, a surgeon named Murphy performed the first successful vascular anastomosis on humans.[125] Although his patients died due to infection, common for the time period, the technique itself was successful.

The man who received the 1912 Nobel Prize for the technique, Alexis Carrel, claimed to have perfected the anastomosis technique using human cadavers.[126] Previously, he successfully sutured dogs' transplanted organs and hence vessels in place, however animals soon destroyed the organs as foreign tissue. This is another example of animals being neither necessary nor sufficient to establish groundbreaking technique. Carrel himself commented that mice and rats have "only very remote analogies with man."[127] Interestingly, Carrel's work, by his own admission, "came into existence nine years ago from the study of the technique of Payr and of Murphy [on humans]."[128] The vascular anastomosis procedure was a milestone, an avenue to an array of operations.[129,130,131]

As early as 1728, physicians had reported that a connection between a vein and an artery, an arteriovenous (AV) connection, occasionally occurs naturally in humans.[132] This knowledge lay untapped until the early 1900s when a surgeon perceived that since AV connections crop up in some humans, perhaps veins could tolerate the pressure of the arterial system. This hypothesis was marginalized by animal experimentation, which "proved" that veins could not support arterial flow, but still clinical observation suggested otherwise.[133,134]

Study of hearts at the New York City Mortuary, among other places, persuaded surgeons that bypasses were possible. They conjectured that by bypassing proximal lesions in the coronary arteries with a section of vein, if the remaining artery was free from obstruction, the heart should benefit from normal blood-flow, and therefore function normally. In 1906, surgeons placed a piece of vein between the two cut ends of an artery. The procedure came off without a hitch and paved the way for coronary artery bypass graft (CABG) operations today.[135,136]

Today the blocked artery is not cut out, but rather "bypassed" by the insertion of a vein. A bypass may be single, double, or even quadruple depending on the number of vessels replaced. After two or three heart operations, some patients literally exhaust their own supply of vessels needed to revascularize the heart. If not harvested from the patient, normally a vein comes from a cadaver, or an artificial vessel is inserted.[137] Arteries may soon be made from a patient's own tissue thanks to *in vitro* research.

Another application of anastomosis is the femoral-popliteal bypass or "fem-pop." Frequently older adults and smokers experience a blockage of the femoral or popliteal artery resulting in claudication and walking becomes quite painful. The corrective procedure is to cut the artery above and below the obstruction, and replace it with a real or synthetic vein. A fem-pop is similar to a heart bypass in that a vein or other substance is connected to the two ends of the artery. It was first performed in 1948.

Typically, the ball and chain of animal experimentation slowed development of the fem-pop. It was at first denied to many patients based on dog studies. In dogs, the venous graft dilates and aneurysm develops. When an aneurysm distends to the bursting point, the patient risks bleeding to death. So, initially, surgeons grafted artery to artery in humans instead of grafting vein to artery. Removing a section of artery is much more dangerous than removing a section of vein. Even after the vein to artery graft succeeded in humans some surgeons refused to abandon the arterial graft.[138-42]

Angioplasty—dilation of occluded vessels with a catheter—sometimes precludes bypass grafting. The technique was discovered by accident when a physician named Dotter inadvertently placed a catheter into an occluded iliac artery when aiming for the aorta. The iliac gained blood flow and the idea of angioplasty was born. Afterward the technique was finessed on humans and cadavers. They also tested it on dogs and pigs. Hence, the animal experimentation lobby can, with justification, say that animal experiments figured in the development of angioplasty. What they omit to say is that no further knowledge was gleaned from the experiments.[143]

Heart Surgery

Battlefield surgeons have always occupied a vanguard position for developing surgical procedures on the heart. Many innovative techniques emerged in last-ditch attempts to save soldiers' lives.[144] Napoleon's surgeon, Baron Dominique Jean Larrey, performed the first operation to remove pus from around the heart, a very aggressive surgery of the time.

Physicians used to believe that any puncture wound to the heart would kill. However, Bartholemy Carbol of Montpellier performed two autopsies showing the deceased had scars on their hearts from penetrating wounds, proving that wounds to the heart need not be fatal.[145] In 1872, Dr. George Callandar successfully removed a needle that had penetrated the heart from a man's chest, proving again that humans could survive puncture wounds to the heart.[146] These revelations suggested that the heart itself was operable.

During this same era, Dr. Ferdinand Sauerbruch, a famous German surgeon, operated on a patient for what he thought was pericardial adhesions. Upon opening up the chest, he found something very different and unexpected. He set about removing what he though was a cyst, only to find that it was a huge aneurysm. The patient began bleeding to death as soon as Sauerbruch cut into it. Left with no options except to sew it back up, this now-famous German surgeon became the first to repair an aneurysm of the heart. The patient survived.[147] However, another step withheld development of coronary artery bypass grafting (CABGs), the operation used to relieve chest pain and other symptoms of blocked arteries in the heart. What would conduct the blood through the blocked section?

Animal studies in the 1930s, 1940s, and 1950s indicated that tying off an artery in the chest, named the internal mammary artery, would divert more blood through occluded coronary arteries. The detoured circulation worked great in dogs ... but not so in humans.[148–51] This was just one of many failures in humans that had worked in dogs.[152]

Another problem facing heart surgeons was the technical difficulty of operating on a beating heart. Especially when the operation was not on the surface of the heart but rather inside it. Clearly, a heart-lung bypass machine was needed to perform the crucial functions of these organs during surgery. Using it, surgeons would be able to stop the heart while they worked on it, then restart it after the repairs were made. In 1938, Dr. Alexis Carrel, Charles Lindbergh, and a Dr. Theodore Tuffier successfully bypassed the heart and lungs in an animal, but they never tested the device on humans.

The premier human heart operation done with a cardiopulmonary bypass (CPB) machine was April 5, 1951, in Minnesota. Though the machine had been extensively tested on animals, the patient died.[153] Another surgeon named John H. Gibbon attempted the same, again on animals first and then on humans. Gibbon demonstrated the CPB machine at Thomas Jefferson University in Philadelphia in 1954. Two out of the first three of Gibbon's patients died from complications caused by the heart-lung machine. After the second death Gibbon was so distraught that he gave up on the idea.[154] It is nonetheless Gibbon that history credits with the heart lung machine invention.

Fortunately, surgeons at the Mayo Clinic and the University of Minnesota did not throw in the towel. As it turned out, another surgeon in India elucidated their course. Word of this Dr. Anthony Andreasen, who had noticed that patients with very low blood volumes, soldiers injured in war, could live for a prolonged time, reached the west. His observations debunked the animal-based notion that the CPB machine needed to pump large volumes of blood in order to keep the patients alive. Andreasen's studies of human circulation contributed the low flow theory of circulation to science. With reduced blood volume, human patients can successfully survive connection to a heart-lung machine.

Many talented people contributed to perfecting the heart-lung machine and the ensuing cardiac surgical techniques. Dr. Walter Lillehei, a cardiac-surgery pioneer at the University of Minnesota, made many contributions. It was Lillehei who communicated with Andreasen and found his clinical observations compelling. He and others operated in a dog lab at the university, practicing on hundreds of animals. Of Lillehei's first twenty-seven operations for ventricular septal defect in humans, eight patients succumbed. The rate plummeted after he gained clinical dexterity with human patients. In his biography, the writer, also an innovator in heart surgery, states,

> Now it should be remembered that in the late 1950s there were no 'road maps' for the conduct of intracardiac surgery. Although there was considerable literature on the clinical presentation of patients with congenital heart disease, there were few and incomplete treatises on the intracardiac anatomy of this form of heart disease. Furthermore, these did not take into consideration the details necessary for the surgical repair of such defects. Therefore the learning process was one of trial and error [on humans], recognition of new unanticipated complications and the development of methods to manage these.[155]

Thus, despite numerous operations on animals, the human patient once again proved quite different. Surgery advanced because of human clinical observation. The Minnesota group was also responsible for perfecting a way of oxygenating blood.

Dr. John Kirklin, a surgeon at the Mayo Clinic and others further revised the bypass machine. They also perfected the surgical skills to perform the operations while the patients were on the CPB machine. Kirklin performed the first bypass operation at the Mayo Clinic in 1955. Despite extensive animal testing, only four of his first eight patients survived.[156] The operations on human patients revealed errors that had occurred as a result of extrapolating from animal experiments. It was human data that guaranteed the operations and CPB machine's success on humans. In Kirklin's own view, the operating room was the instructive arena.[157]

Blood clotting in the CPB machine was an immediate problem, and the need for blood thinners, or anticoagulants was obvious. Heparin, discovered through *in vitro* research, is today still the anticoagulant of choice.[158] Other anticoagulants such as citrate, which is used in banked blood, were also discovered without animals.[159]

Another discovery that paved the way for modern open-heart surgery was the realization the heart could be stopped and restarted. Kolff, inventor of the artificial kidney, describes how this procedure had been done many times in animals but failed in humans when first tried:

> Then this [stopping the heart] was tried in the operating room on three children with congenital heart defects. And the first baby died, although the second and third lived. You see, no matter how many successful animal experiments you have, you can still lose your first patient when you attempt something new clinically.[160]

Despite success in animals, the procedure needed to be modified for humans. As is the common scenario, animal experiments only indicated the operation's relevance for that particular species and breed of animal, nothing more. As one internationally renowned surgeon reflects,

> The abolition of vivisection would in no way halt medical progress, just the opposite is the case. All the sound medical knowledge of today stems from observations carried out on human beings. No surgeon can gain the least knowledge from experiments on animals, and all the great surgeons of the past and of the present day are in agreement on that.[161]

We use less oxygen when our body temperature drops. This "hypothermia" seemed to suggest applicability in heart surgery. Shivering dogs actually required more oxygen to survive, so canine operations using hypothermia went poorly for the dogs and most died.[162] However, humans, as physicians like Bill Bigelow were convinced, could survive with oxygen levels far below normal and would not react like the dogs. The first heart operation with the aid of hypothermia was on a little girl suffering from an atrial-septal defect in 1952. The concept proved true.

For operations where blood flow is compromised—such as those involving a CPB machine wherein the heart is isolated from the rest of the body—the heart remains alive because it is cold and not requiring much oxygen. (The same is sometimes true of the brain and other organs.)

Similar refutation of the animal model pervaded other aspects of the profession. As a stop-gap measure for patients awaiting transplant, engineers worked up an artificial heart using calves as a model. The first artificial heart, the Jarvick 7, kept one calf alive for nine months, so doctors hooked up the Jarvick 7 to a human. Despite its bovine success, the Jarvick 7 was disastrous, bringing on kidney failure, stroke, and many other devastating complications. Efforts since have been equally calamitous. Although any common house pump can pump blood, a serviceable artificial heart has not yet been designed that can overcome these complications. Dr. De Vries, the surgeon who performed the operation stated, "You can't know the answer to strokes by looking at animals."[163]

The heart beats at a pace determined by a region of the heart known as the pacemaker. This region sends electrical impulses down the heart, causing contractions that push blood flow out of the heart. If the heart beats abnormally, we call it a dysrhythmia. Most dysrhythmias are treated with medications, but some require surgical ablation of the pathway that is misconducting the electrical signal, thus causing the dysrhythmia. Technology enables surgeons to locate the aberrant tissue exactly and to kill it selectively with a very precise instrument.

Sometimes neither medications nor surgery can stabilize patients, so surgeons implant a defibrillator that automatically discharges when it registers a life-threatening rhythm.[164]

Pacemaker development provides a good example that those with a vested interest will attempt to claim that animal experimentation was *responsible* for a medical discovery. Millions of people, whose hearts would not otherwise beat, have extended their lives with cardiac pacemakers. This small device produces an electric signal that makes the heart beat regularly. In 1929 Mark Lidwill, an Australian anesthesiologist engineered the first pacemaker. Lidwill tried it in dogs prior to human patients hence the vested interest groups' claim. This was neither necessary nor sufficient for successful trials in humans.

Real advances in pacemaker science came from the advance of technology, not improved dog tickers.[165] Probably the biggest boon was the invention of the silicone transistor. This put pacemakers under the skin, eliminating the risk of infection from wires going from outside the body to the heart. Other advances were mercury-powered batteries and miniaturization.

Just as many of the medications, surgical procedures, and diagnostic tools are used in both humans and animals, pacemakers can be and are used in animals. This does not mean that the animal experiments were necessary or that they predicted what would occur in humans. They happened; but they contributed nothing new.

Today new computer models illustrate why failing hearts have diminished contractility and increased susceptibility to rhythm disturbances that may prove fatal. This steady weakening of the heart muscle is known as chronic heart failure. The computer simulations mimic the interplay of different proteins that deliver messages, in conjunction with calcium, about heart muscle contraction. These models, representing human cardiac conditions, suggest that if researchers can boost the amount of calcium available to cardiac cells, the risk of chronic heart failure will lessen.[166] Eventuality this will narrow the need for pacemakers and defibrillators.

Other surgical procedures, designed to correct congenital heart anomalies rather than conditions brought about later in life, ran amok because of the animal-model. Pro-vivisectionists cite the surgery for *Tetralogy of Fallot* (TOF) to justify funding more animal experimentation. Babies with insufficient oxygen in the blood to provide the healthy pink skin color are called "blue babies." In infants with TOF, blood bypasses the lungs, receiving no oxygen because of a malformation of the heart. Cardiologist Helen Taussig suggested a surgical correction of the problem to Alfred Blalock, a surgeon at Johns Hopkins. She based her suggestion on clinical observation and autopsy findings on the affected infants. Dr. Blalock attempted to simulate the condition in dogs by cutting out lung tissue. His results were poor, to say the least. Many animals became paralyzed. Trying to surgically mimic what is a naturally occurring disease in humans, Blalock's animal model was fundamentally flawed from the start. Dr. Blalock's experience led him to state to Dr. Taussig, "The experiments are suggestive but not very conclusive. But if you are convinced the operation will work, I am convinced I know how to do it."[167]

Despite his lack of success, Dr. Blalock felt the operation might be possible in humans based on Taussig's observations and his surgical expertise. Contrast his actual statement above with this quote from those profiting from animal experimentation, "The (animal) experiments were so successful and confirmed Dr. Taussig's theory so completely that Blalock felt he could venture to operate on one of the poor children."[168]

Typically, though Dr. Blalock's animal experimentation was a flop, promoters still credit it for the success, and throw in the plaintive term "poor children" for good measure! One of the animal experimentation lobbies' historical battle cries, "Which would you rather save—one blue baby or one brown dog?" refers to this sloppily rewritten version of history. This sort of hyperbole is not convincing to well-informed scientists. One outspoken cardiothoracic surgeon, Moneim A. Fadali, commented against continued use of the animal model, "I agree that for the benefit of medical science, vivisection or animal experimentation has to be stopped. There are lots of reasons for that. The most important is that it's simply misleading, and both the past and the present testify to that."[169] Misleading *and* dangerous.

There exist many other congenital human heart defects that have been corrected, experiments on animals to the contrary. Russell Brock developed a device to correct the cardiac anomaly known as right ventricular outflow tract obstruction by studying cadavers.[170] Coarctation of the aorta was corrected after a procedure was attempted in dogs but failed in humans. It was only after surgical serendipity that the correct procedure was discovered.[171,172] For another syndrome, mitral stenosis, there were no "animal models" but surgeons tried to "approximate" one. The technique they developed for mitral stenosis using animals resulted in three out of the first four patients dying. Despite this poor outcome, they went on to try what they had learned on other humans with equal failure. Not until surgeons approached the problem through clinical observation and experimentation on cadavers was a successful operation developed. Valvuloplasty, as it is called, is still used today. As long ago as 1902, Sir Lauder Brunton suggested mitral valve dissection based on cadaver work. But support for his idea was nonexistent, and the mitral valvotomy was postponed. After World War II, the concept was resuscitated by information gathered through autopsies.[173,174]

As new heart operations were conceived, they were practiced on animals. All had to be revised for humans. Nowhere is this concept more evident than in the hobbled development of the artificial heart-valve.

The development of the artificial heart-valve, which has helped tens of thousands of people, was delayed by imagined parity between dog and human systems. In experiments, dogs tended to produce blood clots around the new valve. In humans clots of this type would lead to stroke, pulmonary embolism or other complications. Therefore, enthusiasm for artificial heart valves was tepid, and many people died for the want of this technology. Come to find out humans do not clot as dogs do, and therefore would not have suffered from the severe complication that killed the experimental dogs. Humans do require anti-coagulants, but this is a surmountable problem. Note what Drs. B. C. Paton and J. H. Vogel said about the animal model with regards to the development of artificial heart valves, "Few dogs survived the valve replacement, usually because the valve clotted in the first few weeks."[175]

Dr. George H. Clowes stated this when discussing valve research,

Lots of competent people . . . have worked on it. They found that the great problem was not that they could not put valves in that would work, but that they always produced thrombi in dogs . . . For that reason, many of us have been very reticent about putting in these artificial prostheses . . . but Dr. Starr has . . . proved the point that was brought out at the NIH meeting in Chicago last fall concerning artificial heart valves, that probably man does not react as violently as the animal does in producing a clot at the interface between myocardium and the artificial prosthesis. It may be that man is a better candidate for this type of thing than the animal.[176]

The inventors of the valve, Drs. A. Starr and L. Edwards stated, "the marked propensity of the dog to thrombotic occlusion or massive embolization from mitral prosthesis is not shared by the human."[177]

To date, many people have the artificial valves implanted each year and veterinary cardiologists are still struggling to apply this technology to dogs.[178-82]

Valves harvested from pigs can be used in humans; however they do not function as well as human valves or artificial valves. (We will discuss the risks of using animal parts in Chapter 11.)

In conclusion, it is glaringly evident that achievements in the cardiovascular field are entirely attributable to human-based research, not animal experimentation. This is not surprising to anyone who regards the facts instead of distorted publicity. As cardiac surgeon Moneim Fadali put it, "Animal models differ from their human counterparts. Conclusions drawn from animal research, when applied to human disease, are likely to delay progress, mislead, and do harm to the patient."[183]

And no matter how innovative and life-saving surgeries may be, it is important to remember that most heart conditions are avoidable in our efforts to avert cardiovascular-related deaths. Dr. Caldwell B. Esselstyn is the surgeon in charge of the longest study ever undertaken and completed examining cardiac patients on low cholesterol diets. Eighteen subjects joined his trial as a last hope of staving off lethal heart disease. Combined, they had experienced forty-eight cardiac events (heart attacks, heart failure and so on) prior to joining the study. Most had undergone angioplasties and bypass surgeries. Some had even been told to go home and "wait to die." For twelve years on the program they consumed less than ten percent of their daily calories from fat—a percentage common in countries where heart disease is virtually nonexistent—and took cholesterol-lowering medications. Only one of his subjects, who was non-compliant, had another cardiac event.

The availability of admittedly incredible surgical techniques assures that the consequences of high-fatted couch potato lifestyles can often be rectified under the knife. But we should not overlook our own complicity. The reason cardiovascular disease is our greatest killer is because humans commit slow suicide. As Dr. Esselstyn says in an *American Journal of Cardiology* article, modern cardiology has "given up on a cure," and is instead fixated on stopgap measures such as bypass surgery and variations of angioplasty that "treat the symptoms, not the disease."

chapter 10

AIDS and Humbled Science

What good does it do you to test something [a vaccine] in a monkey? You find five or six years from now that it works in the monkey, and then you test it in humans and you realize that humans behave totally differently from monkeys, so you've wasted five years.

—Dr. Mark Feinberg, a leading AIDS researcher

Like no epidemic in recent memory, Acquired Immunodeficiency Syndrome (AIDS) has catalyzed public fear. Its specter has altered sexual and even social relationships. It has changed the way we parent and the way we educate. It has transformed workplaces and cityscapes. It has varied the practice of medicine. And, despite resistance to abandoning animal experimentation, AIDS may overhaul medical research in that direction.

Unheard of only twenty years ago, AIDS is now one of the leading causes of death in Americans aged fifteen to forty-four. To date, approximately 11.7 million people have died from it globally, including two million children. Almost 400,000 of the fatalities were in the United States. The World Health Organization estimates that the cumulative total infected is thirty-four million, with 99 percent of all infections in developing countries and two million people dying of AIDS each year.

Since AIDS was first identified, science has rallied resources toward extinguishing this terrible disease. But, is AIDS stoppable? No one yet knows. However, we do now know that animal experimentation has sent research off on trajectories as removed from this planet's fearful millions as moon dust.

What has animal-modeled research of AIDS yielded? Wealthy primate researchers and dead ends, as this chapter will demonstrate.

There is still no vaccine and there is still no cure. Arguably, this is due partially to nonhuman research. Grant-hungry animal experimenters have depleted AIDS research funds with highly dubious animal studies. The fact is that non-humans do not get AIDS. Hence, researchers must induce animals with diseases that mimic AIDS in some ways. But the diseases differ so fundamentally that no extrapolations to humans are valid. Some prevention strategies and therapies have emerged over the last twenty years, and as we will illustrate, these owe nothing to animal experimentation.

Notably, even people who stand to benefit most from developments in AIDS research, those who have or will develop AIDS, now vocally oppose animal-modeled research. The AIDS community knows animals do not get AIDS. Frustrated and legitimately angry that research dollars are being wasted, AIDS groups recognize that the research status quo is not helping them. Many blame pharmaceutical industry profiteers for exploiting their plight with expensive and ineffective anti-HIV medications.[1,2] In December 1995, this led ACT UP San Francisco to agree by consensus to support a ban on animal experimentation.[3]

Animal experimentation's poor showing in regard to AIDS does not surprise anyone with knowledge of medical history. Animal models have always been notoriously inaccurate in human immunologic studies. There are two reasons for this. First, immunologic response is intensely complicated and concerns those billions of dissimilarities between humans and other animals that science is just beginning to recognize, differences as minute as a mote on the surface of the cell. As we have already said, these infinitesimal disparities are the result of millions of years of speciation, nature itself working to make a human a human, a dog a dog, a rat a rat.

Second, viruses are species-specific. That is, the same virus affects each species differently, mutating to adapt to new surroundings. These microcosmic titans, each with different "superpowers," either clash or mesh. To wit, pigs do not die of "swine flu" but humans sometimes do. Monkeys do not die of AIDS and humans do. There are viruses that cross species barriers, such as rabies, and affect both species similarly. Even then, a vaccine that prevents the disease in one species must be modified to protect another species. Species-specificity is evidenced by the fact that we vaccinate different species against very different diseases—cats for panleukopenia, dogs for distemper, and kids for measles.

Ironically, much of the data science has accumulated about species-specificity and disparate immunologic response is a direct result of animal experimentation for AIDS. In other words, we have learned how *unlike* our systems are. You will read that the epidemic dumped more dollars into research institutes, snowballing the number (and cost) of animal experiments. As scientists continued to coerce animals' systems for humanlike responses, they failed over and again. This feckless activity has made the imprecision of animal experimentation all the more evident, glaringly so.

The Human Immune System at Work

Before we examine the nature of AIDS, let us review its target, the human immune system. What within us launches a full-scale offensive against every incursion from the common cold to cancer? Our systems are genetically wired to distinguish between most harmless and harmful intruders. When a dangerous protein enters our body, we have an immediate immune response at what is most often an adequate level. This is called our "innate" immune response. It is always present, even prior to infectious exposure, and exposure does not change its intensity.

More complex is our "acquired" immune response, which deals with protein sequences not vanquished by our innate immune system. The acquired immune response responds to more aggressive diseases by producing more white blood cells. Plus, it has a memory. Every microbe or foreign substance the acquired immune system encounters, the acquired immune response "remembers." As it spots more remembered substances, it stimulates increasingly strong defense mechanisms.

This elaborate internal defense system includes many different types of blood cells, tissues, organs, and physiological processes. Its main cellular components are white blood cells of several varieties. Among these are B-lymphocytes (B-cells), T-lymphocytes (T-cells), natural-killer cells, and macrophages.

Each of these has a job. B-lymphocytes combat viruses and bacteria that float freely in bodily fluids (blood, semen, mucous). B-lymphocytes are like weapons manufacturers. They make antibodies, the proteins that attack invading bacteria and viruses. Most of the antibodies they produce are made of gamma globulin. We call this the antibody response. The presence of particular antibodies in the blood is called seroconversion and it is our indicator of the presence of that disease in the system.

If foreign substances get beyond the free-floating phase and actually start infiltrating cells, the body launches an additional line of defense—the cell-mediated response. The T-cell phalanx organizes to dispense with invading pathogens themselves, without producing antibodies. There are two distinct types of T-cells—helper T-cells and killer T-cells—which work together. Helper T-cells communicate between parts of the immune system, letting the body know what is intruding and whether to attack. Killer T-cells are the soldiers that surround invaders and kill them.

Helper T-cells have the added function of presenting pathogens to the macrophages, which perform immune functions outside the blood. Macrophages reside in many organs and tissues including the lymph nodes and bone marrow. Like killer T-cells, they fight infection by attacking and ingesting invading viruses and bacteria.

Natural-killer cells and killer T-cells are not the same. Natural-killer cells bind to aberrant cells, such as cancerous cells, and destroy them.

Human studies, not animal studies, revealed the secrets of the immune system. In 1952, researchers discovered that some patients lacked gamma-globulin in their blood, accounting for chronic illnesses. The scientist who discovered this condition, Dr. Good, relied on human observation not animal experiments. He stated that this discovery "provided a new and clear-cut opportunity to gain insight into the nature and significance of the immune system in man."

Until the early 1980s, we thought that all white blood cells produced antibodies in response to pathogens. Then, the discovery of T-cells enlarged our understanding of the immune system. This information established a valuable direction for research of a newly emerging epidemic—AIDS.

Learning about AIDS

The horror began in the late seventies and compounded. Incidents of patients suffering from weakness, fever, chills, night sweats, and predisposition to diseases such as pneumonia, thrush, meningitis, encephalitis, and tuberculosis increased dramatically into the eighties. Many contracted cytomegalovirus (CMV), a herpes pathogen that can lead to bone marrow suppression, necrotizing adrenalitis, and blindness. Other varieties of herpes were also common. The patients were vulnerable to certain types of cancer, visual disturbances, weight loss, chronic diarrhea, and anemia. Their central nervous system also suffered attack. Multiple bacterial, protozoal, and fungal infections occurred.

What was going on? Historically, people exposed to these malignancies and opportunistic infections would have intercepted and neutralized them at the acquired-immune phase, as described previously. But in these patients, diseases from which healthy patients would easily recover became life threatening. Most cases were adults whose immune responses were previously normal. Severely compromised immune systems made them fair game for any attack. They were now demonstrating the "acquired immunodeficiency syndrome," which we began calling "AIDS." (The reader should not confuse the word acquired as in acquired immunodeficiency syndrome, with the word acquired as in innate versus acquired immunity. AIDS is an "acquired" immune disease versus one that is passed along via genes—a genetic disease. AIDS is not named such because of its effect on what we call the acquired immune response but because of how it is transmitted.)

For the most part, these first cases were in gay, promiscuous men who often also abused drugs. This pattern provided epidemiological proof of the vulnerable population. The U.S. Centers for Disease Control was the first branch of the medical establishment to acknowledge the epidemic in the early 1980s, and CDC's Dr. Mary Guinan theorized that AIDS must be transmitted via blood or other bodily fluids. This hypothesis propelled investigations into its cause.

Two scientific groups, one in France and one in the U.S., led by Drs. Luc Montagnier and Robert Gallo respectively, conducted *in vitro* research to isolate the causative agent of AIDS. In his book, Dr. Gallo credits test tube research, not animal experimentation, for the advances that made the study of AIDS possible.

> The development of *in vitro* systems greatly facilitated progress in this field [virology], enabling scientists to make better quantitative estimates of the amount of virus in a sample, to determine the target cells of a particular virus, and to see whether the virus produced a cytopathic effect . . . Although techniques for tissue culture were a development of the 1930s, the techniques have been continually refined up to the present. A big advance came in the 1950s when John Enders grew the polio virus in cell culture. The 1950s and 1960s became one of the greatest periods of medical virology because of these cell culture advances.[4]

Gallo and Montagnier found several immune system-crippling human viruses, but only one of them killed T-cells. In May 1984 the International Committee on the Taxonomy of Viruses designated the name "HIV," (human immunodeficiency virus) as the causative agent for AIDS. (AIDS is the condition caused by HIV, not the name of the virus.)

Basic chemical and *in vitro* research soon provided methods for measuring the amount of virus in patients. With chemical assays, scientists could evaluate the virus's presence both qualitatively and quantitatively. Today, new assays are increasingly sensitive, allowing the detection of ever-lower viral levels. We now know that frequent measurement of viral levels is critical in treating AIDS patients. It facilitates earlier diagnosis and more accurate evaluation of therapeutics.

Throughout the last twenty years, test tube research and human epidemiological studies have been responsible for the great breakthroughs in AIDS and have given us an ever-more complete picture of its actions within the human body.[5,6] Human tissue and technology provided the following description of the virus:

> Electron microscopy has long been the primary source of information about the overall structure of HIV. Such studies have firmly established that the virus particles are: (1) generally spherical in shape, (2) heterogenous in size, (3) surrounded by a lipid bilayer, (4) initially produced in an immature form with an electron-lucent cone-shaped center that later matures to produce an electron-dense, cone-shaped core.[7]

This portrait of the virus is a monumental achievement, crucial for the creation of a vaccine.

HIV, How It Works

This spherical assassin, this HIV, is a *retrovirus*. Adopting again the warfare metaphor, retroviruses are infiltrators. Streamlined, retroviruses store genetic information on a single-stranded RNA molecule instead of the more usual double-stranded DNA. This single-strandedness makes retroviruses highly adaptable. In a sense, they travel light and therefore farther. In large part, this is also why it is so difficult for the body to locate the virus. If the body cannot find it, the body cannot kill it.

The HIV retrovirus is a protein capsule containing two short single strands of genetic material (RNA) and three enzymes. As such, HIV is simple. What makes HIV so deadly, in large part, is the target cell's participation in its own demise. HIV's most common target is helper T-cells, though it also threatens macrophages.

HIV commandeers the contents of those helper T white blood cells when it enters the cells via distinct "receptors" (proteins) on their surface. The white blood cells that are vulnerable have receptors called CD4 (The CD stands for *cluster designate*, and these helper T-cells may be called CD4 cells). HIV commandeers the CD4 receptors and forces the white blood cells to throw open the cell gateways. These open gateways effectively invite the virus in.

To get an idea of how this occurs, picture gateway-like CD4 receptors on the surface of the helper T-cells. Then picture a tube, in the form of a "glycoprotein" called GP120, extending from the outer shell of the HIV envelope. The GP120 and those receptors fit together neatly and fatally. The HIV's contents flow into the host cell, via the GP120.

There is a hitch, though, a hitch that has proven fatal to animal-modeled extrapolations, as we will soon explain. The CD4 is like a gateway but it requires a key. For HIV to penetrate human cells, a *co-receptor* must be on the cell surface with the CD4. Unless CD4 and the co-receptor work in conjunction with each other, HIV will not bind to the cell surface. The gateways are the CD4 receptors, and the co-receptors are the keys.

The more we learn about HIV, the more complications reveal themselves in the penetration process. The most common HIV co-receptor on the white blood cell surface is CCR5 (standing for chemokine co-receptor). However, there are less common strains of HIV that require other co-receptors. These are classified into two families—CXCs and CCs. Those recognized thus far, via *in vitro* research of human cells, are CXCR4, CCR2, and CCR3. These various lessor co-receptors are critical to understanding the way HIV works, and their existence points out just how intricate and variable activity on the cellular level really is. And remember, those intricacies are the very points at which animal models fail.

Once HIV is inside the cell, the real problems begin. Left to its own devices, our cells' own DNA is a smoothly functioning replication machine. But the virus supersedes the DNA's protocol. The virus's components manufacture a renegade strand of DNA that integrates into the CD4 cell's chromosomes and makes the original blueprint run amok. That perverted DNA becomes part of the host cell's genetic material and directs its deranged contents to replicate new strands of viral RNA. This turns the white blood cell, the CD4 cell, into a viral factory—a well-camouflaged virus factory that is hidden from immunologic attack inside the host cell.

The three enzymes—reverse transcriptase, protease, and integrase—enable the formation of new HIV particles. Specifically, reverse transcriptase (RT) constructs DNA from the RNA template. The second HIV enzyme, integrase, integrates the DNA into the host cell's chromosomes. Thirdly, protease acts as a chemical scissors, pruning the newly-formed virus particles into proper configuration as they emerge from the host cell. As these new particles burst from the host cell, they kill it, then float off to infect other CD4s in a snowballing rate.

As mentioned, helper T-cells are HIV's greatest target. Since helper T-cells are responsible for letting the body know what is intruding and whether to attack, HIV can effectively shut down the acquired immune system. With an ever-diminishing number of helper T-cells to guide them, killer T-cells become disorientated, unable to locate and attack invading bacteria, viruses, and so on. The lack of helper T-cell guidance makes it appear that everything is fine, even when the body is under siege from bacteria and other viruses. Resistance to disease begins to buckle.

Once a person is infected with HIV, his or her immune system may take several days, weeks, or even months to recognize the foreign substance and begin manufacturing antibodies. The process by which the HIV-antibody status converts from negative to positive is called *seroconversion*. Gradually, HIV infects all white blood cells and the immune system crumples. This may take years or even longer than a decade. The condition of the patient at this point is then referred to as "AIDS." Once the patient's immune system is neutralized, it does not take long for them to contract and die from infections that would pose no problem to healthy people.

Researchers did not learn about HIV from experiments on animals. *In vitro* research combined with technology illuminated each phase of HIV progression described. Specifically, it showed that the virus depletes CD4 cells, the subgroup of helper T-cells.[8] *In vitro* research revealed that the CD4 cell was the cell responsible for binding the virus.[9] This led to the knowledge that a co-receptor was needed for HIV to bind to the CD4 cell.[10] *In vitro* research also confirmed that the GP120 protein was involved in viral penetration into the cell.[11] It determined the shape of GP120 and its sequential interaction with another glycoprotein and chemokine receptor, thus identifying a possible blocking site.[12,13,14] The implications of this discovery for vaccine development are monumental. Finally, the sequencing of the genome of HIV was accomplished via *in vitro* research.[15]

Clinical observation indicated that HIV and HIV-infected cells amass in the lymph nodes of people with HIV, even those with abundant anti-HIV antibodies. This suggested that the critical events in the progression of AIDS occur in human lymphoid tissue—lymph nodes, bone marrow, thymus, tonsils, spleen, Peyer's patches and lymphocytes aggregated on mucosal surfaces. In a 1995 *Nature Medicine* article, Dr. S. Glushakova et al. explained:

> Primary cultures and co-cultures of isolated cells cannot mimic the full cellular repertoire within lymph tissue, nor their functional relationship with lymphoid tissue structures. Animal models do not fully mimic the characteristic tissue pathology of human HIV infection. For this reason, we have developed a tissue culture method that retains the complex three dimensional spatial cellular organization found in normal human lymphoid tissue.[16]

Plainly, researchers now had a challenge to which animal experimentation could not possibly equal.

Jungle-Safe, the Folly of SIV

Where did HIV and AIDS come from? No one really knows. However, one theory prevails. Most believe that humans became infected with a simian virus from Africa, through contact with blood or other body fluid. (*Simian* means primate, and includes apes and monkeys.) The hypothesis is that because of close association with primates, such as the killing and eating of monkeys, humans were exposed to a monkey-specific virus. Once inside a human, this virus mutated, resulting in the new virus HIV, and ultimately, AIDS. Simian researchers, always eager for grant money anyway, applied this theory, which is still conjecture, to launch an immense, expensive, and unending investigation of simians.

It should be noted that research on a previous viral threat, that of polio in the early part of the twentieth century, was many times derailed by the simian-model. This should have taught the valuable lesson that viruses behave very differently in different species.

Importantly, one will never find, under natural conditions, an HIV-infected primate in the wild. Only Simian Immunodeficiency Virus (SIV) occurs naturally in primates. But this serious anomaly did not slow the course of animal experimentation. In order to test vaccines and drugs, laboratories tooled up to grow HIV that researchers could transfer back and forth between animals. Researchers whipped out their syringes and started pumping chimpanzees full of concentrated HIV and HIV-infected blood. The strain of HIV used to infect chimpanzees differed from SIV and any naturally occurring virus that would influence them.[17]

Scientists injected thousands of chimpanzees with HIV over dozens of years, but none of the animals has developed classic human AIDS. This becomes all the more amazing considering the enormous viral load given to these animals and the convoluted attempts to stymie the animals' natural immunity. No matter how many immunosuppressing drugs, virus particles, and research money thrown at caged simians, no one can make a chimp get classic human AIDS.

Apparently, one chimp did become sick with AIDS-like symptoms.[18] However, the incident has not occurred again. Needless to say, this lack of substantiation casts doubt on the event and undermines its significance. Given the pharmacologic manipulations these animals have undergone, the single illness that ensued seems a testimony to their hardiness, and their lack of suitability as a model for the human disease. Chimpanzees were not dying of AIDS all over the world. They were not even dying in cages, despite huge doses of the virus. Humans were. Researchers soon began to find out. And that—why chimpanzees do not succumb to AIDS—is all they found out.

In chimpanzees, HIV does not reproduce well for many reasons.[19] The numbers and ratio of helper T-cells to killer T-cells in chimpanzees is much different. Chimpanzees have higher baseline levels of killer T-cells and a lower ratio of helper T-cells to killer T-cells. In other words, in chimps, it takes fewer helper T-cells to organize the killer T-cells into combat. Remember, HIV selectively attacks helper T-cells, not killer T-cells.[20-23] Killer T-cells are the white blood cells that actually annihilate the HIV. Helper T-cells are just alerting the immune system to the virus's presence. When killer T-cells kill HIV-infected cells, they secrete soluble factors called beta-chemokines. These suppress HIV replication in blood and lymph nodes. So the higher the number of killer T-cells (as in chimpanzees), the more resistant the system.

On numerous occasions, researchers thought they had made progress. As always, there was a media blitz and raised hopes, only to discover that the "advances" were not applicable to humans. For example, animal experimentation suggested that HIV progressed slowly with long latency periods. In humans, however, it was found that HIV progressed rapidly with short latency periods. Nevertheless, researchers chose to believe animal data over human data and therefore did not recommend aggressive therapies from the inception of the disease. Many people died.

That is not all. Unlike humans, chimpanzee-helper T-cell counts do not drop to zero with infection. They go down, but not as dramatically.

Furthermore, chimpanzees lack some of the killer cells that humans have.[24, 25, 26] B-lymphocytes produce more antibodies in chimpanzees and they produce them earlier, thus stopping disease spread.[27] Humans drop their antibody count prior to systemic illness. Chimpanzees do not.[28]

Furthermore, HIV-virus particles are far more ubiquitous in humans than in chimps. Chimpanzees seem to confine HIV to blood cells, while in humans it is also in the plasma, saliva, and cerebral spinal fluid.[29] Imagine the transmission implications these differences could make! Certainly, the pathophysiology differs in the extreme.

Chimpanzees exhibit only a flulike illness in response to being infected with the virus, whereas humans go on to full-blown AIDS. Humans also develop opportunistic infections and cancers associated with HIV, which chimpanzees do not. Nor do infected chimps manifest classic changes in the central-nervous system that infected humans do.[30–33]

Even scientists who have ardently supported chimpanzee AIDS research are acknowledging that little scientific merit derives from it. Refutations of long-supported sacred cows by those whose careers rely upon them is powerful refutation indeed. *The Scientist* published an article in summer 1999 wherein Steven Bende, coordinator of funding for preclinical AIDS vaccine studies at the National Institute of Allergy and Infectious Diseases, admitted that HIV replicates differently in chimp cells than in human cells. Thomas Insel, director of the large Yerkes Regional Primate Center, said "I just don't see much coming out of the chimp work that has convinced us that that is a particularly useful model."[34]

At the same time, some scientists are holding out. Mohammad A. Javadian, director of research at the Coulston Foundation, still feels that "the most suitable primate for an AIDS vaccine animal model is chimpanzee."[35] Part of his tenacity may be due to the fact that the Coulston Foundation has one of the most sizable collections of chimpanzees in the world.

One can begin to fathom the billions made by outfits such as Coulston. At the same time, fathom the billions *spent* to uncover these significant disparities between species. Any single such disparity is enough to render AIDS research on chimpanzees meaningless to humans. The sum is insurmountable and reveals the complete fruitlessness of primate AIDS research. Over the last two decades, researchers have used tens of thousands of primates for AIDS research. They have been supplied by a robust industry of animal procurers and farmers, whose interests are supported by fierce lobbyists and shrewd marketers. Yes, thousands have made money; but their discoveries are unserviceable in the human arena.

So much for the chimpanzees. Other simian research, using monkeys in lieu of chimpanzees, and SIV in lieu of HIV, attempted to establish parity with humans. It was dizzyingly off course for two reasons. First, the monkey's immune system is even more different from humans than the chimp's is. And second, SIV and HIV are not the same. Even one percent differences are enormous, and SIV and HIV have only about a sixty percent similarity of the virus. Pretty blatant peculiarities, but not enough to keep the vested interest groups at bay.

Many scientists acknowledge that animals do not suffer from AIDS-like illnesses the way humans do.[36,37] For a start, monkeys do not produce antibodies against the V-3 loop portion of a glycoprotein on the virus's outer covering, as humans do.[38] SIV, the immune-assaulting virus that apes and monkeys might naturally acquire, does not cause Simian Acquired Immunodeficiency Syndrome (SAIDS). SAIDS is entirely a manmade monkey illness. It only develops when SIV is transferred artificially to a new species of monkey . . . and then only sometimes. SIV does not affect all primates in the same manner. For example, the African green monkey can carry SIV around without getting sick. The strain of SIV that infects sooty mangabey monkeys does not result in illness. It does, however, cause rhesus monkeys to become sick.

Neonatal infection—infection of offspring by a virus-positive mother—differs between species. Whereas human mothers can transmit HIV through breast milk and *in utero*, SIV in rhesus monkeys can be passed in breast milk but not *in utero*.[39,40] Obviously, the immune systems of the various primates are so diverse that data gathered from one species does not even translate to other nonhuman primates, much less to humans.

Immune-system contrarieties between host species are just part of the problem. HIV and SIV have their own discrepancies. Under the microscope, SIV is noticeably different than HIV-1, the cause of most cases of AIDS, particularly in the important envelope area. It is somewhat similar to HIV-2, which causes far fewer, and much less aggressive, cases of AIDS. This also distorts data.

A passage, from the journal *Science*, emphasizes the problem: "[Drs.] Tsai and Sarver are quick to point out, however, that there is a big leap from monkeys to humans: For starters, HIV-1, the main AIDS virus that infects humans, differs significantly from SIV, the simian relative that was used in the tests."[41]

The viruses have distinctions at what is known as the *hypervariable* region; the molecular level. SIV enters the cells of rhesus monkeys by binding to the CCR5 receptor without binding to the CD4 receptor. In humans, HIV must bind to both CCR5 and CD4 receptors. The researchers found that a single amino acid difference in the CCR5 terminus was responsible for the difference in binding.[42] Only a single amino acid. (Remember, single amino acid differences are responsible for devastating diseases such as sickle cell anemia and cystic fibrosis.)

It is no surprise then that the study of SIV has not helped treat HIV. The crux of the ineffectiveness is the utter lack of homology. *Homology* means "fundamental similarities based on common descent." Conclusions based solely on very high homology—close to a hundred percent—qualify. Note, the magnitude of differences in viruses HIV-1, HIV-2,

SIV$_{agm}$ (affecting African Green Monkeys) and SIV$_{mac}$ (affecting macaque monkeys): HIV-1 shares only a forty percent genomic homology with the other viruses. HIV-2 and SIV share seventy-five percent homology. Viruses with only forty to seventy-five percent homology lack adequate similarity from which to draw conclusions.[43] SHIV, a combination of SIV and HIV [which means it is more similar to HIV] differs in the rate of CD4 cell loss.[44] In sum, SIV test results "vary greatly according to the strain of the virus used for challenge."[45]

Suffice to say, researchers can study SAIDS, but it is not like AIDS and the monkeys do not respond as humans do. The following was published by researchers in *Science,* "A molecular clone of the prototype SAIDS virus . . . *has no notable similarity in either genetic organization or sequence* to the human AIDS retrovirus."[46] (Emphasis added.)

All these years later, our knowledge base about SIV in rhesus monkeys is vast. Much, much narrower is the scope of our understanding of HIV in humans. Meanwhile, millions more humans have died. Scientists are now admitting that the study of SIV in animals has contributed little if anything to our knowledge of AIDS.[47]

However, as long as agencies award research dollars to animal labs, the deception continues. Ever busy and always for profit, scientists have doused other species with immunodeficiency too.

The gene engineers manufactured mice with Severe Combined Immunodeficiency (SCID). Their lack of functioning B- and T-cells means these mice will not reject transplanted human immune cells, including those infected with HIV. But they do not develop AIDS either. Not surprisingly, the human virus replicates poorly in the SCID mouse.[48,49]

Cats too suffer from an immune-deficiency disease, caused by FIV (feline immunodeficiency virus). But like the other AIDS-like diseases, FIV does not resemble HIV. Scientists have stated that it is "more closely related" to non-primate lentiviruses than HIV.[50] (HIV is among other lentiviruses in the retrovirus family.) Whereas HIV binds to the CD4 receptor, FIV binds to the CD9 receptor. Also, it is usually transmitted via saliva not via sexual contact, unlike HIV. (HIV is not transmitted via saliva.) Furthermore, artificially induced FIV, unlike the naturally occurring virus, does not lead to immunodeficiency.[51] And research has not led to an FIV vaccine either. These non-conformities reinforce one profound truth, evident throughout the course of animal-model research for humans—*inapplicability.*

In light of the inadequacy of animal models for AIDS, animal experimenters have to hustle to justify their research grants. As clinical and *in vitro* study of humans pieces together the AIDS puzzle, animal experimenters rush to mime those results in apes, monkeys, rodents, and even other species. Sometimes their efforts work; sometimes they do not. Never is anything original revealed and never is the research necessary.

For example, in 1993, Dr. Gerald J. Nuovo and colleagues demonstrated that HIV is passed into female sex partners of HIV-infected men via the cervix and from there into the lymph nodes.[52] This was a clinical and *in vitro* study. The animal experimenters then duplicated this study by placing SIV into the vagina of female monkeys. In 1996, they stated that HIV in rhesus monkeys is transmitted from the vagina to the cervix and on to the lymph nodes.[53] Obviously, no new knowledge was obtained but that did not stop vested interest groups from claiming that another animal model had helped reveal AIDS-related information.

Toward the beginning of AIDS research, in 1988, scientists stated,

> To date, adequate animal models have not been developed for HIV-related research. An appropriate model is one in which the animal can be infected with HIV and can develop diseases similar to that produced by HIV infection in humans . . . Difficulties with animal models persist. Chimpanzees for example, can be infected with HIV, but, to date, have not developed AIDS. . . . The lack of appropriate animal models for HIV research makes the application of animal research to humans uncertain.[54]

And in 1995,

> No animal models faithfully reproduce human immunodeficiency virus type 1 (HIV-1) infection and disease in humans, and the studies of experimental vaccines in animal models of disease caused by lentiviruses have yielded disparate results, making it difficult to determine what is required for a successful HIV-1 vaccine.[55]

The facts are these. AIDS is a human disease. Only humans are susceptible to it.[56] Animal models do not work.[57]

According to one scientist, there is no way of knowing if an animal model is useful until "we understand the pathogenesis of AIDS, and when we have the vaccines and therapies to prevent it."[58] In other words, we can only know which animal is like a human with respect to a particular disease, medication response, birth defects, and so on after we understand the phenomena in humans. And after we have knowledge of the human manifestation, the animal study is unnecessary.

How many ways is animal experimentation for HIV unsound? It is needless, inaccurate, unreliable, repetitious, and improperly motivated. It makes special-interest groups rich while people become sick and die.

Despite this knowledge, primates and other animals continue to be experimented upon, at great cost to the taxpayer, and at great misappropriation of charity dollars, with results that have been disappointing at best and lethal at worst. However, this disappointment and its expense are just part of the picture.

There is potential for an outcome far more terrifying than AIDS. Experimenting with viruses in living animals is potentially catastrophic. That viruses mutate in a flash makes moving them from live species to live species exceedingly dangerous. The study of AIDS has made us aware that benign viruses in one species can become deadly assassins in another. Every time researchers inject viruses into new animals, the viruses have the potential to mutate. It is not feasible to anticipate the course of a virus's contagiousness. Viruses are transmitted incongruently and unpredictably, either through body fluids or through the air, as we explain more thoroughly in Chapter 11, Animal Organ Donors.

Scientists have isolated airborne viruses in monkeys. These are benign to monkeys but lethal to other species, and they spread as quickly as the common cold. Already injecting a type of HIV into a strain of mice resulted in a mutation that seemed to spread by air. Fortunately, this turned out to be incorrect, but had the original fear proved correct— which is not impossible—the new virus could then infect humans just like the flu. Just because the alarm, in that instance, was unfounded, does not suggest that it always will be. Obviously, millions of people, billions perhaps, could be infected.

This is not science fiction. Scenarios like the one in the movie *Outbreak* are not impossible. One need only read the history of the Ebola virus or examine the protocol for virus control at disease research centers to know that grafting viruses between species puts the whole planet in jeopardy.

In sum, for advances against AIDS that are accurate and safe, we must rely on the same methodologies that have worked in the past: *in vitro*, clinical research and epidemiology.

Treatments

As described, animal-model research suggested that the disease progressed sluggishly. Hence, in the early years of the epidemic, patients did not receive treatment until they broke out with pneumonia or a Kaposi sarcoma or exhibited other AIDS symptoms. Unfortunately, by that time, the patients had a rampant killer coursing within them. Whereas caged monkeys refused to get sick from a virus that may have issued from their home turf, humans were dying in droves.

A conflicting view of the virus's progression was steadily growing among researchers who were working with humans, men like David Ho, MD, of the Aaron Diamond AIDS Research Center in New York City. Dr. Ho's work with HIV patients has led him to many important contributions, for which he was eventually named *Time* magazine's 1996

Man of the Year. Dr. Ho and others insisted, based on clinical observation and *in vitro* studies, that the virus replicated very rapidly in humans right from the start of infection. Their human-model data helped
persuade physicians to disregard animal studies and abandon the earlier
practice of withholding treatment until the patient had clinical signs.

As soon as scientists discovered the role of HIV's three enzymes (reverse transcriptase, protease, and integrase) through *in vitro* research
they went to work fashioning enzyme inhibitors to interrupt the virus's
replication. One of the first medications used to treat AIDS was originally an anticancer drug, a reverse transcriptase inhibitor named AZT
(3'-azido-3'-deoxythmidine). AZT's efficacy against HIV was demonstrated in 1985, in test tube research that showed it inhibiting the virus's
metabolism.[59] Animal models did not contribute to this revelation. AZT
bypassed animal trials and went directly to AIDS patients. AZT has two
forms. *In vitro* research indicated which of these two forms is effective
against HIV. Drug developers manufactured medications with that specific effective shape, thus limiting side effects and enhancing potency.

AZT was already known from cancer research. This, and political
pressure brought to bear by AIDS advocacy groups, sent AZT directly
to clinical trials bypassing the usual animal tests.[60,61] AZT offered the
first real hope to AIDS patients and is still the primary combatant against
HIV. Grievously, reverse transcriptase inhibitors such as AZT only stave
off the inevitable, slowing the course of HIV but not eradicating it. After
a period of months viral resistance to AZT and other reverse transcriptase inhibitors increases. Also they are toxic and replete with devastating
side effects.

Scientists began exploring protease as another target for inhibitory
drugs. As described, protease snips newly formed HIV into particles as
it emerges from the host cell. Protease inhibitors were computer-designed
and then tested on human cell cultures *in vitro*.[62,63,64] These effectively
dulled protease's blade. Newly formed HIV could still emerge from the
host cells, but without protease it was not viable.

Political pressure pushed protease inhibitors directly to clinical trials,
circumventing the usual animal trials. This rapid assimilation of an AIDS
treatment was a watershed. For subsequent drugs, this incident, together
with the growing number of people at death's door, led to a shortening
of the lengthy period of animal testing that usually precedes a drug's
release, although the tests were performed retrospectively.

Animal models did not bear on the development of other enzyme inhibitors. Additional reverse transcriptase inhibitors (ZDV [Retrovir],
3TC [Epivir], ddI [Videx], ddC [HIVid], d4T [Zerit], ABC [Ziagnen],
Combivir, Rescriptor, EFV [Sustiva], Viramune and Preveon); protease
inhibitors (Indinavir [Crixivan], Ritonavir [Norvir], Saquinavir [Invi-
rase], Nelfinavir [Viracept], and Amprenavir [Agenerase]); and medications like hydroxyurea were all developed from test tube methods,

198 □   Sacred Cows and Golden Geese

mathematical, and computer modeling.[65,66,67] *In vitro* tests led directly to human testing with "little supportive efficacy data" from animals.[68] Michael Wyand, a respected primate researcher, stated,

> Candidate antivirals have been screened using *in vitro* systems and those with acceptable safety profiles have gone directly into humans with little supporting efficacy data in any in vivo [animal] system. The reasons for this are complex but certainly include . . . the persistent view held by many that there is *no predictive animal model* for HIV infection in humans.[69] (Emphasis added.)

Evidently, skepticism such as Wyand's did not bring the animal experimentation machine to a standstill in regards to AIDS and HIV research. Rather, researchers retooled to mine this new threat for more profits. Scientists who were studying white blood cells for other reasons repositioned their grant applications to take advantage of AIDS research funding dollars.[70,71,72]

In 1985, the National Cancer Institute began testing medications for possible anti-HIV activity. Of three hundred chemicals which tested positive in mice for inhibiting mouse retroviruses, only twenty-five were effective against HIV in cell culture. (Remember, HIV is a *human* retrovirus.) In HIV patients, only one, AZT was effective. AZT had been available for cancer treatment since 1964 when it was developed *in vitro*. And anyway, as noted, AZT was already in use as an AIDS treatment.[73-76] Nonetheless, the animal experimentation community still claims that AZT and other anti-AIDS medications were developed as a result of animal experiments.[77]

As always occurs, researchers continued borrowing therapy protocols from other diseases. In cancer therapy, oncologists had already found that attacking the disease on several fronts simultaneously makes it more difficult for drug resistance to develop. This suggested that combination therapies, also known as drug "cocktails," might produce better results than single medication therapies in AIDS too. This theory, in part based on mathematical modeling, proved correct.

Dr. Ho combined protease inhibitors with other anti-AIDS medications early in the course of HIV, before AIDS actually developed. In some patients, T-cell counts rose and the virus actually began disappearing as a result of this new drug cocktail treatment. Giving antiviral medications to patients very soon after exposure to HIV, before symptoms emerged, seemed to lead to long-term nonprogression of the infection. Our present therapeutic arsenal for management of HIV includes fifteen agents.[78] Early implementation of combination therapy has greatly reduced the mortality from AIDS.[79]

Dr. Ho developed the therapy through test tube and human clinical research. Epidemiological studies showed that the combination of antiretroviral medications reduced the risk of death by sixty-two percent and reduced the likelihood of HIV progressing to AIDS by seventy-three percent.[80] All these discoveries were not possible in animals. Indeed, Ho's remarkable success deriving from clinical observation of patients is a classic example of what can happen when physicians actually try to learn about disease from humans.

P24 is one of several proteins that make up HIV. When p24 is there, HIV is there. Scientists developed a laboratory test called the p24 antigen test, to detect p24 in the blood. A strong immune response directed against antigen p24 indicates that combination therapies are working.[81] This development was the result of technology and *in vitro* work with humans suffering from AIDS.

Recently, *in vitro* researchers discovered a new class of drugs known as *antisense medications*. Antisense medications inhibit the proteins produced as a result of AIDS. Developers are optimistic about their beneficial effect as a treatment for cytomegalovirus retinitis, an AIDS complication.[82]

Sharpened Understanding through Human Studies

We have already posited that the only true contributions to our knowledge of AIDS and HIV have come from clinical observation, mathematical and computer modeling, epidemiology, and *in vitro* research. That all advances issue from human-based studies renders meaningless the animal model.

Over the years since AIDS and HIV were first identified, epidemiology slowly revealed the virus's idiosyncrasies in humans. HIV behaves differently in different people. Most often, those infected die of AIDS within twelve years. But some people die sooner. Others live on with no apparent symptoms. Most astonishing are the "exposed uninfecteds." These are people who are frequently exposed to the virus but are never infected. By studying these different groups, and patients' fluids or tissues, researchers have garnered very useful data that has contributed to our growing defense against this terrible disease: "Many clues about the pathogenesis of HIV-1 have come from the study of patients with unusually rapid or unusually slow progression of the disease."[83]

This study continues to unveil a complex cast of cells and cell features, each influencing HIV's progression to AIDS either positively or negatively. On the surface of it, HIV is simple; it destroys resistance to disease. In trying to figure out how and why, researchers have found myriad determinants shaping HIV virulence and mortality.

At first, human study found that early in the course of HIV, patients resist the infection, not through antibodies, but through cell-mediated immunity, earlier described. Certain white blood cells themselves destroy the foreign pathogens. Three cell types are involved—macrophages, natural-killer cells, and killer T-cells. As explained, HIV usually seeks out helper T-cells and kills them by turning them into HIV factories. Some of the variability in responses to HIV exposure appears to revolve around mutated cell-surface receptors on those T-cells. We have already explained that CD4 is the common HIV receptor. Thanks to *in vitro* research, scientists have identified numerous mutations. Observing human cell cultures, researchers discovered how co-receptors govern the disease transmission and their mutations can either delay the onset of AIDS or even prevent infection entirely.[84,85,86]

Another element contributing to resistance is the cell-antiviral factor. We have already described that some T-cells, the CD8 cells in particular, are simply resistant to HIV infection. Why does HIV attack CD4 cells and not CD8 cells? By discovering why, researchers hope to alter CD4s so they behave as CD8s. Using human tissue, Robert Gallo and his colleagues discovered that beta-chemokines may be responsible for these T-cells' ability to ward off HIV attack. These chemokines direct white blood cells to the infection site.[87,88]

This detailed *in vitro* research begins to elucidate the exactitude required for HIV to permeate human cells. We now know that unless chemokines work sequentially with glycoproteins (the GP120 and CD4 glycoprotein), the HIV cannot enter the cell. As mentioned earlier, this kind of knowledge, by determining the pathway to infection, could lead to an effective HIV vaccine.[89]

Researchers learned that AIDS progresses significantly faster in patients with low levels of vitamin B12, A, and E.[90] The protective effect of thiamin, niacin, and vitamin C as well as riboflavin, iron and vitamin E was shown in HIV-positive men when they did not progress to AIDS as quickly as their counterparts.[91] Clinical studies revealed the fact that patients who lost a large amount of weight had an increased risk of death regardless of helper T-cell counts.[92] AIDS patients with normal levels of the body chemical albumin live longer than those with low levels.[93]

In vitro research has also shed light on genetic differences that create better immunity to AIDS. One promising area is in the study of HIV-infected humans who do not progress to AIDS.[94] These groups were epidemiologically derived, then *in vitro* research on their cells isolated a gene that seems to protect against AIDS because it lacks one of the co-receptors.[95]

In some people, genes that cause a defect in the production of co-receptors (receptors other than CD4)—the CCR5, CCR2–64 and CXCR4 receptors—are mutated too. These mutations alter the protein coding regions on the cell surface which "exerts a very strong protective effect on disease progression."[96] Obviously, animal tissue would not have provided illuminations at this level.

People infected with HIV who do not progress to AIDS have taught another valuable lesson in HIV-resistance. Scientists observed these individuals' more active helper T-cells in cell cultures. They determined that by secreting a specific protein—interleukin-2—helper T-cells locate HIV. Interleukin-2 works like an antenna to tune into HIV. As the disease progresses, interleukin-2 supplies decrease. Combination therapy early in the course of HIV seems to bolster the helper T-cells in destroying the virus.

All relatively new discoveries of co-receptors and other discoveries from long-term nonprogressors (people infected with HIV who do not get AIDS) have been accomplished via the combination of clinical and *in vitro* research.[97–102] Another common genetic variation that influences HIV progression turned up in a National Cancer Institute clinical study. When people inherit certain mismatched gene pairs from each parent, it produces discrepant versions of human leukocyte antigens that stave off HIV progression.[103]

Approximately 7,000 infants are born each year to HIV-infected mothers, and HIV is one of the leading causes of death for children between the ages of one and four.[104] Tracking the history of these tragedies has opened the scope of our understanding of the disease. First, pregnant HIV-positive women suffer fewer flare-ups of HIV symptoms, such as Kaposi sarcoma, than non-pregnant patients. Using gel permeation chromatography and urine from the pregnant women, researchers were able to isolate a molecule that suppresses HIV activity in them.[105]

We know that HIV can be transmitted to an infant during pregnancy, delivery, or during breastfeeding.[106] Human clinical research has delineated these risk factors for transmission to the infant—high maternal viral load, prolonged rupture of membranes (as occurs during a very long labor, after a patient's water breaks), premature delivery, low maternal CD4 count, and a symptomatic HIV-infected mother. Mothers with low HIV levels were less likely to give HIV to their fetus than mothers with high levels.[107]

Sometimes infants do not acquire HIV from infected mothers due to distinct markers on the surface of cells that differentiate self from nonself. The major histocompatibility complex (MHC) is a group of genes that code for this recognition. Infants who have MHC discordance with their mothers will not contract the virus.[108]

Clinical trials showed that the use of AZT during pregnancy decreased the transmission of HIV from mother to fetus by two-thirds.[190] Receiving zidovudine during pregnancy, then having elective caesarean delivery, may further reduce the risk of transmission. While HIV-infected mothers low in vitamin A have a thirty-two percent chance of infecting the fetus, mothers with normal vitamin A levels have only a seven percent chance.[110] In children, as in adults, the levels of plasma HIV and helper T-cells are predictive of disease progression.[111]

Likewise as with adults, infants who have a variation of the CCR5 receptor, the delta-32 mutation type, do not progress to full blown AIDS as quickly as those without it.[112] This was found via epidemiology and clinical observation. Such knowledge reinforces the belief that viral load levels should be kept as low as possible through the aggressive use of antiretroviral medications.

Hematopoietic stem cells, cells that do not issue from the lymphoid system, are resistant to HIV infection despite expressing the receptors CD4, CCR5, and CXCR4. This new knowledge in the field of cellular immunity furthers our understanding of the disease and could lead to new treatment options.[113]

Recently *in vitro* studies uncovered thrombospondin 1 (TSP 1) in the saliva of patients infected with HIV. This is significant because HIV is not readily found in saliva. Scientists have often wondered why. TSP 1 may prevent HIV from adhering to cell surfaces, thus explaining why it is difficult to find in saliva. This discovery may yield a method of preventing HIV from adhering to all cells.[114]

In vitro research uncovered "*nef*," an HIV-regulatory protein. The HIV-1 *nef* protein protects HIV-infected cells from being killed by other white blood cells. If that protein could be targeted by medications, HIV may be controlled after infecting a patient.[115] Exposed uninfecteds tend to develop clusters of anti-HIV antibodies on mucosal surfaces such as those in the vagina and rectum, possibly due to a confluence of these HIV-resisting characteristics. Their remarkable imperviousness may suggest a viable avenue of virus research.

All these characteristics, garnered *through human observation*, have built a more comprehensive picture of AIDS and the virus that causes it. Its details have helped doctors prevent transmission of HIV and stave off its progression into AIDS. And they have left researchers better prepared to design a vaccine tailored to human consumption. Exploring human cellular immunity is a much more rigorous science than checking vital signs on monkeys. But unlike the dead ends from animal experimentation, it produces hard data, and offers real hope of finding a way of combating or preventing AIDS on the genetic or molecular level in the species that it afflicts—humans.[116]

All these discoveries are recent, their ultimate ramifications unknown. However, they build a more detailed picture of the virus and the cellular characteristics that either enable it or deter it. Scientists will use these descriptions like signposts to determine how to pattern therapies and, potentially, a vaccine.

The Path to an AIDS Vaccine

The federal government has devoted billions to discovering a vaccine to protect against AIDS. As already indicated, too much of that money has been utterly wasted on animal experiments. Dr. Mark Feinberg, a leading AIDS researcher wrote,

> To make an AIDS vaccine, we really need to know more about the basic human immune system and how it works. They knew next to nothing about it when they made the polio vaccine, but that's not going to work here. We need to understand more about how the immune system recognizes and deals with HIV antigens. Clearly few, if any, people can deal with HIV once they're infected with it; nobody that we know of has ever cleared the virus from their bodies after infection. Somehow we have to demand that the vaccine be better than that. I think the way of doing that is doing studies on human beings at very early stages of the development of vaccines to test whether certain ideas work; then you go back to the laboratory to modify them and then back to human beings . . . What good does it do you to test something in a monkey? You find five or six years from now that it works in the monkey, and then you test it in humans and you realize that humans behave totally differently from monkeys, so you've wasted five years.[117]

Of course, because Dr. Feinberg has a vested interest in animal-models he went to say that animal models are "incredibly important." He explained quite well why they are useless but did not go into d   as to why they are so "incredibly important." Could money ha   to do with why they are so important?

Whether or not scientists are successful in inoculating an. cies against immunodeficiency disease, human tissue is the c medium for human vaccine. Unless vaccine development is ca. with *in vitro* research and based on human physiology and path plainly there will be no AIDS vaccine.

Dr. Margaret I. Johnston of the International AIDS Vaccine Initiat. states that regardless of what animal studies reveal about the vaccine the first recipient will still be "making a leap of faith."[118] Knowing the incompetence of animal models, Dr. Johnston probably appreciates the message of this chapter: Because viruses are so species-specific, humans and humans alone can test vaccines.

It is obvious where we should be directing our research efforts and it is not in animal experiments. Human-based *in vitro* and *in vivo* research has cobbled an identifiable path. AIDS kills at the cellular level and that is where it needs to be studied.

Opposition to using animal models for vaccine development is growing. The facts have disabused even the NIH, which is historically pro-animal testing, of animal models for AIDS research. The institute has recommended basic research, which does not require animals, aimed at identifying: AIDS pathogenesis, HIV gene-coded products and their function, a means of interrupting the life cycle of HIV, and many other nonanimal methods.[119]

Vaccine researcher Dr. N. L. Letvin stated, "It is now clear . . . that a strategy for an effective HIV vaccine can be devised only with a thorough understanding of the biology of HIV and the immunopathogenesis of AIDS."[120] One of America's top medical journalists, Lawrence K. Altman, a medical doctor, confirms, "If those goals [curing AIDS, cancer and other diseases] are to be realized, human experimentation will continue to be mandatory since medical progress hinges on learning how humans respond to cutting edge therapies."[121]

This is a true epiphany, and were it not for two obstacles that create inertia, science would pivot one hundred and eighty degrees on this news. First, there is the obstacle of "convention"—the ubiquity of animal experimentation in the research community and its profitability. And second, there is the drug companies' reliance on animal experimentation as a legal safety net. Recently, Bristol-Myers Squibb, Co., maker of three AIDS drugs, announced that it will spend $100 million over the next five years to fund extensive research trials in sub-Saharan Africa. What does this mean? This region is home to seventy percent of the world's HIV-infected population. On the surface of it, this looks like altruism, considering few African HIV patients can afford the $600-plus-a-month drug cocktails. But what else is going on? Has Bristol-Myers realized the inefficacy of animal models and turned instead to a clinical situation involving millions of people? In South Africa alone the infected population doubled to four million in just the last two years. Does this not signal the animal model brought to its knees, albeit by the back door of Africa? The drug manufacturer has, in effect, a captive test bed of humans who have no other options and will not sue.[122]

chapter 11

Animal Organ Donors

Seldom, if ever, have we had as much knowledge to prevent
a future epidemic. What is lacking is the wisdom to act upon
that knowledge.

—Dr. Jonathan Allan, Virologist, Southwest Foundation in
Nature Medicine

On the surface, the ready ability to replace our defective or worn-out parts sounds like a worthwhile objective. Knowing that these parts could come to us as easily, and in the same way, as chops and rump roast, may be only a bit off-putting. However in reality, xenotransplantation—transplanting live animal organs, tissue, or cells into humans—is one of the most frightening goals in contemporary medicine.

There exists a very persuasive argument in favor of xenotransplantation, and that is organ shortage. Fifty-five times a day someone in the United States gets a new organ, but the need is almost twice that figure. Every sixteen minutes another name is added to the waiting list for organ donations. One hundred thousand people die every year because they cannot qualify for organs. If organs were accessible, many lives would be saved . . . and a lot of money would be made by organ and immunosuppressant vendors, surgeons and hospitals. Yes, the philosophical and financial support for xenotransplantation research is immense, and would be untrammeled were there not also huge downsides.

Xeno is Greek for "foreign" or "alien," and deadly, contagious diseases reside, potentially, within animal tissue. All organisms host other organisms, many without ill effect. They have achieved a state of symbiosis. However, when these same bacteria, parasites, viruses, prions, and fungi are arbitrarily introduced into a new organism, such as a human, through tissue or organ transplantation, the symbiosis often does not continue. Without previous exposure and built up immunities, the host often has very adverse reactions. We will go into more detail about the possible contagion that could threaten the recipient and through the recipient, every other human.

The organs themselves are different from species to species, a discrepancy which donor animal developers overlook, not surprisingly considering the maniacal zeal for inserting animal parts into humans throughout time. Much is missing from the historical records, but there are stories of a Russian doctor replacing a piece of human skull with that of a dog in 1682. In the 1800s, doctors reportedly stitched frog skin onto patients suffering from burns. The patients may have withstood the transplants, but it is doubtful they survived the contamination or that the outcomes were otherwise successful.

Because the patient is still breathing when leaving the operating room, one cannot conclude that the organ is an enduring, functional replacement. In 1905, a French surgeon named Princeteau plunked rabbit kidney pieces into a child and declared the operation a total success, stating the "immediate results were excellent." The child died two weeks after the operation. About the same time, other French surgeons including Mathieu Jaboulay tried goat and pig kidneys in humans, and again the patients succumbed.[1] The surgeons ignored the fact that pig kidneys secrete uric acid whereas human kidneys reabsorb it.[2] In 1923, a lamb kidney/human combination took place, likewise without success.[3] In the 1920s, French surgeon Serge Voronoff laced monkey testicles to elderly male patients hoping for "sexual rejuvenation."[4] Ultimately, the organ-rejection problem sent the institution of xenotransplantation into dormancy.

But in 1963, Dr. Keith Reemtsma, of Tulane University, transferred kidneys from chimpanzees to humans. Also in 1963, Claude Hitchcock attempted to transplant a kidney from a baboon into a human.[5] An Italian surgeon named Raffaelo Cortesini placed a chimpanzee kidney into a human later that decade.[6] All but one hardy soul died more or less immediately. That one survivor, one of Reemtsma's patients who survived approximately nine months before succumbing, fed hope that xenotransplants would eventually work.

In 1964, Dr. James Hardy, of the University of Mississippi, attempted to transplant a chimpanzee heart into a human. The operation failed. Later, in Houston, Denton Cooley performed sheep and pig heart transplants into humans, again, without success. Pig heart xenotransplants were unsuccessful in Great Britain too. Christiaan Bernard, of human heart transplantation fame, also jumped on the xenotransplantation bandwagon. He, too, failed.

Animal-to-animal transplant hodgepodge continued throughout those years, but the next animal-to-human transplant to catch the media attention is still perhaps the most famous. In 1984, a baby girl media-named "Baby Fae" entered the world with left ventricular hypoplasia, a severe congenital cardiac malformation that is invariably fatal without treatment. Baby Fae became our most well publicized lab human, thanks to a surgeon named Leonard Bailey.

The standard treatment for this condition is a heart transplant. Failing that, there is a surgery available that will stabilize these children while they await a donor heart. In Baby Fae's case, a human heart was at hand, however Bailey did not even inquire as to its availability. Bailey had no transplant experience in humans, although he had attempted 160 cross-species transplants with animals and 100 goat-to-goat organ transplants, all failures.[7,8] Nevertheless, he arbitrarily performed a baboon transplant on Baby Fae at Loma Linda University in California.

By some physiologic miracle, had the little girl's system embraced the heart, her problems would not have been over. The mature baboon heart would not have grown with the child, and therefore, she would have required a human heart transplant at a later date anyway. In the meantime, she would have been at extreme risk for any diseases borne into her system with the donor organ. Her immune system did spurn the organ and Baby Fae died twenty days after the operation.

Not surprisingly, Bailey did not choose the child of malpractice attorneys for his foray into animal-to-human transplantation. Baby Fae's parents were un-wed, poor, uneducated teenagers who were willing to try anything to save their little girl. In a post-operative interview, reporters asked what options had been offered for Baby Fae. The parents replied that Bailey had told them that the baboon transplant might save Baby Fae, otherwise she would die.

Bailey went on record stating that public health risk will not prevent him from performing more heart xenotransplants.[9] Thankfully, time has swallowed Bailey whole. Yet, the push for successful xenotransplantation has not abated.

And in the meanwhile, animal experiments for xenotransplants continued to consume resources. In the United States in 1992, dogs had pig kidneys implanted, all of which were rejected within hours. Researchers in Italy placed sheep livers into pigs, and rat hearts into chickens. The latter is a particularly bizarre experiment as the rat-circulatory system differs greatly from that of the chicken. All the animals used for this organ swapping died. At the University of Minnesota, pig hearts were placed into baboons, with the best results being a survival of 96 hours.

Baby Fae is the best-known xenotransplant recipient, and Thomas Starzl of Pittsburgh is the most famous xenotransplant surgeon. In 1963, Dr. Starzl performed six baboon kidney xenotransplants; all failed. Between 1969 and 1974 he transplanted livers from chimpanzees into three children, all of whom died within two weeks. Ever determined, Starzl continued experimenting in the laboratory until the 1990s when he recommenced experimenting with humans, all aglow from the promise of new immunosuppressant drugs.

Surgeons elsewhere were doing likewise. In 1992 in Los Angeles, Cedars Sinai Medical Center hosted a pig-to-human liver transplant. The patient survived less than two days. Pig livers lack the enzyme guanase required by humans and metabolize uric acid to allantoin whereas human livers secrete it unchanged. Also in 1992, a pig heart xenotransplant was performed, with the same results.[10]

In early 1993, Starzl placed a baboon liver into a human at the University of Pittsburgh. Starzl's theory, for which he has received over $8,000,000 in grants thus far, is this: hepatitis is a common cause of liver failure. Patients are still infected with this virus, even after their diseased liver is removed. Baboons do not acquire hepatitis and Starzl's hope was their livers would resist re-infection with hepatitis. However, even he admitted that, "a baboon liver could impose on a human recipient lethal interspecies metabolic differences."[11] And another advocate of xenotransplantation, Harvard's Dr. Hugh Auchincloss, stated, "survival rates reported for allotransplantation [human to human] in those patients with hepatitis B are superior to that which we could expect from xenotransplantation."[12]

The patient died within twenty-six days, never regaining consciousness. At autopsy, Starzl's transplanted baboon liver was infected with hepatitis. It also bore cytomegalovirus, Simian Agent 8, H.Papio, and other diseases that are deadly to humans.

Dr. Marian Michaels of the University of Pittsburgh told participants at the 39th Interscience Conference on Antimicrobial Agents and Chemotherapy that in 1992 a man received a baboon liver in an experimental transplantation and that baboon-specific CMV was found in biopsy samples taken from the patient twenty-eight days after the transplant. Although the event occurred in 1992 it was not until 1999 that this announcement was made. This was the first time that researchers acknowledged that they had cultured a virus that crossed the species barrier during a transplantation.[13]

Open season on baboon livers continued with two more transplants occurring in 1993. One patient died within four weeks and the other after ten weeks. Cases of SFV (simian foamy virus) infection from baboon liver transplants also appeared.[14]

Rejection of organs is an ever-present problem, xenografts obviously posing more of a problem than human transplantations. One way to gauge the impact of a transplant is by measuring matched antigens. There should be as many antigens in common as possible. This is why family members are better donors than non-family members. Baboons have no antigens in common with humans. Even if the rejection problem could be overcome, there are worse worries, particularly with primates.

The Southwest Foundation in San Antonio is a major supplier of animals for xenotransplantation experiments, and Starzl's University of

Pittsburgh is a big customer. Dr. Jonathan Allan, a virologist at Southwest, remarked,

We assume, as a given, that these primates carry pathogens that are infectious to humans. You assume that it's something that can kill you. But then in the next breath we turn around and ship a baboon up to Pittsburgh, they open it up, probably every human in the OR [operating room] is exposed to whatever is in there, and they stick it into a human. Does that seem rational?[15]

The Case of Jeff Getty

The most recent xenotransplantation-media event occurred in 1995. Dr. Susan Ildstad was taking care of an AIDS patient, Jeff Getty, whom she thought might benefit from a bone marrow transplant from a baboon. Since primates can be infected with HIV (as explained), and still not develop AIDS, Ildstad reasoned that baboon bone marrow would offer Getty protection against the AIDS virus. She experimented with rodents and primates first. Undeterred by her limited success, Ildstad decided to experiment on humans. She reported that she had isolated a new type of cell that would make the operation possible. Several respected scientists were unable to discern her so-called facilitator cell. Unimpressed with Dr. Ildstad's proposal, Stephen Rose, director of AIDS funding at NIH, stated that "having seen her data . . . there are no underlying data to make me believe this is going to be successful."[16] Dr. Auchincloss remarked, "successful rodent experiments do not make an adequate scientific basis for human experimentation."[17] David Sachs of Harvard agreed, stating, "there was no evidence from the data she presented to show that facilitator cells were present in primates."[18]

The rationale for Dr. Ildstad's enthusiasm for this ill-thought-out project became more clear when she and a biotechnology firm, Genetic Sciences, patented the "facilitator cells." Dr. Ildstad then had a vested interest in experimenting on Mr. Getty.[19] Prior to this procedure, moved by animal rights groups and scientists who had begun speaking out about the pandemic potential from a single transplant, the FDA conducted hearings on whether or not to approve the transplant. The thought of transplanting a baboon's bone marrow into a human made many infectious disease experts more than a little timorous. Dr. John Coffin stated that, "infection is a virtually inevitable consequence" [of xenotransplantation]. He added that, "This is a very serious worry because the animals that have been chosen for doing this, the baboon and pig, are both known to carry endogenous viruses, replication competent, but very poorly studied, that are capable of infecting human cells." [20]

Dr. Louisa Chapman, of the CDC Xenotransplant Working Group, was at the hearing and explained at length that there was great danger involved in the procedure. Describing previous examples of non-human viral diseases being transmitted from primates to humans, she stated,

> Baboon endogenous retroviral proviral DNA can be detected in tissues of all baboon species, as well as those of many other monkeys . . . [These] retroviruses may have pathogenic potential under conditions associated with xenotransplantation.

We will explain *endogenous, retroviral* and *proviral* in a minute. For now, suffice to say as Dr. Chapman cautioned, "Periodic emergence of new pandemic influenza strains can occur by a process of reassortment between human and animal influenza viruses." She continued to spell out that xenotransplants pose a very real risk to public health because of the "long period of clinical latency associated with all known human retroviral infections . . . and "these infections are latent organisms and are often clinically silent in the donor."[21]

Even scientists at the University of Pittsburgh, the bastion of xenotransplantation thanks to the aforementioned Dr. Starzl, had reservations about the procedure. Dr. Marion Michaels stated before the FDA committee, "the donor organ, the tissue or the accompanying hematopoietic cells can also be a source of infection. Most often these infections are latent organisms and are often clinically silent in the donor."[22]

The most outspoken critic was Dr. Jonathan Allan from Southwest, the very outfit that supplies baboons. As an expert on primate viruses, he emphasized that, "Any agent or pathogen that a baboon may harbor is also going to be more likely to be transmitted to humans. [He went on to state that it is] well established that most new emerging human infectious diseases have their origins in other species."[23]

Allan also underscored the important point that a new virus may not be detectable by current means. The safety issue involved in xenotransplantation does not end with the patient, he explained. According to Allan, one of the world's top authorities on the subject, and others, the entire population may be at risk. Is the benefit worth it? Dr. Allan concluded that,

> to proceed with this kind of procedure in the face of knowing how AIDS is transmitted, is to repeat the past because none of the types of screening processes, none of the registries, none of the archiving of samples, none of the surveillance, none of that would pick up on an AIDS-like virus. If you proceed with this, you need to understand there is going to be a risk that you are not going to eliminate the risk of transmitting another virus that could be as deadly as the AIDS virus. [These experiments] constitute a threat to the general public health and not merely a complication of the risk/benefit cal-

culation for the individual xenogenic tissue recipient . . . Do not use non-human primates as organ donors if you don't want to infect the human population.[24]

That is pretty straightforward. Experts like Dr. Allan believe xeno-transplants offer much danger, not just to the recipient, but also to the general public.[25-32]

However, the only members of the public allowed to testify at the hearing were hand-picked by Jeff Getty, and the public health risk was minimized. The hearing was a formality, and a deceitful one at that, because the panel members from the National Academy of Sciences Institute on Medicine was composed primarily of individuals with either a vested interest in, or known to be supportive of, the procedure.

For the first time, it was not individual scientists or surgeons, hell-bent on personal glory and fooling Mother Nature. Getty's hearing was the first indication of the atmosphere of mass greed, unaccompanied by scruples, thickening around the topic of developing xenotransplantation. This venal force now wends and wields influence in ways every bit as deadly and unstoppable as a virus.

Economic pressure to allow the use of animal organs is great. Nextran of New Jersey and Imutran of Great Britain have both spent substantial money getting pigs ready for the procedures. In the words of Mae-Wan Ho, "it is bad science working together with big business for quick profit aided and abetted by our government for the banal reason that government wishes to be re-elected to remain in 'power.' "[33]

We should point out that not all members of the Getty panel were entirely without conscience. One member of the committee admitted, "We were heavily influenced by emotional pleas on the part of the family of the recipient."[34] Hence, the operation was performed; an attempt to save one man put all humanity at risk.

Within weeks, Getty had no living baboon-bone-marrow cells in his body because they were overwhelmed by his immune system. The surgical team initially tried to persuade the public that the operation had been a success as Getty had an increase in the number of white blood cells after the operation. Massive chemotherapy and radiation prior to the transplant had depleted his white blood cell count. Once the chemotherapy and radiation were stopped, Getty's white blood cell count went up anyway. The increase was unrelated to the baboon bone marrow. Furthermore, Getty began taking protease inhibitors at the same time as the transplantation. The blood boost he manifested is characteristic of what happens when protease inhibitors are administered.[35] There is no way of telling whether, where or when any infectious particles borne into Getty's system with the baboon bone marrow transplant will crop up. Depending on their contagiousness, they may move from Getty to other humans. Or they may not.

Given the obstacles Getty faced in getting his bone-marrow transplant, it seems probable that other xenotransplant candidates would be more discreet about their intentions. Therefore, there are likely xenotransplant recipients other than Getty whom we do not know about, and they too may be percolating new infectious diseases. Frederick Murphy, Dean of Virology at the University of California, Davis, School of Veterinary Medicine, states,

> It will not be easy to determine which viruses represent a risk to society as a whole as a result of species jumping and which may be dismissed as representing minimal risk . . . Despite our incredible power to diagnose viral disease and detect viruses, it would be a mistake to think that methods in common use are all that sensitive and specific for the purpose at hand . . . the question of risk has been expanded to cover the whole population that might come into contact with the xenograft recipient. The questions now asked include: What is the risk of novel viral diseases stemming from unique opportunities for species jumping? Will xenotransplantation be the cause of 'new' viruses? Will the immunosuppression induced in xenograft patients amplify this risk? Here, another HIV-like virus/AIDS-like epidemic replaces prion diseases as the ultimate threat.[36]

In other words, one of the viruses in the baboon, hitherto unknown to humans, may mutate in a human recipient and become the next AIDS or Ebola. Or worse, a prion-based disease like Mad Cow (bovine spongiform encephalopathy) may emerge in people distantly connected to these patients, years from now, so removed that it will reveal no known trail to its origins.

Nonetheless, there seems to be no dampening the xenotransplantation fervor. Diacrin, Inc., implanted neuronal cells from pig fetuses into twenty-four Parkinson's and Huntington's disease patients to study whether the cells may perform like human fetus implants, which in experiments have signaled brain improvement. Cytotherapeutics, Inc., implanted cow adrenal cells into the spinal cords of thirty-six dying cancer patients with untreatable pain. The cells make substances that block pain signals. Neocrin, Inc. encapsulates pig pancreas cells to avoid the immune system while stimulating insulin production in diabetes patients. It plans to test fifty patients. Boston doctors announced that they have injected 400,000 fetal-pig cells into the brain of a middle-aged man with severe epilepsy—the first time an animal-to-human transplant has been tried to treat the disease.

There are no restrictions yet put on the sexual activity of animal tissue recipients. Assuming that the impact of the infection is not immediately apparent, and progresses as HIV or Mad Cow disease does, recipients can continue as normal with their lives, having intercourse, sneezing, coughing, and so forth. With no surety regarding how the infection will spread, the disease may spread to hundreds or hundreds of thousands of people, each of whom will likewise harbor a slow killer. Though this may sound alarmist, it is not inconceivable given what we know about disease contagion.

The Piggy Incentive

Although no xenotransplants have yet succeeded, a combination of genetically engineered animal donors and improved antirejection drugs will probably soon result in successful animal-to-human organ transplants. Not surprisingly, the very companies that manufacture antirejection drugs are also genetically engineering donor animals. Their goal? The full-service transplant—donor parts, plus pharmaceuticals.

More than 53,000 patients are presently waiting for organs. If people come to believe that they can scarf French fries and knock back whiskies with impunity because an inexhaustible supply of piggy parts can replace their own abused organs, that number will grow astronomically.

Today organs are essentially free, but that would not be the case if they were engineered and marketed. Speculatively but conservatively, organs might cost $100,000 to $500,000 each. Surgery and hospital charges would also, just off the bat, be anywhere from $600,000 to one million. The anticipated glint of all those zeros is compelling incentive for biomedical-engineering companies, hospitals, and transplant surgeons.

So, the vested-interest groups have joined ranks to rally for this new source of revenue. Even speculative figures are staggering. According to a Salomon Brothers' report, the xenotransplant market could exceed six billion dollars per year. Others consider that to be a conservative estimate. Novartis is prepared to invest one billion in the near future.[37] Sandoz the owner of Imutran, Baxter the owner of Nextran, and Alexion Pharmaceuticals, along with companies like U.S. Surgical, could reap the lion's share of this.

Not since the invention of the wheel has any development seemed so versatile. The number of uses for xenotransplantation is almost as unlimited as the risks. The editor of *Nature* stated,

> The momentum toward clinical trials of xenotransplantation is seemingly unstoppable, powered as it is by . . . multimillion dollar investment by biotechnology companies . . . politicians would do well to err on the side of caution, and agree on an international moratorium on clinical trials.[38]

Some countries are balking, but not the U.S. The only snag here is, as indicated by Starzl's handiwork and Jeff Getty's xenotransplant: animal organs are not yet up to snuff. Primates are an obvious choice for organ cultivation, because of their genetic similarity to humans. However, our "all in the family" proximity with the great apes is also a hindrance, since it allows easier cross-species transfer of diseases too. A virus, at home in a pig, might not survive in an environment as dissimilar as a human. However, simian viruses regularly adapt to a human and proliferate. Case in point is the virus HIV-2 and a primate virus, SIV, so similar that it is thought that the human version may have arisen from contact with monkeys as expressed in Chapter 10.[39,40] We know that SIV crosses the species barrier.[41] Lab workers exposed to blood from animals infected with SIV have tested positive for the virus.[42,43]

In addition to SIV, some scientists postulate that hepatitis B may have come to humans from chimpanzees since chimps harbor the virus asymptotically. HTLV-2, which causes leukemia in people, is thought to have originated as STLV in monkeys. The monkey-transmitted Marburg virus killed seven people in 1967.[44] The patients became demented, bled from all orifices, went into coma, and eventually died secondary to heart failure. The survivors did not fare much better. Chronic liver failure, impotence and insanity were long-term consequences.

Ebola victims, featured in the movie *Outbreak,* also bleed from all apertures before dying agonizing deaths. Ebola is also believed to have originated in monkeys. (Everything we know about Ebola was diagnosed clinically and with laboratory aids. The electron microscope demonstrated the particle responsible.) Many refer to Ebola as the next plague.

Type-D simian endogenous retrovirus, a new virus recently found in baboons, is harmless in baboons but "scary," as Jaap Goudsmit of the Academic Medical Center in Amsterdam put it. He feels that, "it's one of those viruses that might be activated in a new host."[45]

Robin Weiss, virologist at the Institute of Cancer Research in London, remarked that this new discovery, "adds to the argument that these kinds of primates are perhaps not useful for transplantation."[46] Jonathan Allan explained,

> I would strongly urge that non-human primates not be developed as a donor species for human transplantation at the present moment because of the relatively large and unknown risks associated with these procedures. Implicit in the use of baboons or other non-human primates is the fact that they carry an inordinate number of herpesviruses and retroviruses. Based on current technologies it is virtually impossible to provide a clean animal for use in humans. Recent studies indicate that baboons harbor several endogenous retroviruses, one of which is remarkably similar to a virus that causes simian AIDS. This virus is apparently expressed in baboons and antibodies have been detected to this endogenous type D virus. What this means is that we cannot expect to safely provide baboons

for these procedures due to both known and unknown persistent viruses harbored by non-human primates.[47]

In other words, the closer a donor species is, genetically, to humans the more likely it is to transmit lethal viruses.

Ironically, considering how many profiteers are snorting around this potential trough, our next-best nearest cousins are hogs. Pigs appear to be the most promising animals for mining human replacement parts. Still, there is a trick. Scientists must "fool" the human recipients' immune systems into thinking the donor organ is human rather than porcine.

No one says much about how these pigs are engineered. Perhaps that is because too many people remember *The Island of Dr. Moreau.* Anyway, here's the often-glossed-over method: Genetic engineers insert a bit of human DNA into a pig fetus. (The fetus's system does not attack the foreign DNA, because immune response is unformed in fetuses.) Once born, pigs mature quickly and propagate. More human DNA is introduced into the next generation's fetuses, and so forth. Gradually, the pig organs grow to resemble, in terms of immune recognition, human organs.

Let us, for the sake of medicine, overlook the very disconcerting reality of people in lab coats cooking up batch after batch of *Porcus sapiens.* The hope of the vested interest groups is that the response of human recipients to such organs will be something on the order of, "It looks like pork, it smells like pork, it tastes like pork, but it is human enough that we will let it pass."

Death by Donor

No more organ shortages. No more rejected organs. But can you hear the hinges creaking open on a Pandora's box of infectious disease? The problem is that individual bodies are not just individual bodies. Each is its own microsystem filled with additional smaller organisms. When you move an animal organ into another species, you also move communities of unseen, unpredictable other living microorganisms. These might take the form of bacteria, viruses, parasites, fungi, or most idiopathic of all, prions.

Bacteria are their own story. We treat bacterial infection with antibiotics, and unless the bacteria has fortified in response to antibiotics, like methicillin-resistant *staphylococcus,* antibiotics will wipe it out. *Yersinia enterocolitica* is a bacterium that uses pigs as a reservoir and can infect humans. It is currently spread via pork. Symptoms in humans range from abdominal pain, mimicking appendicitis, to severe septicemia. Yet pigs harboring the disease appear healthy.[48] So pig engineers have that to cull out. Bacteria are becoming more robust, in response to antibiotic treatment, and it is likely that there will be increased numbers of antibiotic-resistant strains.

Viruses, as we know from AIDS, are another matter. They are shape-shifters, quickly mutating to adapt to different environments, sometimes under the right circumstances jumping between species as hepadnavirus, papillomavirus, retrovirus, aterivirus, togavirus, adenovirus, parvovirus, hantavirus, papovavirus, and others cross from animals to humans. They can work quickly to deplete systems and bring on disease and death. Or they can work slowly, unperceived and even lie dormant for years, then suddenly become deadly. Until a patient manifests symptoms, we may not know he or she has a virus. By then the patient may have infected many other people, and they in turn may have infected more. That is how viruses reach epidemic proportions and go global.

So far, approximately 4,000 viruses have been identified that occur in humans, animals, plants, and other organisms. As yet unidentified numbers are, conservatively, in the millions. Suffice to say, we can presently detect only a fraction of a percentage of the world's viral species and we can combat hardly any of them. Beyond that, even if we could know all of the viruses in existence and could adequately test for them, viruses still mutate and result in totally new viruses within milliseconds.

Retroviruses, of which HIV is the most notorious, pose the greatest concern to scientists. Because they can take over the host cell and inject their own genetic material into the DNA of the cell, retroviruses are impossible to remove from all the cells that they infect. Readers can find more about retroviruses in the AIDS chapter. Robin Weiss cautioned, "AIDS was absent from humans thirty years ago, and HIV almost certainly originated as an extremely rare sporadic event from an animal to a human host."[49]

As we know from AIDS, when a retrovirus takes hold in a new species, the consequences can be pandemic. And why should our immune systems have the capacity to combat a virus that they should never have encountered in the natural order? In 1957, the Asian Flu killed one million and in 1968 the Hong Kong Flu killed 700,000. Originating in either birds or pigs, these mutated viruses traveled between humans in the air. A virus brought about the Spanish Flu epidemic of 1918, which killed twenty million people. There is strong evidence to suggest that it began as an avian influenza virus that passed to pigs and then on to humans.[50,51] Do not let the fact that this epidemic was almost a century ago assuage your fears. If this same flu reappeared today, we would be no better prepared to eradicate it than we were then. And it would kill many more people. Air travel was not common then; world communities were more isolated. Today, after a few sneezes in a single airport, the mortality might be in the hundreds of millions.

Recently, scientists postulated that hepatitis E crossed the species barrier from pigs, which carry it asymptomatically.[52] Hepatitis E kills about ten percent of the people it infects. Pigs can also transmit Japanese encephalitis virus, and many other diseases to humans. More killers, borne to humans through pigs, each still without cure.

Some viruses are "endogenous," meaning they are actually programmed into our genes. Pig endogenous retroviruses (PERVs) have been discovered that can infect human cell cultures.[53] The ubiquity of PERVs in pigs makes it extremely unlikely that they can be eradicated from the pig genome.[54] Pigs have also been shown to harbor endogenous C-type or oncovirus retroviruses capable of infecting humans.

Other even more devastating diseases may be possible. Proviruses are strands of DNA that can bring about virus production in other strands of DNA. These proviruses have evolved over time with an animal, the pig for example, and do not harm the pig. However, if inserted into a new host via a xenotransplant, a human for example, they can activate latent retroviruses. Researchers have found two different classes of porcine endogenous proviruses that can infect humans thus far, with multiple copies of the virus within each cell. For them, this discovery reinforced the likelihood that these proviruses are in pigs currently being considered for donor organs for humans.[55] Jonathan Stoye, who led the study, said, "The existence of twenty to thirty copies per cell will make it very much harder to remove the virus from pig cells. It may be impossible . . . We ought to know more about the pathogenic potential of these viruses." [56]

Some scientists are concerned that the surface molecules on the pig's organs will mutate and attack the human host. These concerns are not purely theoretical. This type of phenomenon occurs regularly in nature. Since pigs are more genetically removed from humans than baboons, scientists hope this will slow the virus hopping. However, it is equally likely that we will have fewer defenses. Normally our bodies have tremendous reserves for fighting off foreign invaders. However, for a transplant to take, doctors suppress those defense mechanisms with drugs. The immunosuppressive medications given to transplant patients will make it easier for the pig proviruses to manifest and reproduce. The immune systems of transplant recipients, disabled by immunosuppressants, will relax their defenses. The pig tissue may also have its own retrovirus that could activate in the human patient, or the pig retrovirus may combine with a human retrovirus to create a new virus. The possibilities are almost limitless and *horrifying*.

How can we screen for viruses before symptoms appear? We cannot. We do not even know they are there. But even once we know the virus is there, what then? It takes a long time to develop tests for even identifying a virus, much less combating it. The AIDS test took more than five years to develop. Vaccines that inure us to specific viruses take even longer. Viruses we have known about and thrown money at for years, such as herpes and AIDS, still have no vaccine. Billions of dollars have gone into AIDS research over the last twenty years worldwide and we are nowhere near eradicating or even really controlling it.

In developing pigs as donors, scientists face major challenges to expunge diseases such as pseudorabies, leptospirosis, erysipelas, and wabah babi, which are endogenous to pigs. Each disease presents its own problem. Take the case of pseudorabies, which pigs carry asymptomatically. When it infects other animals, they die agonizing deaths, frequently attempting to self-amputate their infected limbs. Fortunately, we can now screen for pseudorabies, but new viruses emerge on an almost daily basis, as we have explained, and some certainly go unnoticed because they are harmless to the host animal.

Nevertheless, some of the early backslapping over donor pig development features "pigs without virus." Which virus is that? One of the 4,000 we already know about? What about the other million we have not yet discovered or experienced. Presumably, organs could be screened for viruses, as blood now is for HIV. However, as an Australian discoverer of a new virus pointed out, "you can't screen for disease agents that you don't know about."[57] The virus he discovered affects pigs and has spread to bats and humans. No one knew about SV40 when they were cooking up the polio vaccine, and the SV40-infected monkey tissue they used for the vaccine is still turning up in humans, generations later, as a harbinger of disease. It is not possible to breed virus-free animals.

If the possibility of viral catastrophe is not sufficiently chilling, consider *prions*. Prions are responsible for that infamous killer, Mad Cow disease, one of several transmissible spongiform encephalopathies (TSE) that also include kuru and Creutzfeldt Jacob disease (CJD) in humans and scrapie in animals. All TSEs are progressive diseases of the central-nervous system. Dementia, seizures, and ultimately death result as prions turn the brain to "sponge." We know that transplanting tissue such as corneas, kidneys, livers, and dura from those infected with TSE infects others. All blood products derived from Mad Cow disease-infected humans are a source of CJD.[58]

The manifestation of prions is tantamount to the discovery that the world is not flat. Scientists peered through microscopes for over three hundred years before they found prions. Prions change everything. Scientists now feel prions are neither bacterium nor virus, but a completely different infectious substance. Prions lie dormant in systems for years before bringing on lethal disease. So far, they cannot be arrested. They cannot be killed. They were probably always there, but not until 1982 were they "discovered." *Prions may be in pigs.*

All this research and we still really know very little about why animal exposures can negatively influence human health. People who work around animals, who use animal-derived products, and/or who eat animal-derived foods sometimes get sick, often inexplicably. If these slight exposures result in sickness and sometimes death, imagine the kind of toll inserting an animal organ directly into a human might exact. Cavalier disregard to the risks of xenotransplantation could result in a disaster of biblical proportion.[59]

Stop Them Now

Pig breeders can never guarantee bacteria-free, virus-free, and prion-free donors, though they might certainly maintain that they can since the profit potential is so great. Certainly, one feels great sympathy for patients who need new organs. But the reality is that even if animal-donor organs should reach the market, the cost to the recipient and to mankind as a whole is very large.

The public must be made aware that surgeons and organ purveyors are not beyond manipulating patients and families by offering xenotransplantation as the only way out of an awful situation. As in Baby Fae's case, the patients or their guardians are desperate and usually uninformed. Individual cases aside, exposing the population at large to the risks is ethically unacceptable. The risk to other humans from xenotransplantation is real and immense.

For this reason, many scientists and physicians have encouraged caution in dealing with this potentially catastrophic situation.[60–76] Recently, the World Health Organization warned that proceeding with xenotransplants could result in new diseases thus endangering humans.[77] Dr. Weiss stated, "It is the fear of triggering a new human epidemic . . . that has led to a call for a moratorium on xenotransplantation of animal tissues into humans."[78]

Harvard University xenotransplantation researcher Dr. Fritz Bach, a leader in the field of cross-species transplants, and Dr. Harvey V. Fineberg, Harvard University's provost and former public health dean, led a nine-member group calling for a temporary halt to animal-to-human transplants before the pressures to do such experiments become "well-nigh irresistible."

> This is a very unusual situation. It is a situation where what we the medical establishment . . . want to do puts the public at risk "of new diseases possibly as bad as AIDS . . ." have they [scientists experimenting with xenotransplants] got the right, the moral right, to put the public at risk? The public needs to be not only educated but must participate in this decision, I don't think we scientists have the right to make this decision for the public . . . We propose a moratorium on xenotransplantation including those procedures that could be practiced at any time, such as using a pig organ as a temporary 'bridge' until an allogenic organ is found.[79]

Kathryn C. Zoon of the FDA emphasized, "Public awareness and understanding of xenotransplantations is vital because infectious disease risks posed by cross-species transplantation ... go to the public at large."[80]

Dr. Prentice of the University of Nebraska disclosed what is a common approach to the experimentation: "We approved a xenoperfusion protocol at my institution ... and quite frankly we didn't know what we were doing."[81]

Together with this candid admission in mind, consider this from Dr. Allan,

> It only takes one [non-human primate] transplant to start an epidemic. Only one. You are playing Russian roulette betting that a [nonhuman primate] transplant won't transmit a virus. Once you focus on containment, you are already behind the eight ball in terms of containment.[82]

A moratorium on xenotransplants would leave us with the task of increasing the availability of human-donor organs and encouraging more healthful living. If even half the money now being spent on pig organs were going to education and prevention, the need for organs would plummet. As noted earlier, lifestyle accounts for most diseases including those that lead to the need for transplants.

To augment the availability of human donor organs elsewhere in the world, governments are reevaluating their donor policies. It is frequently difficult to persuade people to fill out a donor card for the same reasons that it is difficult to get them to make out a will. It is not comfortable to deal with our own deaths. It is also difficult to ask the survivors of a patient to donate the loved one's organs. Caregivers may not ask and on other occasions families may be too emotionally overwrought to remember to suggest this. To overcome this resistance, Sweden mandated citizens to decide what to do with their organs in 1996. This resulted in 600,000 new donors. A similar situation occurred in Denmark. Using this method, millions of new donors could be identified in the United States alone.

The implementation of a transplantation coordinator—an individual responsible for contacting the family of the deceased and promoting community awareness—at medical centers in Spain resulted in the growth of organ donations by seventy-five percent since 1990. Instead of assuming that one would not donate unless otherwise specified, Austria, Belgium, and France, take the opposite track. That is, citizens of these countries may specify that they do not wish to donate their organs. But unless they make that effort, governments assume that they do not object to their organs' donation. If this were instigated here, donors would increase to the point that xenotransplants would not be necessary.

Increasing the number of donors could also be accomplished by decreasing the restrictions on donor organs, at least for those organs needed for bridges or short-term survival. Some of the organs may actually last as long as the currently used organs.

We could also implement laws linking eligibility for organ donation to willingness to donate. In this case, those who have a donor card would automatically be eligible to receive an organ should they need one. Those who refuse to donate would not be eligible.

Donor card alterations do not suggest profit in the way merchantable animal organs do. Hence, stern warnings to the contrary, countries are allowing development of pig organs. British transplant patients will have to sign a pledge that they remain childless and use "barrier contraception consistently and for life."[83] That means that the fate of humankind depends on the trustworthiness of these recipients in regard to characteristically dicey practice of "safe sex." And it also banks that an unknowable reservoir of viruses, bacteria and prions will not become transmissible through blood or through the air, an altogether chancy investment for which we have no guarantee whatsoever.

chapter **12**

Call to Action

Animal experimentation is not necessary. It is expensive. It is inaccurate. It is misleading. It consumes limited resources. And further, it is detrimental to the very species it professes to be working to help—humankind.

We have presented only a portion of the thousands of ways using the animal-model misleads human medical researchers. There are many more. There will always be more, too many more for one book. The plethora of insults to health and pocketbook we have uncovered has spilled into a second volume of material and onto an informational web site, *www.curedisease.com*.

This sequel volume will review the role of animal experimentation, or lack of it, in the fields of surgery, anesthesiology, neurology, psychiatry, pediatrics, and infectious disease. It analyzes every Nobel Prize for Medicine or Physiology, demonstrating that animals were either not used or used unnecessarily for the twentieth century's greatest achievements. Our web site offers evaluations of the animal model as it bears on current medical news.

Our hope is that *Sacred Cows and Golden Geese* will be well used by many dissatisfied contingencies—those who suffer from incurable illness or know people who do; those who have lost loved ones to disease; those who work to stop cruelty to animals; and the many who are frustrated by the hobbled pace and expense of medical development. It is a point of departure for change, for radically improved medical research.

We live in a country where change is possible, but this book attacks one of America's most *sacred* sacred cows. And those who live handsomely off the golden eggs laid by the goose of animal experimentation will not suffer attack quietly. The overthrow of animal experimentation will require voluble and unrelenting communication from and among common consumers. American patients. Everyone.

Our plea to readers is this: *get involved.*

First, continue to educate yourself about the fallacy of animal experimentation. Having read *Sacred Cows and Golden Geese* will help you
to consider new medical information as it appears in the media more
carefully. If you need more in-depth explanation, please consult our web
site. Second, educate others. Give this book to your friends and relatives.
Third, act based on your education. Rally your friends and neighbors
behind your shared concern.

Write letters to the editor expressing your concern about spending
taxpayer and charity dollars to fund animal experimentation. Educate
the media about why animal models do not lead to cures for human
disease.

Find out about animal experimentation in your own community.
Learn more about medical experiments taking place at nearby universities and corporations. Demand that these experiments be replaced by
more productive methodologies. Although the scientists will say that
their animal models are predictive and will result in cures for human
disease, you now realize that they will not have human application. Insist
on accountability. Challenge researchers to justify publicly their use of
taxpayer money.

Hold press conferences about animal experiments going on locally.
Refer any questions not answered by this book to us. We will be glad
to speak with your local media. Invite animal experimenters in your
community to debate this issue. We would be glad to take part if you
require our participation.

Attend political rallies and ask the candidates about this waste of
money and whether or not they will work for change. Get a thousand
signatures on a petition and present it to your local elected officials, your
congressperson, and senators. Encourage them to read this book or visit
our web site so they are exposed to the other side of the animal-
experimentation story.

Together with other concerned physicians, veterinarians, and scientists, we have created a mechanism for perpetuating and augmenting
the facts presented in this book. This nonprofit organization, Americans
For Medical Advancement (AFMA), disseminates information regarding
the true sources of medical achievement and counters false propaganda
perpetrated by pro-vivisectionists. As an educational organization, it
reaches the public through publications, radio, television and
www.curedisease.com. You can contribute to this worthy effort with tax
deductible donations. (We should also point out that the proceeds from
the sale of this book go to AFMA. The authors do not profit from the
sale. Hence when we recommend you buy another copy of the book and
give it to a friend, we are not doing so because of a profit motive.)

Change requires commitment and a lot of work. As this book shows,
it is not just animal lives that hang in the balance. It is your own life,

your family's lives, your friends' lives. Only by increasing the volume of discussion around the animal-experimentation issue can we hope to break down the conventions that propagate it. Action will contribute to change and the transformation will benefit everyone. Stopping animal experimentation will increase resources for bona-fide science with always applicable results and for prevention that will limit the incidence of disease. And when medical researchers use human-based science, these so-called alternatives to animal experiments, then we can have confidence that we are doing the utmost to ease human suffering from disease.

Postscript

The high standard of medical care we enjoy today was made possible by:

1. Clinical observation and research
2. *In vitro* research with human tissue
3. Postmarketing drug surveillance
4. Serendipity
5. Mathematical modeling
6. Autopsies
7. Computers
8. Epidemiology
9. Pathology
10. Specialization of medical care
11. Specialized areas of hospital care
12. Technology
13. Genetics
14. Basic science research in fields such as chemistry, mathematics, and physics
15. Prevention

We hope we have proved that:

1. Experimenting on animals for human benefit is not *science*.
2. Extrapolating results from animal to humans has misled scientists, delayed therapies, *not* prevented dangerous therapies and techniques from being implemented, and has directly harmed humans.
3. Discoveries made via past experiments on animals could have been found without them.
4. Experiments on animals waste time, money, and personnel that should be devoted to methods that have a proven record of success.

References

Chapter 1: Introduction

1. *JAMA* 1997, vol. 277, pp. 301–6 and *PharmacoEconomics* 1994, vol.5, pp. 482–504
2. Bailey, B. *Clinical Medical Discoveries* 1961
3. *Parade Magazine* April 4, 1997

Chapter 2: How It All Began

1. *Postgraduate Medicine* Vol.101, No.2, Feb. 1997
2. *Companion Encyclopedia of Medical History,* Bynum and Porter (Eds.), Routledge, 1993
3. *Perspectives in Biology and Medicine*, 1990;34:128–33
4. Asimov, I. *Asimov's Biographical Encyclopedia of Science & Technology* 2nd edition. Doubleday & Company 1982
5. Ruesch, Hans, *Slaughter of the Innocent*, Bantam, New York 1978.
6. *Use of Animals in Biomedical Research: The Challenge and Response*, 1992 AMA
7. Hill, R. B. and Anderson, R. E. *The Autopsy—Medical Practice and Public Policy* Butterworth 1988
8. Salen, J. C. W., Animal Models—Principles and Problems in the *Handbook of Laboratory Animal Science* Svendsen and Hau (Eds.) CRC Press 1994 pp. 1–2
9. Ibid
10. Tomkin, O. *Galenism* Cornell Univ Press 1973
11. *New Health* Fraser Harris, D. F., Sep. 1936
12. *A History of Medicine* Guthrie, D Nelson, London 1945
13. *Companion Encyclopedia of the History of Medicine*, (Eds). Bynum & Porter, Routledge 1993
14. Asimov, Ibid.
15. *Perspectives in Biology and Medicine*, 1990; 34:128–133
16. Garrison, F. H., *History of Medicine*, WB Saunders 1929
17. AMA "White Paper" on animal experimentation entitled *Use of Animals in Biomedical Research: The Challenge and Response* 1988 and 1992 Pub. AMA Chicago
18. Tait, L. *Transactions of the Birmingham Medical Society,* 20, April 1882
19. Ruesch, Ibid.
20. Landmarks in Cardiac Surgery, ISIS Medical Media, 1998, pp. 8–11
21. Asimov, Ibid.
22. Ibid.
23. *Postgraduate Medicine* vol.102, no.3, p. 233
24. Asimov, Ibid.
25. Bernard, C. 1865 *Introduction to the Study of Experimental Medicine* Dover Pub. Inc. 1957

26. Ibid.
27. As quoted in Vyvan, J. *In Pity and in Anger* Micah. 1988
28. Kalechofsky, Roberta. *Autobiography of a Revolutionary.* Micah 1991 pp. 30
29. Kalechofsky, Ibid.
30. Vyvan, J. *In Pity and in Anger.* Micah 1988
31. Dr. George Hoggan, *Morning Post,* Feb. 2, 1875
32. Westcott, E. *A Century of Vivisection* C. W. Daniel, England, 1949 pp. 166–67
33. *The Cambridge World History of Human Disease,* p. 51
34. *Memorandum on Rabies* DHSS 1977, HMSO, London
35. Garrison, Ibid.
36. *Lancet* 1909, pp. 250–70
37. *Lancet* 1909, March 20, pp. 848–9
38. *The Study of Medicine* Walker, K 1954, Hutchison, London
39. Guthrie, Ibid.
40. Bynum and Porter, Ibid.
41. *The Cambridge World History of Disease*
42. *Br Med J* 1884, Sep. 6, p. 454
43. Ibid.
44. *The Story of Vaccination,* Riedman, S R, Bailey Bros & Swinfen, Folkestone 1974
45. *Lancet* 1946, ii, p. 99
46. *Fighting Infection,* Dowling, HF, Harvard Univ Press 1977
47. *Explorers of the Body,* Lehrer, S., Doubleday 1979
48. *A Century of Vivisection and Antivivisection,* Westacott, E. Daniel, Saffron, Walden 1949
49. *Lancet* July 20, 1946
50. *Lancet* 1909, March 20, 848–9
51. *Report of the Second Royal Commission on Vivisection,* 1906–1912, p. 31
52. *Br Med J* 2, p 453–8
53. Bynum and Porter, Ibid.
54. Addison T, *On the Constitutional and Local Effects of Disease of the Suprarenal Capsules.* London, Samuel Highley, 1855
55. *Arch Ital Biol* 1884;5:333–340
56. *Arch Gen Med* 1856;8:385–401
57. *Arch Gen Med* 1856;8:572–598
58. *British and Foreign Medical-Chirurgical Review* 1858;21:204–221
59. *British and Foreign Medical-Chirurgical Review* 1858;21:498–510
60. *Arch Physiol* 1894;6:810–815
61. *Trans Path Soc London* 1882;33:340–345
62. *Br Med J* 1948;2:451–455
63. Oliver G. *Pulse Gauging: A Clinical Study of Radial Measurement and Pulse Pressure.* London, HK Lewis, 1895
64. *Clio Medica* 1977;12:57–90
65. *New York Med J* 1895;62:436–437
66. *Medical Record* 1901;59:83–87
67. *Centroblatt für Gynakologie* 1896;20:524–528
68. Asimov, I. *Asimov's Biographical Encyclopedia of Science & Technology* 2nd edition. Doubleday & Company 1982
69. Walker, K. *The Story of Medicine* Hutchinson 1954
70. *Lancet* Oct. 23 1937, p. 950
71. *Companion Encyclopedia of the History of Medicine,* Bynum and Porter (Eds.) Routledge, 1993
72. Guthrie, Ibid.
73. *The Cambridge World History of Disease*
74. Bynum and Porter, Ibid.

Chapter 3: Legislated Ineptitude

1. *Teratology* 1988;28:221–226.
2. *Medical World*, Dec. 1, 1933, p. 335.
3. Ibid.
4. *Teratology* 1988; 38:203–215
5. *Exp Mol Path Supl*, 1963;2:81–106
6. *Federation Proceedings*, 1967;26:1131–6
7. *Teratogenesis, Carcinogenesis, and Mutagenesis* 1982 vol.2, pp. 361–74
8. Mason J., and Wise D. in *Casarett and Doull's Toxicology* 4th ed. McGraw-Hill 1993
9. Schardein, J. L., *Drugs as Teratogens*, 1976
10. Schardein, J. L., *Chemically Induced Birth Defects,* Marcel Dekker 1985
11. McBride in *Lancet* Dec. 16, 1961
12. Arzneimittelforschung, 1956;6:426–30.
13. Ibid.
14. as quoted in Ruesch, H. *1000 Doctors Against Vivisection* p. 107
15. Prof. George Teeling-Smith. *A Question of balance; the benefits and risks of pharmaceutical innovation,* p. 29, pub. Office of Health Economics, 1980
16. *Nature* 1971;232,:634
17. *Lancet*, Setpember 1, 1962
18. *British Medical Journal*, August 18, 1962, and January 26, 1963.
19. *Clin Pharmacol Ther* 1962; pp. 665–72
20. E.K. Marshall, MD. *Baltimore Journal of the American Medical Association*, January 128, 1939, p. 353,
21. *Surg Gyn and Obstet* 1920;31(5):437–448 and Bliss, Michael. *The Discovery Of Insulin* University of Chicago Press 1982 and Opie, Eugene L. *Diseases of The Pancreas. Its Cause and Nature* Lippincott 1903
22. Bliss, Michael. *The Discovery Of Insulin* University of Chicago Press 1982
23. Opie, Eugene L. *Diseases of The Pancreas. Its Cause and Nature* Lippincott 1903
24. Ibid, p. 247
25. Ibid.
26. *Archives of Experimental Pathology and Pharmacology*, 1908;58
27. *BMJ* Aug.4, 1923 165–172
28. Roberts, Ffrangcon. in *BMJ* Dec. 16, 1922, pp. 1193–4
29. Bliss, Michael. *The Discovery Of Insulin* University of Chicago Press 1982 p. 205
30. Ibid, p. 207
31. Ibid, p. 209
32. Ibid, p. 205
33. *Tox & Appl.. Pharm*, 1969;16:498–506
34. Bayly, B. *Clinical Medical Discoveries* National Antivivisection Society London 1961 p. 47
35. *Nature Medicine*, 1999; 5:601–4
36. McNeill, John H. (Ed) *Experimental Models of Diabetes* CRC Press 1999 p 13
37. Ibid p. 55
38. Ibid. p. 177, 250
39. Ibid p. 95
40. McNeill, John H. (Ed.) *Experimental Models of Diabetes* CRC Press LLC 1999 p. 225
41. *Ann Intern Med* 1998; 129:36–41
42. Buchler, M., Friess H., Uhl W., Berger H. G. *European Surgical Research* 1992;24, (suppl 1): pp. 85–88
43. *POSTGRADUATE MEDICINE,* 1997;101, No.2

44. Bliss, Michael. *The Discovery Of Insulin* University of Chicago Press 1982 pp. 189–94

45. Thivolet C, Beaufrere R., Betuel H, et al. Islet cell and insulin autoantibodies in subjects at high risk for development of Type 1 diabetes mellitus. *Diabetologia* 1988; 31: 741–746.

46. Barnard R J, Lattimore L, Holly RG, Cherny S, Pritikin N., Response of non-insulin-dependent diabetic patients to an intensive program of diet and exercise. *Diabetes Care* 1982; 5(4);370–374.

47. *Lancet* 2998;352:837–851, 854–864, 832–833.

48. *BMJ* 1998; 317:691–694, 703–726

49. Fletcher, A. P. in *Proc. R. Soc. Med.,* 1978;71, 693–8

50. Heywood, R. in Lumley and Walker (eds.) *Animal Toxicity Studies: Their Relevance for Man* Quay Publishing 1989 see also *Clinical Pharmacology & Therapeutics* 1962, vol.3 pp. 665–672

51. *J Royal Soc Med* 1978;71:693–6

52. Zbinden, Gerhard, M.D. Testimony given at the hearing before the Subcommittee on Health and Environment regarding H.R. 1635, the Consumer Products Safety Testing Act, May 16, 1988

53. The Clinical Relevance of the LD50, Kaufmann, Stephen R., MD, *Vet Hum Toxicol* 29 (1) February 1987

54. Anita O'Connor of the FDA in personal communication to Andre Menache. Document available upon request

55. Agent Orange Product liability litigation, 611 F. Supp. 1223 E.D. N.Y. 1984, *Turpin v. Merrell Dow*, 959 F. 2nd 1249 6th circuit 1992, *Daubert v. Merrell Dow* 61 U.S.L.W. 4805 June 29, 1993, *Early v. Richardson-Merrell Dow*, 897 F. 2nd 1159, 1163 D.C. Circuit 1990, cert. denied, 111 S. Ct 370 1990, and *Richardson by Richardson v. Merrell Dow* 857 F. 2nd 823 D.C. Circuit 1988

Chapter 4: The "Pathetic Illusion" of Animal-Modeled Drugs

1. *Identification, Characterization, and Control of Potential Carcinogens: A Framework for Federal Decision-Making* Office of Science and Technology Washington D.C, Feb. 1, 1979 p. 14

2. Svendsen, Per Laboratory Animal Anesthesia in Svendsen, P. and Hau, J. (Eds.) *Handbook of Laboratory Animal Science vol. I* CRC Press, p. 4

3. Gad, Shayne C., and Chengelis, Christopher P., *Acute Toxicity Testing*, Academic Press 1998, p. 4

4. *Archives of Toxicology* 1979;43:27–33

5. *JAMA* 1998;279:1200–05, 1216–17

6. *JAMA* 1997;277:301–6 and *PharmacoEconomics* 1994;5:482–504

7. *NEJM* April 22, 1971

8. *J Nat Cancer Institute* vol. 84, 1992

9. *Am J Obstet and Gyn* vol. 66, 1953

10. *The Lancet* Sep. 2, 1978

11. A.L. Cowan, MD, Acting Medical Officer of Health, New Plymouth, New Zealand, *N.Z. Listener*, August 31, 1985, p. 10

12. *J Clin Pharmacol* 1990; 48:65–69

13. *Reuters Health*, May 3, 1999

14. *FDA Talk Paper* T97-34, July 23, 1997

15. Briggs, M. H. *Biomedical Research Involving Animals*, Bankowski and Howard-Jones (eds.) 1984 Council for International Organization of Medical Sciences

16. Lehman, M. et al., in *Advances in Applied Toxicology* eds. Dayan and Paine, pub. Taylor & Francis. 1989 p 52–79

17. *Br Med J*, 1952, July 19, 136–138
18. *ATLA*, 1985;13:38–47
19. *Drug Withdrawal From Sale*, 1988
20. *Ann Int Med*, 1952;36:1526–28
21. *NEJM* 1995;333;1099–1105
22. *J NIH Res*, 1993;5:33–35
23. *Nature*, 1993, July 22, p. 275
24. Institute of Medicine, 1995, *Review of Fialuridine (FIAU) Clinical Trials*, Washington DC: National Academy Press
25. Weatherall, M. *Nature* April 1, 1982, 387–90
26. *Pharmacologist*, 1971;18:272
27. *Br J of Pharm* 1969;36:35–45
28. Inman, W. H. *Monitoring for Drug Safety*, MTP Press, 1980
29. *Am Rev Resp Diseases*, 1972;105:883–890
30. *Lancet*, 1979, Oct.27, p. 896
31. *Toxicology and Applied Pharmacology* 1965;7:1–8
32. *Pharmacologist*, 1971;18:272
33. *Animal Toxicity Studies: Their Relevance for Man*, Quay Pub. 1990
34. *Br Med J*, 1974, May 18, p. 365–366
35. *Drug Withdrawal from Sale* PJB Publications, 1988
36. *Pharmacology*, 1983, vol.27(suppl 1), 87–94 and FDA Drug Review: Postapproval Risks 1976–1985 (US GAO April 1990
37. *Gut*, 1987;28:515–518
38. *Lancet*, Jan 10, 1987, 113–114
39. *Toxicolo Letters*, 1991;55:287–93
40. *Drug Withdrawal from Sale*, PJB1988
41. *Reg Tox & Pharm*,1990;11:288–307 and *Postgraduate Med J*, 1973, vol.49, April Suppl., 125–129 and 130
42. *Drugs*, 1982;24:360–400
43. *Animal Toxicity Studies* Quay, 1990
44. *Lancet*, 1984, July 28, p. 219–220
45. *Matindale: The Extra Pharmacopoeia, 29th edition, Pharmaceutical Press, 1989*
46. *Br Nat Form*, no.26, 1993
47. *Reg Tox & Pharm*, 1990;11:288–307
48. *Br Med J*, 1983, Jan 15, p. 199–202
49. *Br Nat Form*, no.26, 1993
50. *Tox & Appl. Pharm*, 1972;21:516–531
51. *Safety Testing of New Drugs* Academic Press, 1984 and *Drug Discovery: The Evolution of Modern Medicine* Wiley 1985
52. *The Benzodiazepines* MTP Press1978
53. *Drugs and Therapeutics Bulletin*,1989;27:28
54. as quoted in *Activate For Animals* Oct. 1997 The American Antivivisection Society
55. Westport Newsroom 203 319 2700 reporting on an article in the *Wall Street Journal*
56. *Parke-Davis letter dated Oct. 31, 1996*
57. *Reuters, Warner-Lambert Denies Rise in Rezulin Deaths*, March 22, 1999
58. Reuters Feb. 12, 1998
59. GAO/PEMD-90–15 FDA Drug Review: Postapproval Risks 1976–1985
60. Prof. Dr. Guilio Tarro, Head of the Dept. of Virology and Oncology at the Medical Faculty of Naples University and partner of Albert Sabin, in a letter dated 2nd of March 1983 as quoted in Ruesch, H. *1000 Doctors Against Vivisection* Civis,1989
61. *Human Toxicology*, 1987;6:436
62. *Regul. Toxicol. Pharmacol.* 1990; 3:288–307
63. *Thromb Rev.* 1990; 57:909–918.

64. *Lancet,* 1977, March 5, p. 534 and *Lancet,* 1972, August 26, p. 424–425

65. Salen, J. C. W. Animal Models—Principles and Problems. In *Handbook of Laboratory Animal Science* 1994 Svendsen and Hau (eds.) CRC Press 1994 p. 4

66. Hess, R. et al. *Lancet* Aug. 26, 1972 424–5

67. *Nature,* 1982, April 1, p. 387–90 and *Br Med J,* 1983, Jan 15, p. 199–202 and *Drug Monitoring,* 1977 and *Pharmacologist,* 1964, vol. 6, p. 12–26 and *Pharmacology: Drug Actions and Reac* and *Advances in Pharm,* 1963, vol. 2, 1–112 and *Nature,* 1982, April 1, pp. 387–390

68. Reuters News Service, December 3, 1998

69. *FDA Reviewers Say Drug Approval Standards Too Low,* Reuters Health, December 3, 1998

70. Gross, F. *The Scientific Basis of Official Regulation of Drug Research and Development,* ed. De Schaepdryver et al., 1978, pp. 18–20

71. Dr. Roy Goulding, formerly head of poisons unit at Guys Hospital London, in a speech given Nov 12, 1990

72. In the supplement to the *Neue Juristische Wochenschrift* (New Legal Weekly), in the *Zeitschrift für Rechtspolitik* (issue 12, 1975), Prof. Dr. Herbert Hensel, Director of the Institute of Physiology at Marburg University

73. T. Koppanyi and M. A. Avery *Clinical Pharmacology & Therapeutics* vol. 7 1966 pp. 250–270

74. *Lancet,* 1962; 599–600.

75. *Lancet* Oct. 5, 1991,856–7

76. Sneader, W. *Drug Discovery: The Evolution of Modern Medicine* Wiley, 1985

77. Lewis, T. *Clinical Science* Shaw & Sons Ltd. 1934

78. *Federation Proceedings* 1967;26:1125–30

79. *Toxicology In vitro* 1992;6:47–52

80. *JAMA,* 1990, April 4, p. 1766

81. *Lancet,* 1989, July 22, p. 227

82. *Lancet,* 1989, Oct 28, p. 1000–1004

83. *Hepatology,* 1991;13:1259–1260

84. *Pharmacology and Therapeutics* 1988, vol.36, 326

85. Sidhu, R. K. in *Drugs and Pregnancy: Human Teratogenesis and Related Problems* Hawkins (ed.) Churchill Livingstone 1983

86. *Pharmacology and Therapeutics,* 1988;36:326

87. *Drugs and Pregnancy: Human Teratogenesis & Related Problems* Churchill Livingstone, 1983

88. Loomis, *Essentials of Toxicology* pp. 211–12

89. *Surg Neurol* 1982;18:320–327

90. *Am Practioner* 1961;12:169–74

91. *J Neurosurg* 1984;61:124–130

92. *Drugs and Therapeutics Bulletin,* 1990;28:74–75

93. *Anesthesiology: Proceedings of the VI World Congress of Anesthesiology,* Mexico City 1977

94. *Drugs and Therapeutics Bulletin,* 1990;28:74–75

95. *Clinical Pharmacology: Basic Principles in Therapeutics* Macmillan, 1978

96. *NEJM,* 1987, Sep. 10, pp. 653–58

97. as quoted in Ruesch, H. *1000 Doctors Against Vivisection* p. 100 from Koppanyi and Avery *Clinical Pharmacology & Therapeutics* vol. 7, 1966 pp. 250–70 also see next reference

98. Ibid. and BBC Radio 4 broadcast The Discovery of Penicillin August 5, 1981 as cited in Sharpe, R. The Cruel Deception

99. *Mayo Clin Proc* 1997; 72: 683–87

100. *Am J M Sc* 1943;206:642–52 and *Proc Soc Exper Biol & Med* 1956;91:229–30

101. *Lancet,* 1962; 599–600.

102. *ATLA* 1994;22:207–209

103. *Clinical Pharmacology: Basic Principles in Therapeutics,* Macmillan, 1978.

104. *Conquest,* Jan 1953, p. 12

105. as quoted from a court record where Chain was testifying concerning vivisection. Published in *CIVIS International Foundation Report* no.11, p. 3

106. *International Journal of Technology Assessment in Health Care,* Lars Werkö 1993; 9:189–201

107. *Human Epidemiology and Animal Laboratory Correlations in Chemical Carcinogenesis* Coulston and Shubick eds. Ablex, 1980

108. *J Pathology,* 1981;135:301–314

109. *Meyler's Side Effects of Drugs,* Elsevier, 1988

110. *Nature,* 1982, April 1, pp. 387–90

111. Liliefield, A. M. & Liliefield, D. A. *Foundations of Epidemiology,* Oxford University Press, 1980

112. *The Causes of Cancer,* 1981, Oxford Press

113. *J NIH Res,* 1991;3:46

114. *Nature,* 1991, Feb 28, p. 732

115. Dollery, C. in *Risk-Benefit Analysis in Drug Research,* ed. Cavalla, 1981, p. 87

116. Jeffrey P. Cohn, The Beginnings: Laboratory and Animal Studies, *FDA Consumer Special Report on New Drug Development in the United States,* 1995

Chapter 5: White Coat Welfare

1. *Nature,* 1989;398:380

2. Dr. James G. Gallagher, Director of Medical Research, Lederle Laboratories, *Journal of American Medical Association,* March 14, 1964

3. Dr. Irwin Bross as quoted in *Cancer Research on Animals,* By Brandon Reines, 1986

4. *Clinical Research,* 1991;39:145–156

5. Dr. Walter Hadwen as quoted in *1000 Doctors Against Vivisection,* by Hans Ruesch, Civis Publications 1989

6. *1000 Doctors Against Vivisection,* by Hans Ruesch, Civis Publications 1989

7. Solomon, Frank. Error, Fraud, and Misconduct in Science. Conference at MIT April 7, 1990

8. *Human Epidemiology and Animal Laboratory Correlations in Chemical Carcinogenesis,* Ablex Pub, 1980, p. 13, pp. 391–3

9. Ahrens, E. H., *The Crisis In Clinical Research: Overcoming Institutional Obstacles* New York, Oxford University Press, 1992

10. Danforth, William H. and Schoenhoff, Doris. *Academic Medicine* vol.67, no.6, June 1992

11. *Human Epidemiology and Animal Laboratory Correlations in Chemical Carcinogenesis* Coulston and Shubick eds. Ablex, 1980, p. 309

12. *JAMA*1989;261:2543–45

13. IOM Committee Report: A Healthy NIH Intramural Program: Structural Change or Administrative Remedies? Washington, DC, National Academy of Science 1988

14. Ahrens, E. H. *The Crisis In Clinical Research: Overcoming Institutional Obstacles* New York, Oxford University Press, 1992

15. Ibid.

16. *Lancet* 1994;343:1574

17. *Democrat and Chronicle* July 19, 1991, p. 11A

18. *Z Magazine* 1993;April:57–60

19. *Lab Animal Medicine* June 1994, pp. 30–35

20. Letter from D. Barnes as quoted in Ruesch, H. *1000 Doctors Against Vivisection* Civis,1989

234 □   References

21. U.S. Congress, Office of Technology Assessment, *Federally funded research: Decisions for a decade,* OTA-SET-490 Washington, DC: US Government Printing Office, May 1991 as quoted in Bell, Robert. *Impure Science* John Wiley and Sons. 1992
22. Wyngaarden, J. B. *Trans Assoc Am Physicians* 1979;92:1–15
23. Ahrens, E. H. Ibid.
24. Committee on Addressing Career Paths for Clinical research: Careers in Clinical research: Obstacles and Opportunities. Institute of Medicine. Washington, DC, National Academy Press, 1994
25. Clinical Research Study Group: An analysis of the review (POR) of grant applications by the divisions of research grants, National Institutes of Health. Patient Oriented research, Bethesda, MD, Nov 1994
26. *Clinical Research,* 1991;39:145–156
27. U.S. Congressional Hearings on Scientific Fraud and Misconduct April 12, 1989
28. Ahrens, E. H., op. cit.
29. Ibid.
30. *Models for Biomedical Research,* a report from the Committee on Models for Biomedical Research, National Academy Press 1985
31. *BMJ* 1988, Nov 5, 1151
32. *Science* 1994;265:20–21
33. NIH Data Book 1992
34. National Cancer Advisory Board, Minutes: Report of the clinical Investigators Task Force, Bethesda, MD Sep 20–21, 1993
35. *Journal of Clinical Oncology* vol. 1996;14, no. 2, (Feb)
36. *Alternatives to Use in Animal Research, Testing & Education.* United States Congress, Office of Technology Assessment, 1986
37. Ibid.
38. *Scientific Fraud and Misconduct and the Federal Response: Hearing before the Human Resources and Intergovernmental Relations Subcommittee of the Committee on Governmental Operations,* April 11, 1988 p. 108
39. U. S. Congress, Office of Technology Assessment, *Federally funded research: Decisions for a decade,* OTA-SET-490 Washington, DC: US Government Printing Office, May 1991
40. Ahrens E. H. *The Crisis In Clinical Research: Overcoming Institutional Obstacles* New York, Oxford University Press, 1992
41. *Ten Leading Causes of Death In the United States, 1977* US Dept. HHS, July 1980
42. *Br Med J* June 6, 1981, pp. 1847–1851
43. *Br Med J* Jan 5, 1985, pp. 5–6
44. Ibid, pp. 34–37
45. *Public Affairs Quarterly,* 1992;7(2):113–130
46. *Southern Journal of Philosophy* 1993;31:323–333
47. *Behav Br Sci,* Dec 1993
48. Rowan, A. W. *Of Mice, Models & Men.* Albany, Suny, 1984
49. Bross, I. D. *Scientific Fraud vs. Scientific Truth.* Buffalo, Biomedical Metatechnology Press 1991
50. *Stroke* 1990;21:1–3
51. *JAMA* 1989;262:2716–20
52. *Arch Int Med* 1988;148:1710–11
53. Stanford Committee on Ethics. Animal research at Stanford University; Principles, policies and practice. *NEJM* 1988;318:1630–32
54. Bernard, C. *An Introduction to the Study of Experimental Medicine.* Paris, Henry Schuman, 1949
55. Gay, W. I. (Ed.) *Health Benefits of Animal research.* Washington DC, Foundation for Biomedical Research, 1986

56. Kalecholsky, Roberta, *Autobiography of a Revolutionary*. Michah Pub 7
57. Ibid.
58. *Lancet* January 6, 1934
59. Pappworth, M. H. *Human Guinea Pigs* Beacon Press 1967
60. As quoted in Vyvan, J. *The Dark Face of Science* Micah Pub 1989 from *The Medical Case Vol. I* US Government Printing Office available in the Library of Congress pp. 141–42
61. As quoted in Vyvan, J. *The Dark Face of Science.* Micah 1989
62. Grodin, M., and Annas, G. *The Nazi Doctors and the Nuremberg Code* Oxford University Press 1992
63. *Science* 1976, April 9, 105–111
64. *BMJ* 1987, Nov 28, 1404–1407
65. *Science* 1989, Aug 11, 583
66. *Circ Res* 1969;25:501–503
67. *Circ Res* 1974;35:661–669
68. *BMJ* 1954, June 26, 1451–1455
69. *Epidemiological Reviews*, 1985, vol.7, 147–177
70. *Perspectives in Biology and Medicine* 1980, Part 2, S9–S24
71. *Animals Agenda* Dec. 1986
72. Stauber, John C., and Rampton, Sheldon, *Toxic Sludge Is Good for You*, Common Courage Press, 1995
73. Dr. Irwin Bross as quoted in *Cancer Research on Animals*, By Brandon Reines, 1986
74. Dr. Irwin Bross as quoted in *The AV Magazine* Nov.1983, pp. 5–7
75. *Congressional Record-House*, July 25, 1995, H7655
76. *Science* vol. 277, August 8, 1997
77. *NEJM* 1998;338:101–6
78. *Wall Street Journal* Feb. 2, 1999
79. *JAMA* 279;995:1998
80. *Aping Science* Published by the Medical Research Modernization Committee, 1995, pp. 99–100

Chapter 6: Alternatives

1. Congress's Office of Technological Assessment 1986
2. National Academy of Science 1985
3. *Investigational New Drugs,* 1983, vol.1, 297–301
4. Svendensen and Hau (Eds.) *Handbook of Laboratory Animal Science Volume I, Selection and Handling of Animals in Biomedical Research*, CRC Press, 1994, p. 410
5. *BMJ* 1952, July 19, 136–138
6. *The Alternatives Report*, 1989, vol.1, no.4
7. *Mutagenesis* 1989, vol.4
8. *ATLA*, 1988, vol.16, 76–82
9. Panigel, M. in, *In vitro Perfusion of Human Placental Tissue,* Schneider and Dancis, (eds.) Karger 1985 and *Toxicology*, 1980, vol.17, 101–104
10. Ekwall, B. as quoted in Fano, A. *Lethal Laws* Zed Book LTD 1997 p. 155
11. *Trends in Pharmacological Science,* 1988, vol.9, 221–223
12. *Trends in Pharmacological Science,* 1987, vol.8, 289–90
13. Hill, R. B. and Anderson, R. E. *The Autopsy—Medical Practice and Public Policy.* Boston, MA. Butterworth 1988
14. *Arch Pathol Lab Med*, Vol. 120, August 1996
15. *Pediatrics* 1993;92:872–875

16. *Pediatr Clin North Am* 1994;41:967–989
17. *Scand J rehab Med.* 1988:17(suppl):25–31
18. Asimov, I. *Asimov's Biographical Encyclopedia of Science and Technology,* 2nd Edition, Doubleday and Co., 1982
19. *Arch Pathol Lab Med.* 1984;108:518–521
20. Hansch, C., *The Use of Alternatives in Drug Research,* (Eds.) H. Schneider & J. Dancis. Karger 1985
21. *Epidemiologic Reviews,* 1985, vol.7,147–177
22. Liliefield and Liliefield, *Foundations of Epidemiology,* Oxford University Press, 1980
23. *Mayo Clin Proc* 1997;72:726
24. *Morbidity and Mortality Weekly Review* August 15, 1997
25. *NEJM* Nov.20, 1997 p 1524–31
26. *Am J Indust Med* 1997;32:614–619
27. *The Cambridge World History of Human Disease,* Kiple, K., Cambridge, 1993
28. *Br Med J* 283: 1421–22, 1981
29. *Biometrics* 1969;25:95–109
30. *Perspec An Res* 1989;1:83–108
31. *Nature Biotechnology,* Vol. 156, July 1998, pp. 597–8.
32. Reuters, July 30, 1999
33. Melmon, K. Testimony before the Subcommittee of Health and Scientific Research, Committee on Labor and Human Resources, US Senate. Washington US Gov Printing Office, 1980
34. *The Causes of Cancer* Oxford 1981
35. Dollery, C. T. *Risk-Benefit Analysis in Drug Research,* MTP Press 1981
36. *The Denver Post,* Feb 21, 1999, pg. G 1–2

Chapter 7: Real Origins of New Medications

1. Prof. Dr. med. Herdegg, Animal Experimenter, at the Conference on Laboratory Animals, in Hanover, 1972
2. *Ann Intern Med* 1998;129:36–41
3. W. Sneader, *Drug Discovery: The Evolution of Modern Medicine.* Wiley 1985
4. Lewis, T. *Clinical Science* Shaw & Sons LTD 1934 p. 188
5. Williams, Vaughan E. M. *Antiarrhythmic Action & the Puzzle of Perhexiline.* Academic Press, 1980
6. Ibid.
7. Bellet, S. *Clinical Disorders of the Heart Beat* Lea and Febiger 1971
8. *This Week* July 13, 1996 p. 4
9. *New Scientist,* Nov. 22, 1997 p. 18
10. *New Scientist,* July 25, 1998, p. 15
11. Dr. Anthony Dayan, Wellcome Research Laboratories, in. Cavalla (Ed.) *Risk-Benefit Analysis in Drug Research,* p. 97, 1981
12. Gross, F. *Antihypertensive Agents,* Springer-Verlag 1977
13. Dr. Anthony Dayan, Wellcome Research Laboratories , in. Cavalla (Ed.) *Risk-Benefit Analysis in Drug Research,* 1981
14. Caldwell, A. *Origins of Psychopharmacology: From CPZ to LSD.* Springfield, Charles C Thomas, 1970
15. Lehmann and Kline. Clinical Discoveries with Antidepressant Drugs, in Parham MJ, Briunvels J, eds.: *Discoveries in Pharmacology.* Vol. 1. NY, Elsiever, 1983, pp. 209–247
16. *Cancer* 1949;2:943–945
17. *The Post Graduate* 1893;8:278–286

18. Boesen, E. *Cytotoxic drugs in the treatment of cancer*. London, Edward Arnold, 1969, p. 24

19. Schardein., J. L. *Chemically Induced Birth Defects*, Marcel Dekker, Inc. 1993, p 157.

20. *Biological Therapies in Psychiatry Newsletter* 1990;13(11)

21. *Drugs and Therapeutics Bulletin*,1990;28:79–80

22. *Clinical Pharmacology: Basic Principles* in Therapeutics 1978

23. *Am Heart J*, 1973;85:605–610

24. *General Pharmacology*, 1981;12:303–308

25. Leonard 1984 and *Drugs and Pregnancy—Human Teratogenesis and Related Problems*. Churchill Livingston 1983

26. *Biological Therapies in Psychiatry Newsletter* 1990;13(11)

27. Altman, Lawrence K. *Who Goes First? The Story of Self-Experimentation in Medicine*, University of California Press, 1998 p. 99

28. *JAMA* 1950, June 24, 717–720

29. *Pharmacy International* Feb., 1986; pp. 33–37

30. *Lancet* Sep. 23, 1939; pp. 678–681

31. *Pharmacy International* 1986, Feb. 33–37

32. Altman, Lawrence K., *Who Goes First? The Story of Self-Experimentation in Medicine*, University of California Press, 1998, p. xi

33. Reuters News Service, May 6, 1998

34. *BMJ* 1997;315:480–483

35. AMA "White Paper" on animal experimentation entitled *Use of Animals in Biomedical Research: The Challenge and Response* 1988 and 1992 Pub. AMA Chicago

36. *This Drug's for You*, Business Week, January 18, 1999, pp. 98–100

37. Reuters Health News Service, December 8, 1998

38. Sipes, I. G., and Gandolfi, A. J., Biotransformation of Toxicants in *Casarett and Doull's Toxicology* (Amdur, Doull, and Klassen, eds.) 4th edition, McGraw-Hill 1993

39. *This Drug's for You*, Business Week, January 18, 1999, pp. 98–100

40. Prof. Dr. med. Herdegg, Animal Experimenter, at the Conference on Laboratory Animals, in Hanover, 1972

41. *JAVMA* 1979;175:1014–15

42. *Bio/Technology* 1992;10:974

43. Gad and Chengelis, Ibid. p. 332.

44. Brodie, B. B. Acceptance Speech, Torald Sollaman Award Meeting of the American Society for Pharmacology and Experimental Therapeutics, Fall 1963

45. *Nature Biotechnology* 1998;16:1294.

46. *American Family Physician* Nov. 1, 1997 p. 1781

47. *Basic & Clinical Pharmacology* Katzung, Bertram G., Appleton and Lange 1992

48. Hill, R. B. and Anderson, R. E. *The Autopsy—Medical Practice and Public Policy* Butterworth 1988

49. *ATLA*, 1994;22:207–209

50. *This Drug's for You*, Business Week, January 18, 1999, pp. 98–100

Chapter 8: Cancer, Our Modern-Day Plague

1. Higginson and Muir in *Cancer Detection and Prevention I*, Lyon; IARC 1976, p. 81

2. *Science* 1986;231:1055–56

3. *Lancet* Aug. 9, 1952, p. 274

4. "Animals tend to be much more resistant to the ill effects of arsenic derivatives. Caparsolate, an arsenic derivative is routinely used to treat heartworms in dogs, would be

much too toxic for humans to tolerate. The carcinogenic effects of arsenic were suspected in 1801. In 1887, cancer from arsenic was described in the literature. In 1977, scientists stated that 'little evidence in animals' existed to support the conclusion that arsenic was carcinogenic." (*J Nat Cancer Inst* 1969, vol. 42, 1045–52) This was the view until three years later when it was "produced in lab animals." *Br J Cancer*, 1947, vol. 1, p. 192–251; *Advances in Modern Toxicology*, vol. 2, Wiley, 1977; *J Nat Cancer Inst*, 1962, vol. 5, p. 459).

5. "My mentor, Dr. Berenblum, noted there was a considerable discrepancy between the effects of coal tar on the mouse and on the rabbit, the rabbit being much more sensitive. This sensitivity was measured by the rapidity with which skin tumors appeared. Berenblum had become intrigued by the fact that the carcinogen benzo(a)pyrene, isolated from coal tar by Kennaway and Cook and assumed to be the active principle of coal tar, was, in point of fact, more potent in the mouse than in the rabbit. The opposite was true of coal tar. In fact it proved to be quite difficult to induce tumors in the rabbit with benzo(a)pyrene by injection, and induction in the skin was much, much slower than with coal tar." *Human Epidemiology and Animal Laboratory Correlations in Chemical Carcinogenesis* Coulston and Shubick eds. Ablex, 1980

6. *Br Med J*, 1958, June 28, pp. 1495–1508
7. *NEJM*, 1985, Feb 28, pp. 541–545
8. *J Soc Rad Prot* 1987;7:3–15
9. *J Rad Prot* 1988;8:3–8
10. *Agents and Actions*, 1978;8:299–302
11. *Fund Applied Tox* 1994;22: 483–93
12. *Annals of the New York Academy of Sciences* 1965;132:456–488
13. *Cancer Treat Report* 1987;71:71
14. *PPO Updates of Cancer* Dec 12, 1987
15. *PPO Updates* Oct 10, 1989
16. As quoted in *LA Times* Wednesday, May 6, 1998
17. Ibid.
18. *Nature* 1990;348:555–557.
19. *U.S. News & World Report* May 18, 1998 p. 63
20. as quoted in *LA Times* Wednesday, May 6, 1998
21. *The American Journal of Pathology*, 1999;155:739
22. *Fund Appl Toxicolo* 1983;3:63–67
23. *Mutagenesis* 1987; 2:73–78
24. *Fund Appl. Toxicolo* 1983; 3:63–67
25. *Science* 1992;255:141
26. Occupational Safety and Health Administration, *Federal register* 45;15: 5069–70, Jan. 22, 1980
27. International Agency for Research on cancer, IARC Monographs on the Evaluation of the Carcinogenic Risk of Chemicals to Humans, vol. 17, *Some N-Nitroso Compounds*, IARC, Lyon, 1978
28. Occupational Safety and Health Administration, *Federal register* 45;15: 5075–76, Jan. 22, 1980
29. *Reg Tox & Pharm*, vol. 1992;18:115–135
30. *Am J Clin Nutr* 1997;66(suppl):1513S-22S
31. DiCarlo, F. J. *Drug Met Rev*1984;15:409–13
32. Efron, E. *The Apocalyptics*, Simon & Schuster, NY, 1984
33. Shubik, P. "Identification of Environmental carcinogens: Animal Test Models," in Griffin, A. C. and Shaw, C. R. (Eds.) *Carcinogens: Identification and Mechanism of Action*, Raven, NY, 1979
34. *Nature* 1988;336:631–633
35. DiCarlo, F. J. *Drug Met Rev* 1984;15:409–13
36. Ibid.

37. Italian parliamentarian Gianni Tamino, researcher at the University of Padua, in an interview with Domenica del Corriere, No. 48, December 1, 1984

38. *Fund Appl. Toxicol* 1983;3:63–67

39. *Br J Cancer*, 1980;41:494

40. Dr. Ronald Hart in *Business Review Weekly*, April 27, 1990

41. "Many difficulties are encountered in estimating human carcinogenic risk from rodent studies. First, interspecies differences such as uptake, activation, detoxification, and storage of chemicals can influence the process of cancer risk assessment. Abelson (1992) draws attention to the cancer-prone B6C3F1 mouse, which is often used for cancer risk assessment but has a high background incidence (up to 58%) of liver tumors when exposed to large doses of substances MTD, whereas other rodents are less or not at all affected ... Second, testing of chemicals is often conducted at near toxic doses (the maximum tolerated dose (MTD). Ames and Gold (1990) have pointed out that the chronic dosing at the MTD must be seen as *chronic wounding*, which can cause cell death, accompanied by chronic cell proliferation. This may lead to a neoplastic [cancerous] process, which may not be indicative for cancer risks at lower doses." *Regulatory Toxicology and Pharmacology* 25: 94–102

41b. *Am J Clin Nutr* 1997;66(suppl):1506S-12S

42. *Regul Toxicol Pharmacol* vol.21, no. 1, pp. 87–107, as quoted in Fano, A. *Lethal Laws*, Zed Books LTD, 1997, p. 110

43. *Clinical Oncology* 1980;15:1–2

44. As quoted in Ruesch, H. *1,000 Doctors against Vivisection*. Civis 1989

45. See reference 42

46. As quoted in *Vivisection Unveiled* by Tony Page Jon Carpenter Publishing 1997 p. 47

47. See reference 44

47b. *Nature* Nov 26, 1992

48. *Science* vol. 278, Nov 7, 1997 p. 1041

49. Ibid.

50. *Science* 1997;278:1041

51. Beniashvili, Dzhemali, MD., *Experimental Tumors in Monkeys*, CRC Press, 1994.

52. *Science* Sep 21, 1990 p. 1357

53. *Scientific American* Nov 1985, 31–39

54. Boesen, E. *Cytotoxic Drugs in the Treatment of Cancer* 1969

55. *The Cancer Bulletin* 1981;33:40–42

56. *CA A Cancer Journal for Clinicians* 1999;49(no.5):258

57. *J Clin Oncol*, 1998;16:1287–93

58. *Journal of Clinical Oncology* vol. 14, no. 2, (Feb) 1996

59. *POSTGRADUATE MEDICINE* vol. 102, no. 3, p. 235

60. Lewontin, R. C., *Biology as Ideology*, Harper-Collins 1991

61. University of Rochester Cancer Center publication, 1999

62. *Cancer Research*, 1953;13:205–215

63. *Cancer Treatment Reviews*, 1975;2:1–31

64. *BMJ*, Dec 2, 1950, p. 1272

65. *Science* 1979;204;587–5930

66. *Proc Acad Sci USA* 1986;83;4839–4843

67. Veronesi, U. Cancer research in Italy: Present and future. *Italian Journal* 1990;4: 58–59

68. *Mutation Research*, 1984;134:89–111

69. Reuters April 1, 1998

70. *Medical News* Sep 9, 1985

71. *Cancer*, 1980;45:2475–2485

72. *Cancer Research on Animals*, by Brandon Reines in NAVS, Chicago 1986

73. *The Guardian*, July 20, 1991

74. *Occupational Lung Disorders*, Butterworth 1982
75. *Toxicology & Industrial Health*, 1990;6:293–307
76. *Br Med J* 1981;283:1421–22
77. *Crit Rev Food Sci Nutr* 1995;35:175–90
78. Reuters March 6, 1998
79. *J Natl Cancer Inst* 1998;90:150–155
80. *Gastroenterology* 1992;103:1783–9
81. *J Natl Cancer Inst* 1998;90:389–94
82. *NEJM* 1997;337:1350–8
83. *JAMA* 1997;278:1407–1448
84. Reuters Health, May 12, 1999
85. *The Columbus Dispatch* March 20, 1998
86. *Mayo Clin Proc* 1997;72:467–74
87. *Nature Genetics* Jan 8, 1998
88. *Nature* 1998;392:402–5
89. *Proc Natl Acad Sci* 1997;94:13950–13954
90. *JAMA* Nov 1996
91. *Clin Cancer Res* 1997;3:2465–9
92. *Science* Oct 24, 1997 p. 569
93. *Science* 1997;278:1043
94. *NEJM* 1998;338:499–505
95. Centers for Disease Control and Prevention's *Morbidity and Mortality Weekly Report*, July 8, 1994
96. The $50 billion figure is conservative because burn-care from smoking-related fires, perinatal care for low birthweight infants of mothers who smoke, and treatment of disease caused by secondhand smoke exposure were not included in the calculation. Also, the study did not consider indirect costs of smoking resulting from lost productivity and early death. Centers for Disease Control and Prevention's *Morbidity and Mortality Weekly Report*, July 8, 1994
97. *The Consumers Union Report on Smoking and the Public Interest*. Mount Vernon, Consumers Union, 1963
98. *Lancet* June 25, 1977 pp. 1348–9
99. *Epidemiology and Health Risk Assessment* Oxford Univ Press 1980
100. *Cancer* 1980;45:2475–2485
101. *Archives of Pathology* 1926;2:533–576
102. Greenstein, J. P. *Biochemistry of Cancer,* 2nd ed., 1954 pp. 163–167. Academic Press NY
103. *Science looks at Smoking*, NY, Coward-McCann, 1957, p. 133
104. *Human Epidemiology and Animal Laboratory Correlations in Chemical Carcinogenesis* Coulston and Shubick eds. Ablex, 1980
105. *New Scientist* Sep 20, 1997 p. 13
106. *Int J Cancer* 1998;75:335–338
107. *Journal of Respiratory and Critical Care Medicine* vol. 156, p. 358
108. from *The Kansas City Star* Nov 5, 1997 p. A-6
109. *JAMA* July 17, 1981
110. *British Medical Bulletin,* 1996;52:3–11
111. *National Cancer Facts and Figures*
112. Ching Y. Chang, Wayne State University. Mechanisms of bladder tumorigenesis. Grant of 4255,049 from Michigan Cancer Foundation
113. *J Pharmacol Exp Ther,* 1995;275:646–53
114. *Spine* 1995;20:1549–53
115. *Am J Physiol* 1995; 268:G153–160
116. *Acta Medica Polona* vol. VII (1966) pp. 407–8
117. *ALTA* 1989;16:231–243

118. *Health Physics*, 1989;56:256

119. Utidjian, M. *Perspectives in Basic and Applied Toxicology* ed. Bryan Ballantyne, Butterworth, 1988

120. *Reproductive Toxicology* 1995;9:449–59

121. Newcomb, P. A. and Carbone, P. P. The health consequences of smoking. *Cigarette Smoking and Cancer* 1992;76:305–331

122. *Psychopharmacology*, 1994;115:180–4

123. *J Urol* 1987;18:431–8

124. *Scientific American* Sep 1996, p. 59

125. *Scientific American* Sep 1996, p. 82

126. *Br Med J* 1985;290:5–6

127. US GAO *Cancer patient survival: What progress has been made?* Washington DC, GAO 1987

128. *Scientific American* Sep 1996 p. 57

129. *NEJM* 1986;314:1226–1232 & *Scientific American* 1994;Jan:130–138 & Dr. John Bailar former chief of War on Cancer speaking before the presidents cancer panel 1986 and 1996

130. *Quick*, March 15, 1979

131. *Food, Chemistry and Toxicology* 1990;28, 783–788

132. *Use of Animals in Biomedical Research: The Challenge and Response* 1988 and 1992 pub. AMA, Chicago (AMA "White Paper" on animal research)

133. *Lord Dowding Fund Bull* 1984 21;26–34

134. Salen, J. C. W. Animal Models—Principles and Problems. In *Handbook of Laboratory Animal Science* 1994 Svendsen and Hau (eds.) CRC Press 1994 p. 4

135. *Science,* 1992, June 19, p. 1609

136. *NEJM* May 1986

137. *NEJM* 1997;336(22):1569–74

138. *Science* 1998;279:1843

139. "Before 1985, the NCI used mice bearing murine leukemia P388 cells to screen new compounds for anticancer activity. That strategy identified agents active against leukemias but relatively few that were effective against solid tumors, including the most common human carcinomas. Hence, the NCI established a primary screen in which compounds are tested *in vitro* for their ability to inhibit growth of 60 different human cancer cell lines." *Science* 1997;275:343–349

140. *J Nat Cancer Inst* 1990;82;1087

141. *Expressions* 2, New England Antivivisection Society, 1994, p. 22

142. EPA/600/P-92/003C April 1996

143. *Science* 1998;280:1196

144. *Nature Biotechnology* 1999; 17:276

145. *New Scientist*, Nov. 15, 1997, p. 12

146. *Scientific American*, Nov. 1997, p. 44

147. *Fundamental and Applied Toxicology*, Nov. 1982

Chapter 9: Diseases of the Cardiovascular System

1. Friedman, Meyer and Friedland, Gerald, *Medicine's Ten Greatest Discoveries*, Yale 1998, p. 76.

2. Lewis, Thomas. *Clinical Science* Shaw & Sons, Ltd., London, 1934 p. 120

3. *Medical World* Feb. 16, 1940 p. 691

4. Westaby, Stephen and Bosher, Cecil. *Landmarks in Cardiac Surgery*, Isis Medical Media 1998, pp. 13–14.

5. *Lancet* Dec. 13, 1958 p. 1261

6. Wertenbaker, L. *To Mend the Heart* The Viking Press 1980 p. 178

7. Comroe, J. H. *Exploring the Heart; Discoveries in Heart Disease and High Blood Pressure* 1983 W. W. Norton and Co. p. 159

8. Metzler, L. E. *Textbook of Coronary Care* Charles Press Publishers Inc. 1980 pp. 3–4

9. American Heart Association, 1997 heart and stroke statistical update. American Heart Association, Dallas

10. *Mayo Clinic Health Letter,* June 1999

11. Friedman, Meyer and Friedland, Gerald, *Medicine's Ten Greatest Discoveries,* Yale 1998, p. 158–62.

12. *JAMA* 1999;282:725

13. Gross, D. *Animal Models in Cardiovascular Research* Martinus Nijhoff Pub 1985

14. *Current Pharmaceutical Design,* 1998;4:37–52

15. Gross, D. R., *Animal Models in Cardiovascular Research,* Martinus Nijhoff, The Hague 1985

16. *Current Pharmaceutical Design,* 1998;4:37–52

17. *Journal of Experimental Medicine* 1949;89:611–30

18. Sharp, Patrick E. and LaRegina, Marie C., *The Laboratory Rat,* CRC Press, LLC, 1998

19. *Nutrition and Cancer,* 1983;4(4):285–291

20. *J Nutrition* 1991,121:431–437

21. *Nature Medicine,* Vol. 4, No. 8, p. 876

22. *Medical News Tribune* London, Sep 18, 1970

23. *Current Pharmaceutical Design,* 1998;4:37–52

24. *Atherosclerosis* 1972;16:256–272

25. *American Journal of Cardiology,* Jan 1958, pp. 46–50

26. *The Journal of Thoracic Surgery* 1937; 7:113–131

27. *Proc Soc Exper Biol & Med* 1935; 32:759

28. *Ann Surg* 1935; 102:801

29. Westaby, Stephen and Bosher, Cecil, *Landmarks in Cardiac Surgery,* ISIS Medical Media 1998, pp. 187–203

30. Lewis, T. *Clinical Science, University College Hospital, London* Shaw & Sons Ltd. 1934

31. Altman, L. K. *Who Goes First? The Story of Self-Experimentation* Random House 1987

32. *J Physiology* 1985, vol. 358, pp. 509–526

33. *Trends in Pharmacologic Science,* 1987, vol.9, pp. 71–74

34. *Annals of New York Academy of Science,* 1988, vol.524, pp. 133–141

35. *NEJM* 1991;325:1468–75

36. *Circulation* 1992;85:942–9, and 1993;88:492–501

37. *NEJM* 1998; 339; 1810–16

38. *Tr Am Ophth Soc* 1967;65:493–543

39. *Biochemical and Biophysical Research Communications* 1988; 2:530–34

40. *Atherosclerosis* 1998;140:15–24

41. *Am J Med* 1989;87(suppl 4A):4A-28S-38)

42. McGregor, M. Drugs for the treatment of angina pectoris in *International Encyclopedia of Pharmacology and Therapeutics: Section 6: Clinical Pharmacology* (Ed.) Lasagna Pergamon Press, 1980

43. *ATLA* 1985, vol.13, 38–47

44. *Lancet* 1998;351:88–92

45. *American Family Physician* Oct 15, 1997 pp. 1607–12

46. *Wall Street Journal,* October 23, 1998, B-1

47. *NEJM* 1998;338:79–93, 122–124

48. Shannon J. A. Testimony before the Department of Labor and Health, Education, and Welfare Appropriations, Subcommittee of the Committee on Appropriations, United

States Senate, Eighty-sixth Congress, First Session. Washington. United States Government Printing Office, 1959, p. 609
49. *JAMA* 1999,281:1722–1727
50. Hill, R. B. and Anderson, R. E. *The Autopsy—Medical Practice and Public Policy*. Butterworth 1988
51. *AMERICAN FAMILY PHYSICIAN* March 15, 1998
52. *New Scientist*, 1990, Dec 8, pp. 39–43
53. *New York Times* 1990, May 8
54. *BMJ* 1954, June 26, 1451–1455
55. *Arteriosclerosis and Thombosis* 14:214–22
56. *J Am Coll Cardiol* 1993;22(2):459–67
57. *POSTGRADUATE MEDICINE* July, 1988, 231–4
58. *NEJM* Nov 6 1997, pp. 1360–69
59. *Circulation* 1998; 98:731–33
60. *Am J Path* 1969;56:111–28
61. *JAMA* 1998;279:359–64, 393–93
62. *New England Journal of Medicine* 1999; 340: 1449–1454
63. *Science* 1998; 281:32,108–111
64. *Cell* 194; 77:701–12
65. *Nature Genetics* 11997; 16:379–82, and 1996;13:63–69 and 1995;11:438–40
66. *Proc Natl Acad Sci* 1995;92;3864–68
67. *Nature* vol. 392, March 19, 1998 p. 293
68. *Science* 1998; 281:32,108–111
69. *NEJM* 1998;339:915–17
70. *JAMA* 1999;282:724–6
71. Altman, Lawrence K., *Who Goes First? The Story of Self-Experimentation in Medicine*, University of California Press, 1998, p. 50.
72. Forssmann W. T. O. Die sondierung des rechten herzens. Klim Wochenschr 1929; 8:2085–7
73. *Newsweek*, April 6, 1998
74. *JAMA* 1999;281:1175–1188, 1220–1222
75. *JAMA*, 1998;280:1926–1929
76. *Circulation* 1991;83(4):1194–1204 and *Erratum, Circulation* 1991;84(6):2610
77. *Lancet* 1990;335(8692):765–74
78. *BMJ* 1991, April 6, 819–824
79. Sassard, J., *The Importance of Animal Experimentation for Safety and Biomedical research*, Dordrecht: Kluwer Academic Publishers, 1990
80. Gross, F. *Anti-hypertensive Agents* Springer Verlag, 1977 p. 7
81. Fitzgerald, D. The development of new cardiovascular drugs in *Recent Developments in Cardiovascular Drugs* eds. Coltart and Jewitt, Churchill Livingstone 1981
82. *Perspectives in Biology & Medicine*, 1980 Part 2, S9–S24
83. *Pharmacy International* Feb. 1986; p. 33–37
84. *Drug Responses in Man: Ciba Foundation Symposium* Wolstenholme and Porter (Eds.) Little Brown and Co. 1967 p. 113
85. *Recent Developments in Cardiovascular Drugs* Coltart and Jewitt (Eds.) Churchill Livingstone 1981 p. 13
86. Cruikshank, J. M., Fitzgerald, J. D., & Tucker, M. in *Safety Testing of New Drugs—Laboratory Predictions and Clinical Performance* ed. Laurence, McClean and Weatherall, Academic Press, 1984
87. *Persp in Biol and Med* Spring, 1977 p. 417
88. *POSTGRADUATE MEDICINE*, vol.101, no.2, Feb 1997
89. Comroe, J. H. *Exploring the Heart: Discoveries in Heart Disease and High Blood Pressure*. W. W. Norton and Co. 1983 p. 303

90. Gross, F. *The Scientific Basis of Official Regulation of Drug Research and Development*, ed. De Schaepdryver et al., 1978, pp. 18–20
91. *Stroke*, May 6, 1999
92. Whisnant, J. P., *Cerebral Vascular Diseases*, 1958, Grune and Stratton pp. 53–67
93. *Stroke*, 1989;20:699–700
94. *Guys Hosp Rep* 1836;1:458–475
95. *Stroke* 1988;19:1195–1197
96. *Cerebral Vascular Diseases* 1966 Grune and Stratton pp. 3–27
97. *J Neuropathol Exp Neurol* 1952;11:34–43
98. *Cerebrovascular Diseases* 1979, Raven, pp. 19–33
99. Ibid, pp. 73–77
100. Ibid, pp. 87–91
101. *Stroke*, 1990;21:981–983
102. Ibid, 1–3
103. *Postgraduate Medicine* vol. 102, no. 2, Aug 1997 p. 212
104. *Postgraduate Medicine* vol. 100, no. 4, Oct 1996, pp. 58–70
105. *Stroke* 1997;28:1908–12
106. *Nature Genetics* 1997;18:8–10, 45–48
107. *Arch Intern Med* 1997; 157:2413–46
108. *Scientific American*, Feb 1999, pp. 56–63
109. *AIDS*, 1999; 13:399–405
110. *Arch Int Med* 1993;153(5):287–93
111. *Br Med J* 1985;291(6488):97–104
112. *Stroke*, May 6, 1999
113. *Arch Intern Med* 1999;159;285–293
114. *American Family Physician*, May 1, 1999, Vol. 59: Num 9, pp. 2475–2482
115. Mustard, J. F. in *Controversies in Therapeutics* Lasagna ed. W. B. Saunders & Co. 1980 p. 319
116. *British Medical Journal* Feb 19, 1955 p. 474
117. *Ann Surg* 48:10–15,1908
118. *Med Record* 1897;51:73–88
119. *Ann Surg* 1908;48:152–155
120. *Surg Gyn Obstet* 1912;14:246–250
121. *Bull Johns Hopkins Hospital* 1907;18:154–192
122. Ziegler, E. A., *A Textbook of General Pathological Anatomy and Pathogenesis*, Wood Pub., pp. 1883–87
123. *Med Record* 51:73–88, 1897
124. Morris, R. T. *Fifty Years a Surgeon* E. P. Dutton 1935
125. *Med Record* 1897;51:73–88
126. Morris and Schirmer, "The Right Stuff," *Surgery*, op. cit.
127. Carrel, A. *Man the Unknown* Burns and Oates 1961
128. *Bull Johns Hopkins Hospital* 1907; 18: 154–192
129. Ziegler, E. Op. cit.
130. *Ann Surg* 1908;48:10–15 and 18–21
131. Morris, R. T. Op. cit.
132. *Medical Observation Society of the Physicians of London* 1761;2:390–414
133. *Transactions of the American Society of Artificial Internal Organs* 1963;9:305–16
134. *Arch Mal Coeur* 42:371–75, 1949
135. *El Siglio Medico* 1906;346
136. Goyanes, J. San Martin and his work. A lecture delivered at Athenaeum of Madrid, Dec 1920. Academy of the RAN of Medicine, 1920
137. *Federation of American Societies for Experimental Biology Journal* vol. 12, p. 47
138. *Arch Mal Couer* 1949;4:371–375

139. *Surgery* 1953;33:183–189
140. *Trans Am Soc Artificial Organs* 1963;IX:3050308
141. Mavor G. Autogenous vein grafts, in Mackey WA. *Arterial Surgery*. New York, Macmillan, 1964
142. *Surgery* 1959;46:145–161
143. Westaby, Stephen and Bosher, Cecil, *Landmarks in Cardiac Surgery*, ISIS Medical Media 1998, p. 201.
144. The Wellcome Museum of the History of Medicine (Science Museum, London, 1986
145. Westaby, Stephen and Bosher, Cecil. *Landmarks in Cardiac Surgery* ISIS Medical Media 1998 p 13–14
146. Ibid, p. 16
147. Altman, Lawrence K. *Who Goes First? The Story Of Self-Experimentation In Medicine* University Of California Press 1998 p. 39
148. *American Journal of Cardiology*, Jan 1958, p. 46–50
149. *The Journal of Thoracic Surgery* 1937; 7:113–131
150. *Proc Soc Exper Biol & Med* 1935; 32:759
151. *Ann Surg* 1935; 102:801
152. Westaby, Stephen and Bosher, Cecil, *Landmarks in Cardiac Surgery*, ISIS Medical Media 1998, p. 187–203
153. Ibid, p. 55.
154. McLeave, H. *The Risk Takers* 1962 Rinehard and Winston
155. Ibid.
156. *J. Thorc. Cardiovasc. Surg.*, 1989:98:833–45
157. Wetenbaker, L. *To Mend the Heart*, 1980, Viking Press
158. Best, C. H. *Circulation* Jan 1959, p. 79
159. Reines, B. *Heart Research on Animals* American Antivivisection Society p. 52
160. From Weisse, Allan B. *Conversations in Medicine: The Story of Twentieth century American Medicine in the Words of Those Who Created It*. New York University press, 1984. Reprinted in: Weisse: Conversations in Medicine in *Hospital Practice* Nov. 15, 1987
161. Prof. Dr. Bruno Fedi, Director of the Institute of Pathological Anatomy at the General Hospital in Terni, Italy, in a video interview with *CIVIS* in Rome, January 11, 1986
162. Westaby, Stephen and Bosher, Cecil. *Landmarks in Cardiac Surgery* ISIS Medical Media 1998 pp. 52–55
163. *US News & World Report* Dec 2, 1985
164. Westaby, Stephen and Bosher, Cecil, *Landmarks in Cardiac Surgery* ISIS Medical Media 1998, pp. 203–207
165. *The American Journal of Surgery*. Vol. 145, June 1983 pp. 733–39
166. *Science* Vol 284; April 2, 1999, pp. 33–34
167. Taussig H. B. Personal Memories of Surgery of Tetralogy, in *History and Perspectives of Cardiology*. The Hague, Leiden University Press, 1980, p. 159
168. Glaser, Hugo. *The Miracle of Heart Surgery*, London, Lutterworth Press, 1961, p. 59
169. Fadali, Moneim A. M.D. cardiac surgeon
170. Westaby, Stephen and Bosher, Cecil, *Landmarks in Cardiac Surgery*, ISIS Medical Media 1998, pp. 96–99
171. Ravitch, M. *The Papers of Alfred Blalock* The Johns Hopkins Press 1966, p. 21
172. Comroe, J. *Retrospectroscope: Insights into Medical Discovery* Von Gehr Press 1975 p. 50
173. Swazey, J. P. and Fox, R. C. in *Experimentation with Human Subjects* pp. 317–32

174. Westaby, Stephen and Bosher, Cecil, *Landmarks in Cardiac Surgery*, ISIS Medical Media 1998, pp. 139–151.

175. *JACC* Vol. 6 no. 4, Oct. 1985, pp. 897–8

176. *Annals of Surgery* 1961, vol. 154, pp. 726–40

177. *J Thoracic and Cardiovascular Surgery* 1961, vol. 42 pp. 673–682

178. *J Thor Cardiovasc Surg*, 1961, vol.42, pp. 683–695

179. *Annals Surgery*, 1961, vol.154, p. 740

180. *Am Coll of Surg, Surgical Forum*, 1960, vol.11, pp. 258–260

181. *J Thor Cardiovasc Surg*, 1961, vol.42, pp. 673–682

182. *J Thor Cardiovasc Surg*, 1960, vol.40, pp. 1–11

183. Fadali, Moneim A. M.D., Cardiac/Thoracic Surgeon, UCLA Faculty, Board of Directors, Royal College of Surgeons of Cardiology, Canada, UCLA Clinical Staff, as reported by *Fur'n Feathers*, October

Chapter 10: AIDS and Humbled Science

1. *USA Today*, June 20, 1996

2. *Lewiston Sun Journal*, Lewiston Maine, June 30, 1996.

3. Brochure passed out by ACT UP San Francisco at Emory University April 26, 1997

4. Gallo, *Virus Hunters* Basic Books, Harper Collins, 1991

5. *Ann Int Med* 1984;100:92–106

6. *Science* 1984;224:500–503

7. *AIDS*, 1998;12(suppl A):S5–16

8. *Nature* 1984;312:763–7

9. *Nature* 1984;312:767–8

10. *Science* 1996;272(5263):872–7

11. *Proc Natl Acad Sci USA* 1987;84:4601–05

12. Reuters Feb 4, 1998

13. *Nature* 1998;393:648–659, 705–711, 830–831

14. *Science* 1998;208:1949–1953

15. *Nature* 1984;313:450–8

16. *Nature Medicine* vol.1, 1995, p. 1320

17. *Nature* Medicine 1995;1:295–297

18. *J Virology*, 1997;71:4086–91

19. *Science*, vol. 280, June 19, 1998, p. 1876.

20. *J Med Primatol* 1989;18:343–355

21. *Intervirology* 1989;30(suppl 1):51–58

22. *J Virology* 1990;64(6):2751–2758

23. *Animal Models in AIDS*. Amsterdam Elsevier Science Publishing BV, 1990 pp. 27–40

24. *Science* 1984;226:549–552

25. *Nature* 1991;352:434–436

26. *J Immunology* 1990;144(8):2992–2998

27. *Intervirology* 1989;30(suppl):51–58

28. *J Infectious Diseases* 1987;155(2):327–331

29. *J Med Primatol* 1989;18:343–355

30. *Antiviral Research* 1992;19:81–109

31. *Clinical Infectious Diseases* 1993;17(suppl 1):S230–S235

32. *Aids Research Review* New York, Marcel Decker, 1991

33. *FASEB Journal* 1989;3:2593–2606

34. *The Scientist*, Vol. 13, no. 16, p. 7, August 16, 1999

35. Ibid.

36. Institute of Medicine. *Mobilizing Against AIDS*. Washington DC, National Academy Press, 1986

References

37. DeVita, V. T., Jr., Hellman, S., Rosenberg, S. A. *AIDS Etiology, Diagnosis, Treatment, and Prevention.* 3rd edition. Philadelphia, JB Lippincott, 1992
38. *Trends in Bio* 1995;13:142–150
39. *Journal of Medical Primatology* 1991;20:182–187
40. *Antiviral Research* 1992;19:81–109
41. Cohen, Jon. *Science* vol.270, Nov 17, 1995 p. 1121
42. *Science* 1997;278:1470–3
43. *Nature* 328(1987):539–47
44. *Science* vol.280, June 19, 1998, p. 1876
45. *AIDS* 1995;9(suppl A):S137–141
46. *Science* 1987;231:438–446
47. DeVita V. T. Jr., et al. *AIDS Etiology, Diagnosis, Treatment and Prevention* 3rd edition Lippincott 1992
48. *FASEB Journal* 1989;3:2593–2602
49. *AIDS* 1995;9:313–24
50. *J Medical Microbiology* 1995;42:233–236
51. *Trend in Biotechnology* 1995;13:142–150
52. *Am J Pathol,* 1993;143:40–48
53. *Journal of Experimental Medicine,* 1996; 183:215–225
54. Presidential Commission: Report of the Presidential Commission on the human immunodeficiency virus epidemic. Washington DC, Government Printing Office, 1988, pp. 39–47
55. *Science* 1995;270:1811–15
56. *Nature Medicine* 1995;1:295–297
57. *AIDS Research and Human Retroviruses* 1992;8:349–356
58. *Nature Medicine* 1995;1:295–297
59. *Proc Natl Acad Sci USA* 1985;82:7096–7100 and *Nature,* Vol. 398 p. 380, 1999
60. *Proc Nat Acad Sci USA* 1985;82:7096–7100
61. *Nature* 1987;325:773–778
62. *Science* 1996;272:1882–3
63. *Science* 1990;247:454–456
64. *Nature* 1987;325:773–778
65. *Antimicrobial Agents and Chemotherapeutics* 1991;35:1386–90
66. *Proc Nat Acad Sci USA* 1985;82:7096–7100
67. *Science* 1990;248:358–61
68. Wynand, M. S. *AIDS Research and Human Retroviruses* 1992;8:349–356
69. *AIDS Research and Human Retroviruses* 1992;8:349–356
70. *Nature* 1987;325;773–78
71. *Antimicrobial Agents and Chemotherapeutics,* Ibid.
72. *Science* 1990;248;358–361
73. *Proc Nat Acad Sci USA* 1986;83:1911–1915
74. Grmek, *History of AIDS* Princeton University Press, 1990 pp. 184–85
75. *Lancet* March 15, 1986, pp. 575–80
76. *NEJM* 1987;317(4):185–191
77. Committee on the Use of Animals in Research. *Science, Medicine, and Animals.* National Academy Press, Washington DC, 1991
78. Daar, Eric S., MD, *Understanding HIV Pathogenesis: Implications for Clinical Practice,* (r)MD+ULMedscape(r)MD-UL HIV/AIDS 5(2), 1999.
79. Reuters Feb. 4, 1998
80. *BMJ* 1997;315:1194–1199
81. *Science* 1997;278:1447–1450
82. *JAMA* 1998; 280:871
83. *NEJM* 1997;337:1267–74
84. *Nature Medicine* 1997;3:1318–19 and 1369–75

85. *Lancet* 1997;351:2–3, 14–18

86. *Science* 1998 vol. 279, p. 389

87. *Science* Oct. 24, 1997 p. 695

88. McNicholl, Janet M., Smith, Dawn K., Qari, Shoukat H., and Hodge, Thomas, *Host Genes and HIV: The Role of the Chemokine Receptor Gene CCR5 and Its Allele,* Medscape 1999

89. *Nature* Vol. 393, pp. 648–59, 705–11

90. Gordon, Nary, Editor, *Journal of the International Association of Physicians in AIDS Care,* July 10, 1996. Internet version

91. *Journal of Acquired Immune Deficiency Syndromes* 1993;6:949–958

92. *PAACNOTES (Physicians Associations for AIDS Care)* February 1993, pp. 82–85

93. *Journal of the American Dietetic Association* 1992;92(4):477

94. *NEJM* 1994;332:259–260

95. *Scientific American* Sep 1997

96. *Lancet,* 1998; Vol 352; 866–870

97. *New Scientist* April 6, 1996

98. *Nature* 1996;381:647–648

99. *Science* 1996;272 (5263): 872–77

100. *Lancet* 1996;347:1395

101. *Science* 1996;272(5269):1740–1

102. *Science* 1996;273:1856–61

103. *Genes Tied to Rapid AIDS Progression, Science* 1999;283:1748–1751.

104. *MMWR* 1995;44:929–33

105. *Nature Medicine,* 1998; 4:390–1, 428–434

106. *Journal of Infectious Diseases* 1998;177:34–39

107. 1998 Medical Tribune News Service 2/6/98

108. *J Infect Dis* 1998;177:551–6

109. *NEJM* 1994;331:1173–80

110. *Clin Inf Dis* 1994;19(3):489–499

111. *JAMA* 1998;279:756–61

112. *JAMA* 1998;279:277–80,317–18

113. Reuters Feb 4, 1998

114. *J Exp Med* 1998;187:25–35

115. *Nature* 1998;391:397–401

116. *Science* vol. 277, August 15, 1997 p. 959

117. *Atlanta Journal Constitution* September 21, 1997

118. *Scientific American* April 1998 p. 18

119. Report of the NIH AIDS Research Program Evaluation Working Group of the Office of AIDS Research Advisory Council. Washington, DC. Office of AIDS Research, March 13,1996

120. *NEJM* 1994;329(19):1400–1405

121. Altman, Lawrence K., *Who Goes First? The Story of Self-Experimentation in Medicine,* University of California Press, 1998, p. xi.

122. *Wall Street Journal,* May 6, 1999

Chapter 11: Animal Organ Donors

1. Hamilton, D. in Morris, P. ed. *Kidney Transplantation—Principle and Practice* W. B. Saunders 1988 pp. 2–4

2. Simmonds, A. *New Scientist* July 23, 1994

3. Neuhof, H. *Transplantation of Tissues* D Appleton & Co. 1923

4. *Scientific American,* July 1997

5. Sark, A. *Knife to the Heart—The Story of Transplant Surgery* Macmillan 1996 p. 158

6. Ibid p. 231

7. *New Scientist*, p. 7, Nov 29, 1984

8. *Nature* p. 88, Nov 8, 1984

9. *Nature* vol. 391, Jan 22, 1998, p. 324

10. *J Heart Transplant* 11(1992):393–396

11. as quoted in *AV Magazine* Fall 1996

12. Ibid.

13. Reuters Health News service October 1, 1999, Westport Newsroom 203 319 2700

14. *Nature Medicine* 1998;4:391–2, 403–7

15. Garrett, Laurie. *The Coming Plague*, Penguin Books, 1994

16. as quoted in *AV Magazine* Fall 1996

17. as quoted in *AV Magazine* Fall 1996

18. Ibid.

19. Ibid.

20. as quoted in *AV Magazine* Fall 1996

21. *New Engl J Med* 1995;333:1498–501

22. *Transplantation* 1994;57:1–7

23. *Nature Medicine* Jan. 1996 vol.2, no.1, pp. 18–21

24. Allan as quoted in Garrett, Laurie *The Coming Plague*, Penguin Books, 1994.

25. Allan as quoted in *The Coming Plague* New York, Farrar Straus and Giroux

26. *NIH Research* 1993;5:36–38

27. *Science* (Letter) 265:1345–6

28. *Nature Medicine* 2:18–21

29. *ILAR J.* 37:37–48

30. *ASM News* 61(9): 442–443

31. *Molecular Diagnosis* 1(3): 1–8

32. *New Scientist*, p. 7, Nov. 29, 1984

33. Ho, Mae-Wan. The Unholy Alliance. *The Ecologist* Vol. 27, no.4, pp. 152–158

34. as quoted in *Nature Medicine* vol.2, no.1, Jan. 1996 p. 19

35. Locke, M. *Washington Times* Dec. 15, 1996

36. *Science* vol.273, Aug. 9, 1996

37. *Nature* vol. 391, p. 320

38. *Nature* vol. 391, p. 309

39. *J NIH Research* 1992;4:37–40

40. *J Virology* vol. 71, no.5, May 1997

41. *J Gen Virology* 1996 77, 773–81

42. *Lancet* 1992;340:271

43. *MMWR* 1992;678

44. Martini, G. A., and Siegert R. *Marburg Virus Disease*. Springer-Verlag 1971

45. *J Virology* May 1997 as reported in *Science* vol. 276. May 2, 1997 p. 685

46. Ibid.

47. As quoted in an editorial by J. Allan. He cited the following references to support his opinion: Broussard, S. R. et al., (1997) Characterization of New Simian Foamy Viruses (SFV) from African Nonhuman Primates. *Virology* 237:349–359. Van der Kuyl, A. C., et al., (1997) Complete nucleotide sequence of simian endogenous Type D retrovirus with intact genome organization: evidence for ancestry to simian retrovirus and baboon endogenous virus. *J. Virol.* 71:3666–3676. Grant, R. F., et al. (1995) Characterization of infectious type D retrovius from baboons. *Virology* 207:292–296. Van der Kuyl, A. C., et al., (1995) Distribution of baboon endogenous virus among species of African monkeys suggest multiple ancient cross-species transmissions in shared habitats. *J Virol.* 69:7877–7887. Allan, J. S. (1996) Public health concerns take center stage in Nuffield Council on Bioethics' Xenotransplantation Report. *Science and Engineering Ethics* 2(2): 486–490.

Allan, J. S. (1996) (commentary) Xenotransplantation: Prevention versus Progress. *Nature Medicine* 2:18–21. Allan, J. S. (1996) Xenotransplantation and Possible Emerging Infectious Diseases. *Molecular Diagnosis* 1(3): 1–8. Moné, J., et al., (1992) Simian T-cell leukemia virus type 1 infection in captive baboons. *AIDS Res. Human Retroviruses* 8(9): 1667–1675.

    48. *JAVMA*, vol.210, no.5, March 1, 1997
    49. *The Times Higher* Jan 31, 1997
    50. *TIME* March, 16, 1998 pp. 47–56
    51. *Science* vol. 275, p. 1993
    52. *Mayo Clinic Proc* 1997;72:1197–98
    53. *Nature Med.* 3,282–6, 1997
    54. *Nature* 389;681:1997
    55. *Nature* vol. 389, Oct. 16, 1997 p. 681
    56. as quoted in *New Scientist* Oct. 18, 1997 p. 4
    57. From *Infobeat News* (Reuters) Feb 25, 1998
    58. *Nature* vol. 390, Dec. 11, 1997 p. 541
    59. Weshsler, Pat. *New York* Nov. 11, 1996 p. 38
    60. *ILAR Journal* 1995;37(1):37–48
    61. UNOS Update 1993[a]b:11–12
    62. *New Scientist*, Nov 29, 1984, p. 7
    63. *ILAR J* 1995;37:13–15
    64. *ILAR J* 1995;37:9–12
    65. *Emerg Inf Dis* 1996;2:64–70
    66. *Lancet* 1995;346:369–370
    67. *Xenotransplantation* 1994;1:47–57
    68. *Nat Med* 1995;1(11):1100
    69. *Lancet* 1993;328:142–143
    70. *Virology* 1995;212:752–756
    71. *Nature* 1995;377:98
    72. Nuffield Council on Bioethics. *Animal-to-human Transplants, the ethics of xeno-transplantation.* 1996
    73. *Virology* 1995;207:292–296
    74. *JAIDS and Human Retrovirology* 1995;9:429–441
    75. *AIDS Res Human Retroviruses* 1992;8(9):1667–1675
    76. *Science* vol. 273, Aug 9, 1996 pp. 746–7 and Steele, D., Auchincloss, H.: The application of xenotransplantation in humans—reasons to delay. *ILAR J* 1995;37:13–15 and Reemstma, K.: Xenotransplantation: historical perspective. *ILAR J* 1995;37:9–12. And Michler, R.: Xenotransplantation: risks, clinical potential and future prospects. *Emerg Inf Dis* 1996;2:64–70. And Thompson, C.: No cheers for baboon to AIDS patient xenotransplant. *The Lancet* 1995;346:369–370. And Fishman, J.: Miniature swine as organ donors for man: strategies for prevention of xenotransplantation-associated infections. *Xenotransplantation* 1994;1:47–57. And Michaels, M., Simmons, R.: Xenotransplant-associated zoonoses. *Transplantation* 1994;57:1–7. And Stoye, J., Coffin, J.: The dangers of xenotransplantation. *Nat Med* 1995;1(11):1100. And Smith, D.: Endogenous retroviruses in xenografts. *The Lancet* 1993;328:142–143. And Duncan, R., Murphy, R., Mirkovic, R.: Characterization of a novel syncytium-inducing baboon reovirus. *Virology* 1995;212:752–756. And Chapman, L., Folks, T., Salomon, D., Patterson, A., Eggerman, T., Noguchi, P.: Xenotransplantation and xenogenic infections. *New Engl J Med* 1995;333:1498–501. And Plagemann, P.: Virus infection of baboons. *Nature* 1995;377:98. And Nuffield Council on Bioethics. *Animal-to-human Transplants, the ethics of xenotransplantation.* 1996. And Grant, R., Windsor, S., Malinak, C., Bartz, C., Sabo, A., Benveniste, R., Tsai, C.: Characterization of infectious type D retrovirus from baboons. *Virology* 1995;207:292–296. And Allan, J., Ray, P., Broussard, S., Whitehead, E., Hubbard, G., Butler, T., Brasky, K., Luciw, P., Cheng-Mayer, C., Levy, J., Steimer, K., Li, J., Sodroski, J., Garcia-Moll, M.:

Infection of baboons with human and simian/human immunodeficiency viruses. *JAIDS and Human Retrovirology* 1995;9:429–441. And Mone, J., Whitehead, E., Leland, M., Hubbard, G., Allan, J. S.: Simian T-cell leukemia virus type 1 infection in captive baboons. *AIDS Res Human Retroviruses* 1992;8(9):1667–1675. And *Science* vol. 273, Aug 9, 1996 pp. 746–47 And Elswood, B. F., Striker, R. B., *Research in Virology*, 144, 175–177, 1993

   77. *Nature* vol. 390, Nov. 6, 1997 p. 11
   78. as quoted in *AV Magazine* Fall 1996
   79. AP newswire Jan. 23, 1998 and *Nature Medicine* 1998, vol.4, 141–144
   80. *Medical Tribune News Service* Jan 22, 1998
   81. Dr. E. Prentice speaking at an open forum at the NIH conference on Developing Public Health Policy in Xenotransplant, Jan 21, 1998
   82. Reuters News Service Jan 26 1998
   83. Courtesy Weir-Williams, Nicholas, *AFP*, October 25, 1999

INDEX